Museums and Education

At the beginning of the twenty-first century (a period of 'liquid' or 'post' modernity) museums are challenged on a number of fronts. The prioritisation of learning in museums in the context of demands for social justice and cultural democracy combined with cultural policy based on economic rationalism forces museums to review their educational purposes, redesign their pedagogies and account for their performance.

The need to theorise learning and culture for a cultural theory of learning is very pressing. If culture acts as a process of signification, a means of producing meaning that shapes worldviews, learning in museums and other cultural organisations is potentially dynamic and profound, producing self-identities. How is this complexity to be 'measured'? What can this 'measurement' reveal about the character of museum-based learning? The calibration of culture is an international phenomenon, and the measurement of the outcomes and impact of learning in museums in England has provided a detailed case study. Three national evaluation studies were carried out between 2003 and 2006 based on the conceptual framework of Generic Learning Outcomes. Using this revealing data, *Museums and Education* explores the power of museum pedagogy and, as it does, questions are raised about traditional museum culture, and the potential and challenge for museum futures is suggested.

Eilean Hooper-Greenhill is Professor of Museum Studies at the University of Leicester. She is recognised internationally for her work on museums, education and communication.

Museum Meanings

Series editors

Eilean Hooper-Greenhill

Flora Kaplan

The museum has been constructed as a symbol of Western society since the Renaissance. This symbol is both complex and multi-layered, acting as a sign for domination and liberation, learning and leisure. As sites for exposition, through their collections, displays and buildings, museums mediate many of society's basic values. But these meditations are subject to contestation, and the museum can also be seen as a site for cultural politics. In post-colonial societies, museums have changed radically, reinventing themselves under pressure from many forces, which include new roles and functions for museums, economic rationalism and moves towards greater democratic access.

Museum Meanings analyses and explores the relationship between museums and their publics. 'Museums' are understood very broadly, including art galleries, historic sites and historic houses. 'Relationships with publics' is also understood very broadly, incorporating interactions with artefacts, exhibitions and architecture, which may be analysed from a range of theoretical perspectives. These include material culture studies, mass communication and media studies, learning theories and cultural studies. The analysis of the relationship of the museum to its publics shifts the emphasis from the museum as text, to studies grounded in the relationship of bodies and sites, identities and communities.

Museums and Education

Purpose, Pedagogy, Performance

Eilean Hooper-Greenhill

Routledge
Taylor & Francis Group

LONDON AND NEW YORK

First published 2007
by Routledge
2 Park Square, Milton Park, Abingdon, Oxon OX14 4RN

Simultaneously published in the USA and Canada
by Routledge
270 Madison Ave, New York NY 10016

Reprinted 2008, 2009

Routledge is an imprint of the Taylor & Francis Group, an informa business

© 2007 Eilean Hooper-Greenhill

Typeset in Sabon by
Keystroke, 28 High Street, Tettenhall, Wolverhampton
Printed and bound in Great Britain by
TJ International Ltd, Padstow, Cornwall

British Library Cataloguing in Publication Data
A catalogue record for this book is available from the British Library

Library of Congress Cataloging in Publication Data
A catalog record for this book has been applied for

ISBN10: 0–415–37935–0 (hbk)
ISBN10: 0–415–37936–9 (pbk)
ISBN10: 0–203–93752–X (ebk)

ISBN13: 978–0–415–37935–9 (hbk)
ISBN13: 978–0–415–37936–6 (pbk)
ISBN13: 978–0–203–93752–5 (ebk)

Contents

Plates

Plates

Figures

Tables

Acknowledgements

The issues addressed in this book have provided a focus for my work for a considerable period of time; this book may be seen as furthering the intellectual trajectory established in *Museums and the Shaping of Knowledge* and *Museums and the Interpretation of Visual Culture*. The extensive empirical research which underpins this book was shaped by and has extended the conceptual frameworks for the analysis of museums set out in these earlier volumes.

The research on which the book is based was carried out under the aegis of the Research Centre for Museums and Galleries (RCMG) in the Department of Museum Studies at the University of Leicester. RCMG was established in 1999, following the recommendation from the influential Anderson Report to the Department of National Heritage in 1997: *A Common Wealth: Museums and Learning in the United Kingdom*, that 'one or more higher education institutions should establish a centre or centres for museum education, to encourage and enable research, teaching and development in the field'. I acknowledge with gratitude the initial start-up funds of £20,000 which were provided by the Museums and Galleries Commission and the University of Leicester Senate Development Fund.

RCMG research focuses on museums and galleries and their audiences, but has also included libraries and archives and their users. The research discussed in this book focuses on the development of a method to 'measure learning' in museums, archives and libraries, and three national studies that measure the outcomes and impact of learning in museums. Since its inception, RCMG has articulated integrated relationships between research which is conceptual and theory-building, research which is policy-related and research which is practice-related, with a view to contributing to knowledge, encouraging and enabling the emergence of a more theoretically informed and reflective professional practice, and contributing to the development of cultural policy.

I have found it an enormous pleasure to work with a group of talented, hard-working and creative individuals who share my enthusiasms and convictions, and I owe them all a great deal. Not only could the research programmes not have taken place without the teams and the people involved, these programmes have taken the shape they have because of collective discussions and decisions. I have learnt much through working with my colleagues, and perhaps against the odds, we found ideas emerging and maturing during the relentless hurly-burly of complex research programmes with tight deadlines achieved through group analysis, interpretation and dissemination.

The research discussed in the book resulted from commissions and consultancies, but these would not have been undertaken had they not enabled us to take forward the themes pursued by RCMG, which, under a general heading of *Museums and cultural change*, consist of a number of sub-themes:

• The social, educational and communicative character of museums
• The social agency of arts and culture
• Museums spaces and technologies
• Disability cultures and museums

Without a doubt, my greatest debt is to Jocelyn Dodd, who acted as RCMG Research Manager from 2000 to 2006, when she took over from me as Director of the Centre. Jocelyn's perceptive and insightful analysis combines with her deep knowledge, understanding and multi-faceted experience of the museum field; without this and her project management skills, the research programmes would not have got off the ground, let alone been brought to conclusion on time and within budget. I thank her for her endless energy, enthusiasm, determination and management skills. Each research programme involved slightly different teams, but Ceri Jones acted as Research Assistant/Associate on them all; her tremendous hard work, flexibility and perceptions have been very much valued. Team members for the RCMG research discussed here have included Amanda Clarke, Lisanne Gibson, Catherine Herman, Francois Matarasso, Professor Marlene Morrison, Dr Theano Moussouri, Helen O'Riain, Dr. Martin Phillips, Chris Pickford, Llewella Selfridge, Emma Sullivan, Frazer Swift, Dr Richard Toon, John Vincent, and Jenny Woodward. Peter Clarke also worked with RCMG at an early point when it took the form of an inauspicious shelf in my office. I am grateful to them all.

Many of the ideas discussed in this book first saw the light of day in presentations to the staff of museums, libraries and archives, and on each occasion the ideas benefited from critical review. As a major part of the web-based *Inspiring Learning for All* programme (www.inspiringlearningforall.gov.uk) of the Museums, Libraries and Archives Council (MLA), the Generic Learning Outcomes (GLOs) took shape in the context of seminars, discussions, and eventually pilot projects with a considerable number of colleagues in fifteen organisations across England. The three national research programmes that followed using the GLOs to 'measure' learning involved between 36 and 69 museums, and many of the education staff took part in seminars for briefing and the interpretation of research findings. Various presentations have enabled me to expose and refine the ideas in other environments; these include lectures and seminars over the years to students in the Department of Museum Studies at Leicester; to the Museums Group of the British Sociological Association at Tate Liverpool in October 2002; to the ICOM/CECA Conference in Oaxaco, Mexico in November 2003; and to the AAM conference New Orleans in May 2004.

I am grateful to MLA, and especially Sue Wilkinson, for allowing the development of the approach to 'measuring learning' to take considerably longer than was originally expected, and for having faith that the GLOs could work. Sue and her colleagues at MLA immersed themselves in the development of the *Inspiring* framework as a whole, and were fully involved in the emergence and piloting of the GLOs. The consultants in charge of the *Inspiring* programme, Anne Murch and Gaby Porter, were also encouraging and helpful.

I acknowledge with thanks permission from the Department for Culture, Media and Sport (DCMS) to quote freely from the research data in the report entitled *Inspiration, Identity, Learning: The Value of Museums. The Evaluation of the Impact of DCMS/DfES Strategic Commissioning 2003–2004: National/Regional Museum Education Partnerships, June 2004,* and permission to use the illustrations that were prepared for the resulting publication *Inspiration, Identity, Learning: The Value of Museums.* I also acknowledge with thanks permission from MLA to use the research data from the two evaluation studies that resulted in the reports entitled *What Did you Learn at the Museum Today?(2003)* and *What Did you Learn at the Museum Today? Second Study (2005),* and permission to use the illustrations that were prepared for the MLA research summary publications with the same name and those that were prepared for the three flipbooks with the children's work. Thanks to Tom Partridge, the designer of the bulk of these publications, for supplying the PDFs so quickly.

RCMG is embedded within the Department of Museum Studies, and over the years I have been lucky to have had the support and companionship of many colleagues, including Professor Simon Knell, Dr Richard Sandell, Dr Ross Parry, Suzanne McLeod and Barbara Lloyd. I have valued the discussions, challenges and critical reviews along with the laughter and practical jokes. I acknowledge with gratitude the period of Study Leave granted to me by the University from February to June 2006 to write the book; and express here my tremendous thanks to Simon, who, as Head of Department, was able to allow me to take extended leave until January 2007, without which the book would certainly not have been completed. Specific thanks are due for reading drafts of chapters to John Reeve, Simon Knell and Jocelyn Dodd, for preparing figures and charts to Ceri Jones, Jenny Woodward, Emma Sullivan and Gurpreet Ahluwahlia, and for general technical support to Jim Roberts. Any errors, misrepresentations or omissions are my own responsibility.

Finally, I thank my husband, John Eland, for his patience and understanding over the months of writing the book and also the years of never being finished with things that had to be done urgently. In the future (soon) you will find us on the beach.

Eilean Hooper-Greenhill
Langtree, North Devon; August 2007

1

Museums: learning and culture

Towards the post-museum: the challenge of changing times

At the beginning of the twenty-first century, museums[1] are re-orientating themselves through imagining afresh what they can become; familiar practices are being reassessed and tired philosophies are being overturned. New ideas about culture and society and new policy initiatives challenge museums to rethink their purposes, to account for their performance and to redesign their pedagogies.

Bauman suggests that the present period of 'late', 'high', 'liquid' or 'post' modernity is characterised by endless incomplete processes of modernisation,[2] and in this respect the cultural field is no exception. Museums have been subject to innumerable calls to modernise as their purpose and performance have been scrutinised, analysed and critiqued.[3] New ways of thinking about media audiences[4] have confirmed the dynamic character of the relationship between museums and their audiences, and the interpretation of collections is high on the priorities of most museums:

> The role of museums is no longer limited to the conservation of objects: they also have to share and continuously reinterpret them.[5]

Until recently, museums could be described as repressive and authoritarian symbols of unchanging solid modernity[6] and indeed there are still some museums that cling to this out-dated identity, but across the cultural field many others have moved with nimble flexibility and creative fluidity to respond to the conditions of post-modernity. The creative re-imagining and reworking of the identity of the museum is one characteristic of the post-museum.[7] The 'post-museum' is a useful hook on which to hang conceptions that signal a move into a positive and hopeful future for museums.[8] One of the key dimensions of the emerging post-museum is a more sophisticated understanding of the complex relationships between culture, communication, learning and identity that will support a new approach to museum audiences; a second basic element is the promotion of a more egalitarian and just society; and linked to these is an acceptance that culture works to represent, reproduce and constitute self-identities and that this entails a sense of social and ethical responsibility.

1

As museums have renewed their philosophies and practices, they have begun to play a more central social role. This can be seen as part of the 'cultural turn'.[9] Societies are becoming more aware of the significance of representation, and of the power of symbols to carry meaning, to signal identity and to invoke social and cultural alignments.[10] As Hall puts it, there is growing recognition of the centrality of culture and its relation to identity.[11] The acknowledgement of interpretation as a practice grounded in social relationships entails the recognition that the interpretive processes which constitute cultural imagery cannot be perceived as neutral.[12]

The increasing awareness of the power of culture has opened up questions of consumption, subjectivity, meaning and identity, and all of these are central to learning. Museums are active in shaping knowledge; using their collections, they put together visual cultural narratives which produce views of the past and thus of the present.[13] In displays and exhibitions, museums 'condense, dislocate, reorder (fictionalise) and mythologise'.[14] Museum displays combine disparate artefacts and fragments of material culture into coherent, continuous and unified narratives, into what Hutcheon calls 'totalising narratives'.[15] Museums must inevitably select from the collections that *could* be displayed those objects that *will* be displayed, and this selection shapes the visual narrative to be presented. Different contexts of meaning are invoked by the different assemblages that are produced.

Through the activities of display and interpretation, using objects, paintings, photographs, models and texts, museums construct a view, present a story and produce resources for learning. These interpretive processes, which involve the attribution of meaning,[16] make up much of the work of museums and could be described as the constitution of the 'curriculum' of the museum. This raises issues of which interpretations are being made, by whom and to what end. Much analysis of learning in museums focuses on pedagogic method (how to use objects in teaching, how people learn), but there are also important questions to be asked about content, namely what it is that museums set out to teach. Wenger discusses how learning transforms who we are and what we can do. Learning, he states, is not just an accumulation of skills and facts, but a process of becoming.[17] Learning works to shape what Giddens calls 'self-identity'.[18] In considering museums and galleries as educational sites, the relationships between the cultural perspectives that museums produce and the self-identities of learners must not be forgotten.

As museums have reshaped themselves for contemporary times, their educational purposes have become prioritised and their educational provision has increased. Since 1997, this has been driven forward in England by government policies that have insisted that education in museums should be centrally positioned:

> The Government believes that education is central to the role of museums today.[19]

This emphasis has been welcomed by those from within the museum field who have long wished to democratise culture and have found that current government policies have offered opportunities to rearticulate these desires. Museum education philosophies have been influenced by the deschooling movement,[20] and inspired by child-centred teaching philosophies and discovery learning strategies[21] which have remained in use in museums long after they had been overturned in schools.

Along with government policies have come national funding programmes that have been made available for the specific purposes of developing closer relationships with schools and communities, of building partnerships between national and regional museums based on the development of joint educational programmes, of appointing specialist staff and of developing professional structures to support museums as they build their educational work. These government funds have come with the responsibility of providing evidence that the objectives for which they were intended have been met. Where formerly it has been enough to *claim* that museums could have an educational impact, today it is necessary to prove it.

The measurement of educational performance has been experienced as burdensome by many, but the necessity to account for the outcomes and impact of learning in museums has rendered the educational work of museums systematically knowable; by being able to articulate the value of museum education in new ways it has become more visible.[22] In addition, the generation of material to present government and its agencies with evidence to justify the continued funding of the educational work of museums has produced a huge body of research that, as this book will describe, shows how museums have the power to position themselves as key sites for learning in post-modernity. The measurement of educational performance has revealed new possibilities for the post-museum.

Changing views of learning

Education and learning have been prioritised in museums, but there is no single view of what this might mean.[23] The words 'learning' and 'education' are understood by individuals in very different ways, depending on their experience of educational systems and of learning and teaching styles. These systems and styles vary within and between countries, and are underpinned by different theories of learning and teaching,[24] which may lead to diverse perceptions of the purposes, processes and outcomes of education and learning.

From a traditional and didactic approach to educational arrangements, 'learning' is synonymous with 'scholarship' or 'knowledge'. Learning is a noun – that which is or can be known.[25] Educational processes are designed to encourage the acquisition of knowledge and to enable the transfer of this learning/knowledge from the teacher (the expert) to the student (the novice). Within this educational paradigm, it is facts and information that are to be learnt, and the processes of grasping the facts and information are expected to be highly focused, purposeful and rigorous. Increased verbal knowledge is the objective, with resources for learning generally limited to the written or spoken word. Teaching methods are cognitive rather than experiential; they privilege the student's mind, and ignore the (frequently regarded as too active) body. Schools and universities are perceived as places of serious study, environments that are kept separate from the everyday world.

Teachers and educational theorists have argued for a long time against this narrow and prescriptive approach to education, and have insisted on a broader, more learner-centred basis for learning and teaching. Many different and powerful arguments have been made, including the fact that many of those labelled as failures by the formal education system have gone on to live successful and productive lives; that learning occurs in many more locations than simply those of formal instruction, where many people learn very little; and that traditional academic educational arrangements privilege those whose families have been educationally successful in the past, and dis-empower those that are not familiar with educational codes and practices.[26]

In Britain, there has been a major shift from the expression 'museum education' to the expression 'museum learning'. The semantic shift from 'education' to 'learning' represents a major philosophical change in the way in which the educational functions of museums are being understood. The use of the word 'learning' indicates an increased focus on the learning processes and outcomes of users, and a shift away from thinking about the museum and its educational delivery. Attention is to how learning can be facilitated, in an attempt to put the production of a pleasant and useful experience for visitors in front of organisational convenience; in effect thinking from the visitor's perspective.

But the educational role of museums remains ambiguous. For some, this refers to the purpose of the museum as a whole, and for others, 'museum education' means the work carried out by specialist museum staff. There is also a range of ways in which the purposes of museum and gallery education can be conceptualised. Pringle, for example, draws a line between museum education which she characterises (quoting Falk and Dierking[27]) as 'tried-and-true sources of understandable information, places one can trust to provide reliable, authentic and comprehensible presentations of . . . objects and ideas', and education in the art gallery, which she describes as concerned with intellectual speculation, with the sceptical self-conscious questioning of 'truth', authenticity' and 'reliability'.[28] But not everyone would agree with this way of defining learning in museums, or that education is so different in museums and galleries.

The contexts for learning in both museums and galleries are not the same as in schools or in other sites for formal learning. Museums are sites of spectacle and display, environments that can be rich and surprising. They can be overwhelming and difficult to manage, but equally can arouse curiosity or inspire new ideas. Museum-based learning is physical, bodily engaged: movement is inevitable, and the nature, pace and range of this bodily movement influences the style of learning.[29] Museums have no national curriculum – each museum may present a different view of a specific matter; they have no formal systems of assessment and no prescribed timetables for learning. Learning in museums is potentially more open-ended, more individually directed, more unpredictable and more susceptible to multiple diverse responses than in sites of formal education, where what is taught is directed by externally established standards.

This is a dynamic moment in museum and gallery education, at a time of rapid social and cultural change, when many of the old signposts for thought and action have been removed, and social and cultural landscapes are being remapped and rearranged. But museum education in Britain is being expected to develop from a weak base; while there are 25–30 years of good practice to draw on, museum education is under-researched and under-theorised.[30]

The 'educational turn' in museums

Educational provision was slow to develop in British museums during the twentieth century. With the lack of a strong commitment to education in the museum field,[31] development depended on highly motivated individuals such as Molly Harrison at the Geffrye Museum in London, Barbara Winstanley in Derbyshire, and René Marcousé at the Victoria and Albert Museum in London.[32] The first schools officers were appointed in the early 1900s; during the 1930s school services increased from eight to fifteen; 34 museum education services were registered in 1963 by the new Group for Educational Services in Museums, and this had increased to 48 by 1967. In 1983, 362 specialist education posts could be counted across Britain, concentrated in 154 museums.[33]

By the early 1990s, however, in part inspired by the report *Excellence and Equity: education and the public dimension of museums* which was published by the American Association of Museums in 1992,[34] museums in Britain were asking questions about the limited nature of educational provision. A report for the lobbying body National Heritage written by Camilla Boodle in 1992 described how educational and local government legislation during the 1980s had opened up opportunities for museums to work more easily with schools through linking collections to the requirements of the new National Curriculum, while at the same time creating the possibility of museums losing funding for their educational work as the local management of schools meant that educational funds moved from the control of the local authority to the schools themselves.[35] Boodle quotes from an earlier (1984) and very influential AAM report, *A report of the Commission of museums for a new century*,[36] and remarks that these points could also be made of the position in Britain in the early 1990s:

> Despite the obvious commitment of museums to learning, there is
> still confusion in the public mind about the role of museums as
> educational institutions and within the museum world, about the role
> of education in the institutional structure . . . Educational responsibility
> is firmly embedded in the philosophical foundation of museums, but
> there is no clear understanding of how people can learn best in the
> museum environment – a situation which is ironic when one considers
> the quantity and quality of educational programming in museums
> today.[37]

A year later, the Museums Association Annual Report in 1992/3 took the form of a report on museums and education entitled *Responding to change: museum education at the crossroads*.[38] It made the claim, to be heard over and over again in the years that followed, that education lies at the heart of museums and that many museums were founded explicitly for educational purposes. However, the reality that lay behind these claims is exposed in the recommendations that museum management and governing bodies should recognise education as a core function of museums, that management structures should reflect the importance of education, and that every museum should develop an education policy. The rhetoric of museums as 'educational' was not matched by clarity of purpose, staffing structures, sufficient resources or management support. At this time, museum education staff made up 1.8 per cent of all museum staff (including security staff) in the national museums, 3.6 per cent of all staff in museums that were funded by local authorities and 2.1 per cent of museum staff in independent museums.[39]

Soon afterwards, the Department for National Heritage,[40] the government ministry with responsibility for culture and heritage, commissioned a report which was intended to 'review the current activities of museums in the United Kingdom as centres for formal and informal learning, and identify how this function can effectively be developed.'[41] Two surveys were carried out, in 1994 and 1995, and extensive discussions were held. The resulting report was published in 1997[42] and then again, under a slightly different title, in 1999.[43] The Anderson report (as it became known) identified 755 specialist education staff in 375 museum services. It was also found that one-third (37 per cent) of the 566 museums responding to the survey made provision for museum education, defined as on a limited level, and that half (49 per cent) offered absolutely no service at all. Only 23 per cent had a museum education policy.[44] This survey also reported that on average, 3 per cent of all paid and voluntary staff in museums were education specialists, and that there were far more curators and others (11 per cent of all museum staff) who contributed to the organisation and delivery of museum education for schools, adults and communities. Only 37 per cent of museums in the survey sample had received any help from education authority advisers.[45] In 2000, a central government statement on museums and education commented that:

> at present the provision of educational services by museums is patchy, ranging from the outstanding to the mediocre.[46]

Since the advent of the Labour government in 1997, a remarkable development in museum education has taken place. The state has become much more centrally directive, and one of the forms this has taken has been to demand increased provision for learning from museums and other cultural organisations. Since the publication of *A New Cultural Framework* in 1998, there have been consistent and unequivocal calls for museums, archives and libraries to develop their provision for learning, enshrined in a number of different policy documents, where government priorities have established major user-related policy initiatives for museums.[47] This has been driven by the ideological convictions of government that culture must be socially inclusive, accountable and used more by schools.

The development of the educational capacities of museums has moved at a rapid pace, as the demands of government have in the main been seen as opportunities to be exploited. In 2006, a report from the Museums, Libraries and Archives Council (MLA),[48] commissioned explicitly to map change in relation to Anderson's findings, found that, in 2006, there were 1,171 education posts in England, that 86 per cent of English museums were used by formal educational groups and 88 per cent by informal educational groups, that 69 per cent have an educational policy and that 87 per cent of curatorial staff contribute to educational activities.[49]

Much of the development of the educational work of museums has been supported through government funds that have been forthcoming because evidence of the efficacy of learning in museums has been provided. Over the last few years, a method of 'measuring learning' in museums has been developed and this method has been used in three national studies of the outcomes and impact of museum-based learning. It is the task of this book to describe this method and the resulting evaluation studies, to assess the findings of the research, and to review the challenges that these findings present to some aspects of museum culture.

Much has changed during the last ten to fifteen years, and the need to theorise learning and culture, to move towards a cultural theory of learning, is very pressing. The pressure to develop educational capacities and to show evidence of effective learning has led to a flurry of educational evaluations. Evaluation is new to the UK; while well established in the USA, it has not been as well established here.[50] However, much of the educational evaluation being carried out at present takes the form of 'grey' literature;[51] produced as reports, booklets, web-based accounts, and sometimes even posters or postcards. Much valuable work is being lost because it is not being made available through normal publication channels. The push from government for the development of museum education in England is taking place in a context where there is still much to be done in terms of theory-building and research.

This book describes research that grew out of the need to be able to present government with evidence of the outcomes and impact of museum learning. The research has taken place in a febrile, contested and fluid hot-house atmosphere where initiatives have flowed at a rapid pace, and cultural practitioners have been forced to interrogate their long-held views as the cultural map has been redrawn. While the research was commissioned for the purposes of advocacy, the researchers were adamant from the start that the research would be worthless if this was a prime factor in the design of the research process and in the interpretation of the research findings. The research has been carried out by the Research Centre for Museums and Galleries (RCMG) in the Department of Museum Studies at the University of Leicester.[52] The motivations of RCMG in competing for and accepting government-funded commissions were grounded in the desire to better understand and to build theory about learning in museums.

This book aims to add to the evidence base and to contribute to the debates about the purpose, character and outcomes of learning in museums and galleries. The research is concerned mainly with school pupils in active learning situations in art galleries and museums, but some work has also been carried out with communities and young people being educated outside school. A very large number of museums were involved in the research, including regional, independent and national museums in England, with collections which cover all disciplines.

This account can be seen as part of a new phase of research which moves beyond that research which focuses on iconic buildings and large national, often art, museums. In the UK, with increased regionalisation because of devolution, and with programmes of funding for non-national museums, tied closely to education, a new focus on regional museums has emerged.[53] This has deepened and complicated earlier views of museum culture.

From the quantitative and qualitative evidence that the research generated, the power of museum-based learning emerges. This powerful force for learning is shaped by post-modern pedagogic approaches. These contemporary ways of thinking about teaching and learning challenge those nineteenth-century ideas that are still found in museums today. The final chapter of the book reviews the questions that the research raises for museum culture as a whole.

The final section of this introductory chapter sets out the argument and structure of the book.

Inspiration, learning, identity – the potential of the post-museum

At the beginning of the twenty-first century, cultural organisations have to fight hard for survival in a political environment shaped by economic rationalism. An instrumental approach to culture demands evidence of value for public funds, sponsorship and the provision of resources. The calibration of culture can be observed on an international basis, and events in England provide a particularly detailed example. The very early years of the new century saw a deluge of official reports, consultation papers and policy documents from government, many of which addressed social inclusion and education. This was accompanied by a restructuring of the cultural field to link museums, archives and libraries, and the emergence of new national and regional agencies tasked with taking forward government policies. Museums, archives and libraries were charged with working to deliver government agendas, and funding was made available for them to do so. Educational evaluation, formerly not well established in the cultural field, developed rapidly.

A new national strategic body (Resource/MLA) was established in April 2000 to work with museums, libraries and archives across England; this body commissioned RCMG to develop an approach to 'measuring' the outcomes of cultural education. The approach can be used in individual organisations, but it has also been used to gather and interpret evidence on a national basis in the museum field, where it was used to evaluate three government-funded national educational programmes. As the same methods were used in each case, a very large body of evidence has been produced and this forms the basis for this book. It is highly unusual to be able to present a national overview of the outcome of learning in museums. The method of 'measuring learning' was devised in a very public arena; it was explored, discussed, piloted and accepted by a large number of staff in museums, archives and libraries, with all stake-holders in the research being informed of the process as it evolved.

The approach is based on an interpretive scheme, a conceptual framework for the design of research tools, analysis and interpretation, founded on the idea that learning outcomes, while occurring at an individual level, can be classified into generic categories. The approach was designed to be used by practitioners, who were not necessarily researchers, in any museum, archive or library, to map and describe the learning of any of their users. The interpretive framework focuses on the outcomes of learning but avoids any behaviourist approach through asking questions in an open-ended way about the extent to which learning has happened and about the outcomes of this learning.

Chapter 2 discusses the cultural policy context in England and the concomitant demand for evidence of educational performance. It introduces the Learning Impact Research Project (LIRP) which resulted in the framework for 'measuring learning' using the Generic Learning Outcomes (the GLOs). Commissioned to find a way to 'measure the outcomes and impact of learning' in museums, archives and libraries, LIRP began by considering in depth what this actually meant. Chapter 2 describes how 'measure' and 'outcomes' were conceptualised. 'Measure' was understood as meaning both 'count' and 'understand'; 'outcomes' were conceived as open-ended and generic.

Chapter 3 analyses the third term 'learning', conceptualising learning in a post-modern way as a basic human attribute. We are learning creatures; learning processes are continuous, as natural as breathing, and not always specifically educational. Learning is not always purposeful; sometimes we can learn without intending to do so. Learning does not only involve the intellect, it involves the emotions and the body as well; it is both tacit (felt) and verbal. Learning can be experiential/performative; it may have depth or be quite shallow. If culture is understood as a process of signification, a means of producing meaning that shapes world views, then learning in museums and other cultural organisations is potentially dynamic and profound, producing self-identities.

Once the meaning of the statement – 'measuring the outcomes and impact of learning' – had been analysed and negotiated with the research stake-holders, LIRP moved to develop a methodology. It was important to work on the basis of the intellectual analysis while at the same time designing an approach to evaluation research that could be used in the individual organisations in a very diverse field and that would produce evidence that would be acceptable ultimately to the Treasury. The approach that emerged was established at a conceptual level. Rather than design a single research tool, perhaps a questionnaire, that could be used to 'measure learning' in any cultural site, the research team proposed a way of thinking – an intellectual framework that could be used by any researchers who wanted to 'measure learning' in their organisation.

The intellectual framework was based on the concept of generic learning outcomes (GLOs), with learning theorised using socio-cultural and constructivist ideas. It proposed that while learning outcomes can be observed in individuals, generic outcomes of learning can be identified which could be used as broad categories for the aggregation of individual learning experiences. This aggregation was important; as the findings of any research using this new method would be used for advocacy purposes, evidence had to take a form that was acceptable to government accountants, and thus statistical data was required.

Chapter 4 examines the five GLOs that LIRP identified. These are:

- Knowledge and Understanding
- Skills
- Enjoyment, Inspiration, Creativity
- Attitudes and Values
- Action, Behaviour, Progression.

The development, parameters and scope of the GLOs are discussed. This conceptual framework was suggested as a basis on which research could be designed and research tools shaped and research data interpreted.

However, the design of a research methodology cannot produce experience in those who were intended to use it, and piloting the approach across museums, archives and libraries exposed a variable level of expertise in evaluation research. The approach, with its straightforward and recognisable language, and the potential to mix quantitative and qualitative data, was welcomed as a solution to the problem of educational accountability. Following the development of the approach, RCMG was commissioned by Resource/MLA and DCMS/DfES to carry out three national evaluation research programmes between 2003 and 2006.

Chapter 5 describes the background to these research programmes, which include the evaluation of the educational work of *Renaissance in the Regions*, the modernisation programme for regional museums in England, and the *Strategic Commissioning Museum Education Programme* funded by DCMS/DfES to link regional and national museums through educational partnerships. These research programmes can be described as 'impact studies', but they do not focus on economic data as impact studies generally do, and they seek to go well beyond the advocacy purposes that limit the theory-building value of these studies. The research took a risk; had the findings not been as positive as they turned out to be, museums could have been exposed as poor providers of education.

The research used mixed methods, all of which used the GLOs; in all three studies questionnaires which asked about the pupils' learning outcomes were completed by 3,113 teachers and 56,810 pupils immediately after their museum visit and, in addition, case studies, interviews and focus groups were carried out where attitudes and examples were explored in more depth. As part of their questionnaires, pupils were asked to complete an open-ended statement – *What amazed me most at the museum today . . .* – and this proved unexpectedly successful, generating many thousands of spontaneous and dynamic visual and textual responses. The research data forms a vast body of linked quantitative and qualitative evidence of learning in museums and the findings are discussed in Chapters 6 to 10.

Chapter 6 reviews the pattern of school use of museums. It shows that while primary-aged pupils make up the largest proportion of museum visits numerically, primary and secondary schools are represented in proportion to their distribution across England. Special schools, however, are more highly represented as museum users than would be expected and this reflects the effort that museums have made to respond to government policies. A review of the postcodes of all visiting schools reveals that while museums are working with schools across the social spectrum, a disproportionately large percentage of schools using museums can be found based in locations which are defined as deprived. Checking the level of eligibility of pupils for free school meals in these schools (as this is the measure used by DfES in relation to deprivation) confirms that large numbers of these pupils are at risk. Museums made strong efforts to reach schools in deprived areas where child poverty is high in order to comply with government policies, and they have done this successfully. Considered in relation to use by schools, the RCMG evidence shows that museums play a powerful role in working towards an inclusive society by working with special schools and by working with children at risk. In analyses of museum visitors, children and school use are rarely included; the continuing evidence is of use by highly educated middle- and upper-class white society. The evidence from the use by schools paints a very much more diverse picture.

Chapter 7 takes the discussion of the value of museums to teachers a little further. It shows how teachers most value their use of museums because of the pleasure and enjoyment that pupils gain from their museum experiences, and an overview of the pupils' questionnaires reveals that they did indeed experience very high levels of enjoyment, and that many were inspired by the events. Enjoyment–Inspiration–Creativity emerges as the most highly valued outcome of museum-based learning for both teachers and pupils. Teachers valued all the generic learning outcomes highly, although teachers' attitudes varied a little. Primary teachers were more likely than secondary teachers to find all learning outcomes very important, and the importance of learning outcomes varies according to teachers' purposes in using the museum. The more tightly linked to the curriculum, the more likely it is the learning outcomes will be perceived as important.

Chapter 8 explores the teachers' perceptions of the outcomes of their pupils' learning. Teachers are very enthusiastic about museums, and use them because the pleasure that pupils experience opens them up to new ideas. This is important for all pupils, but especially for those that find learning difficult. Teachers felt confident that the enjoyment of the visit combined with the tangibility of museum collections would enable their pupils to retain subject-related knowledge. Teachers responding to questionnaires seemed less interested in whether or not their pupils increased their skills; although they could, when asked face to face, list any number of diverse skills that museum visits could develop, it seems as though this was not the main focus of most visits, unless, of course as one of the case studies showed, skills development was one of the specific aims. As pupils enjoyed themselves and developed their knowledge, teachers expected their attitudes to learning, to museums and galleries, and to themselves as learners to become more positive. Teachers found it difficult in the questionnaires completed immediately after the museum visit to assess the behaviours that museum-based learning might stimulate and it was found that focus groups and interviews produced more confident assessments. Here teachers talked about progression and gave examples. Differences in confidence in using museums were found between those teachers of art in the secondary school, who were the most confident, to those teachers of science in the primary school, who were the least confident.

Chapter 9 presents the pupils' views of their own learning. Straightforward questions about learning outcomes in questionnaires present a statistical overview of their attitudes, and the free writing and drawing that pupils produced at the bottom of the questionnaire sheet proved enormously useful in giving specific details. These visual and written statements provide a remarkable record of the pupils' responses to the often wonderfully exciting things they have just experienced in the museum. Their work is spontaneous, fresh and immediate, capturing their joy and enthusiasm before these are overlaid by events. In the responses to the stimulus question, the rich, immersive, memorable and personal character of learning in museums begins to emerge. It also becomes clear how integrated and holistic learning is; the GLOs, while conceptually distinct for analytical purposes, prove to be integrated in practice; cognition and the emotions are inseparably bound together. Mind and body are found to operate together, with much learning being stimulated by bodily experiences. Learning in museums for these pupils often involved unusual enactive experiences and this demanded an open-minded receptive attention that worked to generate new ideas. Learning did not take the form of a single defined focused intention, but was multiple and kaleidoscopic, such that lateral connections were made.

In Chapter 10, the research findings are assembled into an evidence-based grounded account of the power of museum-based learning. Learning in museums emerges as embodied, immersive, holistic, individualised, performative and identity-related. Museums stimulate the desire to know and to try harder; they stimulate a 'readiness to learn', and success in learning through the 'serious play' experienced in museums enabled learners to feel more confident, to begin to develop resilience and receptiveness and potentially, to develop a stronger self-image. Museums clearly have the opportunity to present themselves as powerful sites for learning in post-modernity.

The generation of evidence has enabled English museums to give an account of their educational value. The evidence enables museums to identify how they can contribute to government educational policy in three very specific ways: through working with teachers to promote creativity; through becoming part of an ongoing conversation about the personalisation of learning; and through working with schools and other agencies to fulfil the potential of every child.

The final chapter considers the research findings in the context of museum culture, where some ways of thinking act as barriers to the realisation of the power of museum pedagogy. The character of the successful learning experienced by the pupils in the research discussed in this book was embodied, enactive and immersive, but this is not the learning experience that most museum visitors encounter. Most learning is based on the nineteenth-century idea of 'learning at a glance', where the use of the body and the senses is restricted. This approach to learning was informed by the Enlightenment view that mind and body were distinct entities, and that mind was superior to body. It was thought that the educational purpose of museums could be achieved merely by putting items out on display in the appropriate order. Learning styles in the museum were thus highly restricted, and it seems likely that only those who understood and felt comfortable with an abstract, intellectual, visual approach to learning found museums easy to use. Museums were proclaimed as educational sites for all but the pedagogic style operated as an excluding strategy. The RCMG research raises questions about which pedagogic approach should be used and how pedagogic styles might influence museum present-day visitor patterns.

Questions are also raised by the research about the curriculum of the museum. Museums have been charged with producing narratives that represent gendered and racialised social hierarchies. The stories told in what Bennett calls the evolutionary museum are one example of this where the 'archaeological conception of the person' linked pernicious ideas about the evolutionary idea and the attainment of 'civilisation'. It was plain in the research that museum-based learning worked to shape self-identities, and thus narratives shaped by intellectual frameworks such as these that denigrate peoples and communities can result in harmful and destructive learning.

Further questions arise about the educational purposes of museums. Up until the end of the nineteenth century, education was seen as integral to the character of museums, although how far and to what end was disputed. Education was based on the mastery of bodies of knowledge, its purpose to fit individuals to their expected station in life. The museum was expected to work towards the good society through inculcating a taste for the arts in the working classes, a civilising mission linked to the growth of citizenship. The educational purposes of the nineteenth-century museum do not hold today when it no longer seems possible to produce a unified 'good' society. Education is no longer expected to fit individuals for fixed stations in life, and instead is shaped around ideas about lifelong learning, flexibility, resilience and self-realisation. Learning is no longer concerned with the mastery of large bodies of knowledge, it is about producing people who, in a fluid and changing society, know how to learn, and who have strong self-identities. And putting things out on display for visitors to learn through looking is no longer enough to achieve the educational purposes of museums. Pedagogic style in museums today uses participative and performative modes of learning, where bodies are seen as potent resources for learning. And many museum programmes open up new knowledge, introducing pupils to black culture, feminist histories and representations of a more egalitarian society.

New ways of articulating the educational value of museums are needed today, at a time when perceptions of learning, the self and social life are changing. In post-modernity, questions of purpose, pedagogy and performance have come together

13

in museums in a swirling vortex that appears confusing, but in fact offers up potential for the future. The research shows that museums already know how to become powerful sites for learning; as the post-museum takes on a clearer focus, the strategies to develop museum-based learning are already in place. Museums enable the integration of mind, body and emotion, in a way that few other sites for learning do. Museums are already producing very effective learning experiences that are highly appreciated by their users. This deserves to be more highly celebrated and I hope that the presentation of the research will enable this to happen. This celebration will hopefully lead to increased appreciation and understanding of how and why learning in museums is as successful as it is. Even though the research shows very positive results, there is still a great deal to do.

2

Calibrating culture

Museums and other cultural organisations operate today in environments that are 'saturated by data'.[1] In Britain, America and Australia, demands to demonstrate social value and to account for the expenditure of public funds combined with the need to present arguments for the maintenance of continued support have resulted in a flood of 'impact studies' which use statistical and numerical data to present value in economic terms.

In England, the cultural field has been reorganised as part of a newly interventionist stance on the part of the Labour government. Museums, archives and libraries have been grouped together and charged with addressing government policies, especially those that focused on social inclusion and education. In addition, they were expected to give evidence of having done so.

The need for evidence of the outcome or impact of education posed particular challenges for museums, archives and libraries. There was very little research-based evidence in England that learning occurred at all in museums, even less in libraries and archives and no obvious method, such as monitoring exam results, of 'measuring' this learning. Approaches to the delivery and even the understanding of 'learning' were patchy and uneven across the sector. A new strategic body, The Museums, Libraries and Archives Council (MLA; formerly Resource), established by government to bring museums, archives and libraries into a single cultural territory, took on the responsibility of building professional structures to enable the development of educational capacity, part of which was the development of a method of providing evidence of learning from culture.

This chapter describes the contexts and part of the conceptual framework for the Learning Impact Research Project (LIRP), the research project that, funded by MLA, was carried out by the Research Centre for Museums and Galleries (RCMG) at the University of Leicester. In an atmosphere of increased emphasis on performance measurement, and with very few models to follow, LIRP began in September 2001. The development and testing of a way of researching the impact of learning in museums, archives and libraries based on 'generic' learning outcomes stretched over eighteen months. It is now used very widely by museums and other cultural organisations in England. The development of the framework led directly into three national programmes which researched and evaluated the outcomes and impact of learning in museums in England. This has produced a very large body of evidence of museum-based learning.

The conceptualisation of an approach to 'measuring' and 'outcomes' will be described in this chapter; Chapter 3 discusses how 'learning' was understood by the research team; and Chapter 4 outlines and illustrates the concept of 'generic learning outcomes', which forms the basis of this approach.

Government and the remapping of culture

At the end of the twentieth century in England, a radical remapping of the cultural field occurred. A key element of this was the new position in relation to culture adopted by central government. During the nineteenth century and the early years of the twentieth, there had been no formal lines of communication between museums in the United Kingdom and central government,[2] and for much of the twentieth century, government had adopted an 'arm's length' position in relation to museums, based on a consensus that culture was a good in and of itself. With the election of a Labour government in 1997, culture became drawn much more centrally into government activity as a view of culture as susceptible to accountability and subject to government priorities emerged. A range of strategic reviews and the establishment of a new ministry, the Department for Culture, Media and Sport (DCMS), set the context for new relationships between government and both the cultural organisations that it subsidises[3] and others at the local government level.[4]

A second important aspect of the reterritorialisation of culture in Britain has been regional devolution, with the establishment of a Parliament for Scotland and an Assembly for Wales, each of which has developed its own cultural policies. England has become a single cultural unit, with its own policies, structures and agencies; culture has begun to be shaped as 'English' rather than 'British'. In addition, English cultural restructuring has emphasised regionality; in each of the English Regions, cultural consortia have been charged with developing a unified cultural policy that both reflects regional issues and integrates all art forms.[5] In the case of museums, however, this regionality operates within the centralised framework of government policies.

In addition to the inauguration of a strongly interventionist approach, the new Labour government attempted to create a new cultural field which was given specific tasks. Museums, libraries and archives, hitherto operating as quite distinct communities of practice, with distinct identities, purposes, ways of making meaning and ways of working[6] were repositioned as a collective group charged by government with contributing to the development of an inclusive learning society. A new body to link together museums, libraries and archives was set up in 2000, replacing the long-established Museums and Galleries Commission and the Library and Information Commission. Resource: The Council for Museums, Archives and Libraries[7] was given the remit of leading the delivery of government policy for these three groups of cultural institutions, working closely with the Department for Culture, Media and Sport. While this enforced interlocking has not been entirely successful, the initial strong emphasis on the development of provision for learning in all three domains[8] underpinned the emergence of a new way to measure the outcomes and impact of learning from culture.

The newly active stance of government towards culture led to a large number of reports, strategies and policies which established clear purposes for cultural organisations; and funding agreements were tied to the delivery of policy-related outcomes. Although there has been no single statement of museum policy,[9] these more general government statements gave direction. In its review of 1998, *A new cultural framework*,[10] the Department for Culture, Media and Sport (DCMS) examined its own role and its support structures for cultural organisations including museums, libraries, archives, film and the built heritage;[11] following this, a range of policies for museums, archives and libraries was quickly developed. The promotion of an increased public use of culture took centre stage, with 'cultural education' and 'more opportunities for the excluded' specified as particular objectives.[12]

The demands of government have been consistent and unequivocal:

> The government believes that education is central to the role of museums today.[13]

> We must place the learner at the heart of a new system . . . Each library is a 'street-corner university', with a vital place at the heart of its local community.[14]

These demands to respond to government priorities were not to be ignored. The Secretary of State for Education and Employment insisted:

> There have been some comments that it is not the business of museums, galleries and archives to be involved in social regeneration by serving a wider and more diverse audience. I cannot agree . . . We believe that libraries, museums, galleries and archives are only likely to be effective as agents of social change if they themselves are accessible organisations, whose culture recognises the role that they, and all their staff, have to play in providing services to all sections of the community.[15]

These demands by government were controversial and have been resisted by some. There were several points of contention, including resentment of 'government interference' in relation to organisational purpose, a reluctance to work collectively with organisations that seemed to have limited affiliation beyond government convenience, and a disagreement with the prioritisation of education and access. Where government policies were seen as essentially democratic and concerned to empower those on the margins of society, they were broadly welcomed. Where New Labour policies were regarded as infringing individual freedom, in reducing culture to the lowest common denominator, and as repetitive and ineffectual ('a monotonous whine' as one critic put it[16]), then the opening up of the debate about culture and social inclusion has been less welcome.

One of the main drivers of government policy for museums, archives and libraries has been the need to establish and articulate a social value for culture, and this desire has been imagined from a utilitarian perspective[17] that has viewed cultural practices as worthy of public support because of their economic value.[18] The opening up of culture and learning from this perspective is in danger of being reduced to seeing education as valuable to the economy and thus quantifiable.

Cultural policies: education and the measurement of social value

A utilitarian perspective, resulting in instrumentalism and the commodification of culture, has positioned the 'museum industry' as subject to economic analysis, managerialism and accountability. The assumption that museums in England are economically significant lies behind many of the policy papers published by the Department for Culture, Media and Sport and its agencies.[19] The requirement for modernisation, increased efficiency and the need to demonstrate value for money has led to a demand to provide evidence of achievement, impact and performance. At the present time, the importance of demonstrating economic value through 'impact studies' which act as advocacy tools has been accepted by cultural organisations, although the value of these studies as serious research has been questioned.[20]

It is not only in England that this tendency can be seen. In America, too, cultural arguments are being made through the provision of quantitative data concerned with economic issues. This has been called 'the statistical tendency' or 'the great American numbers game', which consists of 'a blizzard of data breakdowns'.[21] Similar moves can be found in Australia.[22]

A new practice of cultural economics[23] has emerged and in England there are a number of examples of how the museum community has responded.[24] The dependence of museums at national and local level on public funding entails the need for accountability and the Treasury has underlined both the principle of accountability and the concomitant requirement to deliver in relation to government priorities and to show evidence of having done so.[25]

The measurement of performance has been particularly marked in the educational field in Britain, where the need for data on the educational performance of both individuals and institutions has been described as part of a new mentality of practice.[26] In both adult education and schooling, performance is constantly measured and monitored as education has become increasingly governed by managerialism and the criteria of efficiency and effectiveness as a result of an increasing degree of central control over content, delivery and expected outcomes.[27]

The reorientation of cultural organisations towards educational purposes has opened them up to similar demands as central government has developed the expectation that museums, archives and libraries would not only respond to its priorities, but would also be able to present evidence of the impact of their work. Museums were advised by their professional body, the Museums Association, that if the museum community were to secure increased central funding, then it had 'to prove to the Treasury that they're worth it'.[28] It was explained that 'contemporary education policy is driven by results. Schools have to show results in exchange for their money, so why should museums be any different?'[29]

In 2004, DCMS published an essay entitled *Government and the value of culture*.[30] In this paper, Tessa Jowell, Secretary of State for Culture, opened up the discussion about the value of culture. She pointed out that:

> As a Culture Department[31] we still have to deliver the utilitarian agenda, and the measures of instrumentality that this implies, but we must acknowledge that in supporting that we are doing more than that, and in doing more than that we must find ways of expressing it.[32]

Later in the paper she stated:

> Yes, we will need to keep proving that engagement with culture can improve educational attainment, and can help reduce crime.[33]

This perspective on 'education' is a narrow one, with 'education' signifying state provision for schooling, which means that education within museums is seen as valuable because of what it can contribute to the wider educational system. Museum education is firmly placed within the utilitarian agenda as an instrumental value, presented as an adjunct to schools – a technology for helping to deliver the national curriculum and other government agendas for education and schooling. The broader scope, character and significance of learning in museums are ignored.

The challenge of prioritising learning in cultural organisations

A number of research projects in museums, archives and libraries undertaken since 1997 indicate the challenges that existed for the delivery of the government agenda. These studies seemed to be particularly numerous in relation to libraries.[34] The potential and scope of the social impact of libraries had been identified,[35] but a survey of provision in 2000 suggested that:

> although public libraries are currently modernising their services, this modernisation is unlikely to refocus the public library on excluded communities and social groups.[36]

A review of the collaboration between libraries and education concluded that:

> In many cases, collaborative projects do not yet possess a sophisticated understanding of the needs and aspirations of learners and potential learners. Without this knowledge, it is not possible for library managers to design and deliver services which are focused on learners.[37]

While educational services were well established within museums, the Anderson report exposed the gaps in provision[38] and it was confirmed in 2000 that:

> at present the provision of educational services by museums is patchy, ranging from the outstanding to the mediocre.[39]

Information about learning in archives was very scarce, but the National Survey of Visitors to British Archives in 2001 stated that:

> It is common for archives to undervalue the ways in which they inspire their users and enrich their experience, concentrating primarily on providing intellectual and physical access to records.[40]

The research revealed how far museums, archives and libraries would have to change if education and social inclusion were to be prioritised in any genuine fashion. But the requirements for libraries, museums and archives were not only to work towards the twin policy objectives of education and social inclusion, but also to give evidence of having done this effectively. In 1998, Chris Smith, the Secretary for Culture, Media and Sport wrote:

> The Government has provided the resources and the will, but we know that we cannot just sit back and hope that these are transformed into better and more accessible performances, sporting records, improved cultural education and more opportunities for the excluded. We will give direction, we will set targets and chase progress; and where appropriate we will take direct action to make sure that our objectives are achieved.[41]

The Learning Impact Research Project (LIRP)

Soon after its inauguration, Resource began to develop a powerful and detailed learning agenda across the three domains for which it had responsibility. A commitment to develop a sector-wide education standard by April 2001 was followed by the report *Using museums, archives and libraries to develop a learning community: a strategic plan for action*[42] and the introduction of *Inspiring Learning for All*. Echoing the titles of many of the government reports on social inclusion that have set the policy framework for museums, archives and libraries,[43] *Inspiring Learning for All*[44] was a complex initiative intended to demonstrate how museums, archives and libraries could develop a more professional approach to education and learning, and enable them to do so. One element of the *Inspiring Learning for All* initiative was the development of a method of demonstrating the impact and outcome of education and learning which was achieved through The Learning Impact Research Project (LIRP).

In October 2000, the Department for Culture, Media and Sport charged Resource/MLA with developing a national framework for learning in museums, archives and libraries. Work began with the appointment of a 'Thinktank' which met regularly to monitor and advise on progress. This included representatives from all three of the domains under the Resource/MLA remit.[45] The development of the framework which resulted, *Inspiring Learning for All*, was a very large operation which eventually involved over 700 cultural professionals in consultation and piloting.

As Resource/MLA began the task in 2001 of encouraging the organisations that fell within their remit to prioritise and develop their capacity in relation to educational provision, it was very clear that this was a daunting task. As we have discussed earlier by no means all museums, archives and libraries saw themselves as primarily or even mainly focused on facilitating learning.[46] Attitudes varied across and within each of the three domains, as did the level of educational provision. There was at that time very little research into the potential or character of learning in the three domains in the UK, and virtually none on the outcomes or impact of cultural learning. Museums, art galleries, libraries and archives were certainly aware of some aspects of the experiences of their users; and in many organisations visitors were interviewed or completed comment books or questionnaires. However, often the data that was produced was not analysed, and where it was, there were difficulties in presenting reliable evidence of what visitors have learnt.[47] Although some evaluations of cultural education were being carried out, in contrast to, for example, the United States, evaluation was not a well-established activity in museums, archives or libraries, and these studies were not always very robust.[48] As Selwood points out, much of the literature on the collection, analysis and use of evidence in the cultural sector is made up of what is sometimes known as 'grey literature' – reports, accounts, and other studies whose purpose is advocacy.[49]

A broad understanding of the scope of learning in cultural organisations, and the concepts and common language to talk about learning across the sector was lacking. The question of how cultural learning could be conceptualised (what counts as learning in museums, archives and libraries) can be seen as a sociological question, a question of the sociology of knowledge. It is also, of course, a question that is of crucial significance within current cultural policy. If an understanding of learning is under-developed, this poses a problem for cultural managers when trying to present evidence of the impact of learning. The problem is not unique to the UK; a lively debate has been held in the United States, where similar requirements to deliver learning outcomes can be observed in museums and libraries.[50]

The main thrust of the *Inspiring* framework was to encourage staff in museums, libraries and archives to increase and improve their provision for education through developing their own understanding of what education and learning entailed. The framework included four elements: people; places; policies, plans and performance; and partnerships. It was presented through a website that encouraged discussion and activity in order to develop understanding and experience of learning and it was hoped that the framework would be used in meetings, as part of training sessions, and at other times when the staff got together.

In September 2001 Resource/MLA appointed RCMG to develop a methodology for measuring the impact and outcomes of learning in museums, archives and libraries. It was initially thought by Resource that this could be achieved over a six-month period. However, it became clear as the research team[51] struggled with how this methodology might be conceptualised that six months would not be long enough and the project was extended. By March 2002 a conceptual framework had been developed, based on a system of generic learning outcomes that could be used to shape research into learning in museums, archives and libraries; this was piloted in 15 individual museums, archives and libraries between September 2002 and February 2003 and later formed part of the *Inspiring Learning for All* website.

The focus for LIRP was to find a way of measuring the outcomes and impact of learning for all users of archives, libraries and museums, and these were to include informal users, leisure-learners, people involved in non-accredited learning, and students engaged in formal educational programmes. RCMG was also asked to make recommendations about how the system for measuring learning could, over a period of time, be used to deliver a national picture of the outcomes of learning in museums, archives and libraries.

While the task was clear, the methodology for measuring the impact of educational value was less clear. Although a number of research reports have addressed how 'impact' might be measured from a range of diverse perspectives,[52] none had focused on the measurement of the outcomes and impact of learning across the museum, archive and library sector. And although the language of government and its agencies was framed in the same register as that of economic impact studies, where education and learning in cultural institutions are concerned, serious issues arise if economic studies are to become the model. Discussion of 'outcomes' and 'impact' in the contexts of economics uses the language of accountants and managers and entails a research methodology based on statistics and so-called 'hard data' such as that produced by questionnaires, but once considered in relation to learning, the concept of outcomes becomes much more complex, mysterious, difficult and interesting. The outcomes of learning cannot be separated from individual identity and subjectivity, and in terms of research methodology, the exploration of individual learning demands the use of qualitative methods such as face-to-face conversations and the review of the documents and products of learning. At the same time, impact studies had taken on the character of a kind of currency, a recognisable way of speaking to government and its agencies, and of making a case for recognition and support. For cultural education practitioners, long seen as working in a sub-field of secondary importance, the possibility of increasing the visibility of work to which they were committed, and which they knew in their hearts to be successful and worthwhile, was attractive if dangerous and demanding.

Like much of the research carried out in the cultural sector, the Learning Impact Research Project was carried out in a real-world[53] context that was highly complex, fast-moving, volatile and politicised. The research provided a response to a real and pressing problem – in that sense it was timely. But a number of difficulties presented themselves at the outset. At that time, the collection of data about the impact of the arts and culture was of high priority in cultural policy, and the view in 2001/2 of what could be accepted as 'research' or 'evidence' focused almost entirely on the use of quantitative methodologies using statistics. Qualitative research was virtually unknown in the cultural sector, and any reports based on the views of research participants were dismissed as 'anecdotal'. There were very few models of robust research in the cultural field that used qualitative methodologies, and there were even fewer that linked qualitative and quantitative methods. The development of the LIRP project used ideas from outside the cultural field, and proceeded cautiously. Each step of the research process was negotiated through an iterative process of review and assessment. This included input from the commissioning team at Resource/MLA; the Thinktank established by Resource to oversee *Inspiring Learning for All*; the practitioner organisations (museums, archives and libraries) involved in piloting both *Inspiring Learning for All* and the approach to measuring learning; representatives from the new regional museum, library and archive councils; and participants in three seminars.[54]

The research team began from the assumption that museums, archives and libraries represented open and flexible environments for learning and that they could be used as sites for formal and didactic teaching, but equally, they might be used in informal ways. Self-directed learning is well established in these cultural sites, and the potential for creativity, enlightenment and in-depth learning is well acknowledged. But how could the complex and diverse ways that people use museums, archives and libraries for learning be 'measured'? Work began by analysing the challenge set by Resource/MLA: what did it mean? How could 'measure', 'impact', 'outcome' and 'learning' be conceptualised such that action could follow? And how could research be imagined that would satisfy the commissioners of the research (who were of course Resource/MLA, but also ultimately DCMS, who would want to use any research findings to present evidence to the Treasury as a reason for increased funding for the cultural sector), without compromising an understanding of learning based on contemporary learning theory?

The last section of this chapter considers how 'measure' and 'outcome' were analysed, and the way 'learning' was conceptualised will be discussed in the next chapter.

Understanding 'measuring'[55]

Chambers Twenty-first Century Dictionary defines 'measure' as a noun in a number of ways: as a size of volume in comparison with something else; as an instrument for taking a measurement of something, such as a tape-measure; in the plural, 'measures', as steps to be taken, and in a number of other ways, such as a 'measure' of poetry, or a musical 'measure'. As a verb, 'to measure' is defined as determining the size of something; marking off or dividing something into units ('measuring off', or 'out'); and setting things in competition with one another ('measure' her strength against mine).[56] 'Measure' is also defined as an adjective; as an index of quality (be the 'measure' of something; as something above or beyond what was necessary (for good 'measure'); and as a way of forming an idea or making a judgement about someone (have the 'measure' of someone, or get someone's 'measure').

It became clear that 'measure' could be thought of as a number of different ways of coming to a view about something. This included the process of breaking something up into units and comparing the size or volume, which is perhaps the first meaning of 'measure', but it also included the idea of coming to a better understanding of something – getting the 'measure' of something. This multiple approach seemed to offer a number of ways forward.

The initial fear at the start of LIRP was that the complex processes of learning would need to be reduced to simple mechanical matters in order to be susceptible to presentation as numerical data. This was a challenge to the research team, and was the immediate perception of those cultural practitioners (mainly staff of museums, archives and libraries) who participated in the research. This fear was compounded for cultural practitioners by a lack of awareness of research methods other than questionnaires. The concept of 'measuring learning' was imagined by some people as filling in a questionnaire that would, in their view, be unable to capture the subtlety and open-ended creative character of learning in museums.

There is considerable debate in the educational world about the (im)possibility of 'measuring' learning, especially in relation to informal learning or what are sometimes called the 'soft outcomes' (attitudes, key skills, learning skills, etc.), and these anxieties were shared by staff of cultural organisations. The research team discussed and agreed a number of assumptions with the research stakeholders. These focused on the idea that it is inappropriate to set informal leisure learners specific learning standards to achieve, and, as museums, archives and libraries do not test their users as they enter their institutions, they cannot make judgements about how far their general users have moved forward in their understanding and abilities (although users themselves can and do make these judgements). Nonetheless, it was felt at the start of LIRP that cultural professionals did want to be able to describe the characteristics and dimensions of the learning that occurred in their organisations, and also that policy makers and funders were entitled to be presented with evidence of the depth and extent of this learning. It was agreed that it was important for cultural organisations to be able to call on a useful and appropriate methodology in order to give an account of the impact of learning on individuals and groups, in both the short and the long term.

Thinking creatively about what the 'measurement' of learning might comprise, it seemed that it might be possible to produce both numerical data, by counting units or instances, but also descriptive data that could be used to present a picture of something. Thus perhaps statistical and illustrative data could be combined; the statistical data would provide the kind of material that would be recognised by government departments, and could give a broad overview of learning in museums, while at the same time illustrative data, perhaps in the form of case studies or small-scale descriptions or portrayals, could show the complexity and unpredictability of learning. Linking these two levels of data might enable both breadth and depth, and if a common way could be found to gather data from a range of different kinds of museums, archives and libraries, then a broad picture of learning through culture might be possible.

Before the methods could be taken any further, it became necessary to review the concepts of 'impact' and 'outcome'.

Thinking about learning outcomes

LIRP was charged with finding a way of 'measuring' the impact and outcomes of learning in museums, archives and libraries. It was agreed early in the project that 'outcomes' (including both short- and long-term outcomes) would be understood in relation to individuals, and 'impact' would be seen as cumulative and broader in relation to social structures and organisations (and this would generally be in the long term). The idea of the 'outcomes of learning' led to a thorough literature review on the subject of learning outcomes.[57]

The idea of learning outcomes has been tied to a behaviourist approach to learning, where behaviours are measured and teaching can be criticised for being limited to the production of 'correct' behaviours.[58] There are ethical and moral issues at stake here, and many people are suspicious of learning outcomes when described as specific measurable achievements. The language used in some instances to discuss learning outcomes does not dispel discomfort:

> Learning outcomes should flow from a needs assessment. The needs assessment should determine the gap between an existing condition and a desired condition. Learning outcomes are statements which described a desired condition – that is, the knowledge, skills, or attitudes needed to fulfil the need.[59]

However, the concept of learning outcomes is today routinely used in organisations whose major remit is education. Thus in schools, colleges and universities, the identification of learning outcomes forms a major element of curriculum design and planning. Where specific learning programmes are involved, learning outcomes are generally devised by the lecturer/teacher in relation to a baseline (what students know at the beginning of a programme of study), and students are assessed at the end of the programme (have students achieved the desired outcomes). While learning outcomes might be learner-focused, it is rare in formal education for learners to write their own learning outcomes. The development of learning outcomes, along with the selection of learning materials and their effective delivery, is seen as the responsibility of the lecturer/teacher and part of effective course design. Learning outcomes provide a required standard against which both teachers and learners themselves can measure progress.

Learning outcomes are developed in relation to specific programmes of study or schemes of work. In universities, for example, all course and programme specifications and module outlines include an explicit statement of intended learning outcomes. Assessment criteria for judging students' achievement in respect of these outcomes are indicated. Lecturers write the learning outcomes and judge individual student achievement against these requirements. Aims and outcomes are written to describe the knowledge, understanding, skills and attributes that learners will have achieved upon completion of the course of study.

Learning outcomes, then, are part of the norm in formal educational environments. They are developed, written and assessed by the lecturer/teacher, are assessed against a known knowledge-related baseline, at the end of a specific programme of study, and students are aware that this evaluation will take place.

Where taught programmes are delivered in museums, archives and libraries (as part of a school service, or for adults on focused learning sessions) it is also possible to develop appropriate programme objectives with specific learning outcomes, to assess the baseline knowledge or attitudes of programme participants, and to assess any change in knowledge, skills or attitudes following involvement in the programme. In the USA, funding bodies such as the Institute of Museum and Library Services have developed sophisticated guidelines for what they call Outcome-Based Evaluation, or OBE.[60] This is described as a tool for effective management (and is not seen as 'research'), and it has become a requirement for their funded programmes.

The development of learning outcomes to relate to all users of museums, archives and libraries is more difficult than the development of learning outcomes for those on formal educational programmes. In relation to non-formal learning situations, learning outcomes are more problematic, but during the literature review, many projects were found that addressed the issue of measuring learning in, for example, non-accredited learning.[61] In 2001, for example, the Learning and Skills Council[62] was involved in a project to establish a national system for recognising and recording progress and achievement in non-accredited learning.[63] In the *Position paper on recognising and recording progress and achievement in non-accredited learning*, a 'Staged Process' was proposed that involved a number of different moments when evidence could be gathered, such as when initially assessing the learner's starting point, or at points during the programme when learners reflected on their progress.[64]

While this Staged Process was interesting, it could only be used where learners were known and where they had intentionally entered a learning situation, such as an adult education workshop. The data required to complete the Staged Process could not be completed in situations such as libraries or museums, where people come and go at will, are not known to the staff of the organisation, and do not always have the intention to learn. Much learning in cultural organisations is unintentional, happening in an unplanned way as a result of a chance encounter with a space, a book, an object, or another person. In addition, the data collection process demanded not only that learners be actually identified in a formal way, but also that they took part in an intentional learning process over a period of time. While this does of course happen, especially in museums, it is not the general experience of users of libraries, archives or museums. The challenge for LIRP was to find a system that could be used in relation to all or any user of a museum, archive or library.

In open, informal and flexible learning environments, approaches to learning are very variable and diverse, and are dependent on the intentions and agendas of users. The outcomes of learning may be 'anticipated' and possibly 'expected', but cannot be 'required'. While some users of museums, archives and libraries may look for specific teaching programmes such as art or drama workshops, or reading groups, and some users may wish to relate their experience explicitly to a programme of study, equally, many users will not wish to focus quite so intently on formal learning achievements. In cultural organisations learning may encompass a wide range of forms, styles and approaches and it is this breadth that represents the unique value of learning through culture. It is therefore impossible to define in advance specific learning outcomes for each individual.

It is difficult to know when to assess the achievement of learning. If learning is a continuous lifelong process, it is very difficult to assess the outcome of informal learning at any particular moment in time. If learning outcomes are being researched immediately after a museum or library visit, for example, how do we know that greater learning will not happen after this moment? What is being measured?

What was then called 'goal-oriented evaluation' has been tried and left behind in the museum world. Attempts in the past to assess the effectiveness of exhibitions through evaluating how far museum visitors had correctly assimilated what the exhibitions were trying to communicate was abandoned when it was realised that however well the exhibition was designed, the agenda of the visitors might mean that the exhibition's message was ignored in favour of quite other interpretations.[65] Goal-oriented evaluation was based on a stimulous-response view of learning that was rooted in behavioural psychology, and the failure to find evidence of what was then seen as learning (that is, the correct assimilation (the response) of the curatorial message (the stimulous)) was interpreted as meaning that learning was not taking place. Social learning theory suggests that even though exhibition visitors may not wish to learn the facts the exhibitions may wish to communicate, other forms of learning will be taking place.

In thinking about what might be a useful way of conceptualising learning outcomes for all in libraries, archives or museums a number of basic challenges were identified at this point of LIRP:

- Learning is very broad in scope and approaches may vary in each of these organisations.
- Specific learning outcomes which are written against a baseline in relation to a programme of study are not normally appropriate for all users, although intended learning outcomes could be devised in relation to specific projects and workshops.
- Defining specific requirements in relation to changes in the condition or behaviour of users is not appropriate, although experience of specific skills may be identified as potential learning outcomes for particular activities.
- The formal assessment of the levels of attainment or achievement of users from an external (i.e. institutional) viewpoint is not appropriate.
- Defining a moment in time when an outcome might be identified is problematic, as the end of any visit is not necessarily the end of any learning.
- In most cases it will be the user who defines the objective of the visit and who assesses the successful achievement of those objectives.

These basic challenges set up a number of difficulties for the development of learning outcomes in cultural organisations. The ways in which learning outcomes are conceptualised and developed in formal settings do not fit cultural organisations, especially when the experience of all users, particularly those who do not see themselves as 'learners', needs to be encompassed. It is difficult to identify a moment that can be regarded as an end-point in learning and therefore an appropriate moment for measuring this learning. It is not appropriate for organisations to be prescriptive or judgemental about levels of learning achievement, as users have their own criteria for what counts as successful. In addition, unexpected outcomes may occur, and in fact these surprises may provide the most profound learning.

In spite of all the reservations about 'measuring learning', it was agreed that learning was taking place in cultural organisations. The issue is how to relate this learning to 'learning outcomes' and how to 'measure' these outcomes. In addition, as museums, archives and libraries are used by both informal and self-directed users and also groups engaged in formal learning (such as school or college groups), any scheme must be able to encompass both formal and informal learning.

The literature review revealed a range of examples from disparate sources of a more generalised approach to the concept of learning outcomes. The ERSC Teaching and Learning Research Programme Specification for Phase III, for example, included the following statement:

> Learning outcomes are broadly conceived and include: the development of positive learner identities; the acquisition of qualifications; the acquisition of skill, understanding and bodies of knowledge; the development of attitudes and values relevant to a learning society; and the broader values and commitments relevant to individual and community development and civic concern.[66]

The final report of the Qualifications and Curriculum Authority (QCA) Advisory Group on Citizenship, the Crick Report, contained a rather similar statement:

> The learning outcomes that follow are founded on four essential elements: concepts; values and dispositions; skills and aptitudes; and knowledge and understanding which underpin education for citizenship.[67]

The *Guidelines for preparing programme specifications*[68] suggested that each subject (for example, history, chemistry) should identify intended outcomes which should be expressed in terms of:

- knowledge and understanding
- key skills: numeracy, communication, use of ICT and learning how to learn
- cognitive skills
- subject-specific skills.

A paper entitled *Education for Citizenship in Scotland* produced by Learning and Teaching Scotland discussed learning and learning outcomes in terms that in retrospect seem close to the approach that was eventually adopted by LIRP:

> Education for citizenship should aim to develop capability for thoughtful and responsible participation in political, economic, social and cultural life. This capability is rooted in *knowledge* and *understanding*, in a range of *generic skills and competences* including 'core skills', and in a variety of personal *qualities and dispositions*. It finds expression through *creative and enterprising* approaches to issues and problems. (paragraph 2.2)

Capability for citizenship can be analysed in terms of four related aspects, each of which relates to a set of broad categories of learning outcome. These aspects are: 'knowledge and understanding'; 'skills and competencies'; values and dispositions'; and 'creativity and enterprise'. (paragraph 2.3)[69]

From the literature review and endless rounds of discussions among team members, the idea of 'generic' learning outcomes emerged. It seemed clear from some of the papers reviewed earlier that while each individual learner experienced their own learning, these could be (and have been, as we saw) grouped into generic categories.

The distinction between specific and generic learning outcomes is that the specific outcomes are tied to particular skills, attitudes or knowledge, while the generic outcomes consist of broad general categories. For example, a specific learning outcome might state that at the end of a course of study of Tudor England, students would be able to:

- list the names of three Tudor monarchs
- discuss the fate of Lady Jane Grey.

The generic learning outcome would be:

- an increase in knowledge and understanding.

A second example might be that at the end of six workshops on photography, students would be able to:

- load a film into a camera
- choose appropriate film for various lighting conditions
- successfully expose and develop film.

The generic learning outcome would be:

- an increase in skills.

Generic learning outcomes focus on the broad dimensions of learning such as knowledge and understanding, key skills, how to learn, subject-specific skills, and the development of a positive learner identity. These broad categories of learning provide a framework within which specific programmes of study can develop their own specific learning outcomes. It seemed as though the idea of the generic dimensions and generic outcomes of learning might be a fruitful one for the measurement of cultural learning. To take this forward, it was necessary to consider how 'learning' was conceptualised in the cultural context and the next chapter will review this.

Conclusion

One key characteristic of post-modern society is the demand for performativity, the measurement of performance. With the educational purposes of museums being prioritised as part of ongoing processes of modernisation, it became imperative to evolve new ways of 'measuring the outcomes and impact' of museum-based learning in order to justify and sustain funding. This chapter has described the complex and shifting circumstances that gave rise to the Learning Impact Research Project, and has begun the work of accounting for the approach that was developed. We have discussed some of the conceptual underpinning earlier, and will move to review the ways in which 'learning' was conceptualised in the next chapter.

3

Conceptualising learning in cultural organisations

In trying to 'measure' or understand the outcomes and impact of learning, it is necessary to work on the basis of a theory of learning. In the previous chapter, the concept of 'generic' outcomes was introduced, but in order to recognise those outcomes, clarity is needed about what counts as learning. Different ways of recognising 'learning' entail different kinds of outcomes.

This chapter outlines the theory which underpinned the approach to measuring learning that was based on the concept of 'generic learning outcomes'. It encompasses ideas drawn from learning theory, museum studies and cultural studies. In theorising learning in museums, a cultural theory of learning is needed.

Learning: a problematic concept

Over the past few years the theory and practice of education has changed profoundly. This has been usefully summarised as the change from teacher centred to student centred; face-to-face to distance; education to learning; the few to the many; single discipline knowledge to integrated knowledge; knowledge as truth to knowledge as relative; and rote learning to reflective learning.[1] As Claxton points out, cultures differ widely in how learning is understood, and the way in which learning is conceptualised affects the way in which success and failure can be evaluated.[2]

At the start of the development of a method of 'measuring learning', it was essential that 'learning' was defined and the definition agreed by Resource/MLA. This definition also had to be recognisable, relevant and appropriate to the staff of museums, libraries and archives such that they could use it to underpin their own research and evaluation. It was also vital that this definition took account of relevant educational theory, and acknowledged internal research on learning being carried out by cultural organisations. A key objective of the first phase of LIRP (the Learning Impact Research Project) was concerned with the development of an understanding of learning that could be agreed and accepted by all stakeholders.

Resource/MLA had already adopted the definition of learning developed by the Campaign for Learning for the Inspiring Learning for All initiative:[3]

> Learning is a process of active engagement with experience. It is what people do when they want to make sense of the world. It may involve increase in or deepening of skills, knowledge, understanding, values, feelings, attitudes and the capacity to reflect. Effective learning leads to change, development and the desire to learn more.

This seemed a useful and sympathetic definition, but it was essential to put it to one side at the start of the project while the way in which learning in cultural organisations was fully considered. 'Learning' is a slippery concept, with different meanings according to its context of use. Holmes refers to 'learning' as a 'contaminated' concept, as its meanings in one context can leach into its use in another, confusing communication.[4] But a way of dealing with this had to be resolved in order to move forward. The research team was also determined that the complexity of learning processes and outcomes would not be sacrificed or ignored in order to produce a mechanistic way of 'measuring learning'.

There are significant challenges in defining the outcomes of learning in museums, archives and libraries. Within formal educational systems, learning outcomes are established for each programme of study. Individuals engaged in these programmes are measured at the end of the period against set standards (A levels, GCSEs, etc). All involved in the system (teachers, students, examiners) understand and work to a common system. In the case of non-accredited learning such as evening classes, learning outcomes are agreed by teacher and student at the start of the class, and these may be re-visited at the end of the period for teacher and student joint assessment of the individual student's learning.

Most visitors to museums, and users of archives and libraries, on the other hand, have their own agendas for learning (some of which are very unfocused and undeveloped) and they are not required to disclose these in advance. It is inappropriate for cultural organisations such as museums, archives and libraries to measure their users against external standards. However, visitors and users themselves make their own judgements about the success or otherwise of their visit (whether on-site or on-line). They are well able to articulate whether they feel they have found out what they were looking for, have moved forward in their understanding of something, have been inspired or have simply had an enjoyable time. Users know and can discuss the outcomes of their use of cultural organisations, and frequently (though not always) these outcomes can be seen as learning outcomes.

The research to develop an agreed way of understanding learning reviewed existing work on learning as a generic process, and on learning in museums, archives and libraries. Clearly, there is a great deal of research into learning, but most of this is focused on learning in formal educational institutions with very little in Britain written by educationalists who are working in relation to cultural organisations. The educational and cultural fields are largely separate in this respect. The review carried out for the LIRP research team identified a considerable lack of work on understanding learning in libraries and archives.[5] And, in respect of museums, the vast bulk of the research into learning was known to have been produced in America and has been based in science museums.[6] The approach taken by LIRP to 'learning' was constructed on the basis of relevant contemporary learning theorists, theorising of learning in museums, and the conceptual framework that informed *Museums and the Interpretation of Visual Culture*.[7] The way in which learning was understood, therefore, was drawn more from the museum domain than from the other two domains, but museum learning research was carefully considered for a more general application across all three cultural arenas. This approach was subject to scrutiny by practitioners and policy makers in each of the three domains in the UK.

One of the issues involved in talking about learning in museums is that the discourse itself is under-developed. The concepts that describe the specific characteristics of cultural learning have not been developed and so the words which would be used to discuss these characteristics have not been identified, shared and used to bring a discursive field into being. While rapid movement can be seen at the present time, the lack of research in Britain and Europe has, until very recently, led to a lack of concepts and a paucity of terms to use. This can be illustrated by analysing a rather strange concept, that of 'edutainment'.

Edutainment

As Hein says, it is not easy to understand learning in museums.[8] Partly this is because the amount of time spent in museums is often quite short, takes place in groups and happens infrequently. The results for museum users of these often fragmentary experiences are not easy to pin down and it has sometimes proved difficult for museum staff to find the words to describe the characteristics of learning in a museum environment. One expression that has sometimes been used to discuss the character of museum-based learning and that implies a distinction between education in museums and education in places such as schools and colleges is 'edutainment'. This is a clumsy word. It is a word that has not had a very long life within the museum world. It is no longer used in the UK and has all but disappeared from the current literature on museums and education.[9] But it is still being used in some parts of the world.[10] It is worth spending a little while unpacking this expression as it can help to reveal some of the assumptions still held about education and learning. 'Edutainment' brings together 'education' and 'entertainment', and by implication, positions these as two opposing activities. This is necessary when 'education' is perceived as something different from what happens in museums. 'Edutainment' as an expression is an attempt to find words to conceptualise the characteristics of the learning experience within museums. The assumptions that it appears to embody are revealing (Table 3.1).

The term implies that education is rarely enjoyable, concerned only with serious intellectual matters, and carried out in formal self-contained circumstances. However, ideas about learning and teaching have changed in recent years, and one effect has been to bring the polar opposites encapsulated in the expression 'edutainment' much closer together. The main focus has been a considerable development in the way in which 'learning' is understood. The bringing together

Table 3.1 Education and entertainment: binary opposites

Education	Entertainment
Hard work	Pleasure
Cognitive	Affective
Instructive mode	Discovery mode
Experts and novices	Friends and family
School days	Holidays

of education and entertainment and the recognition that learning and enjoyment work very well in conjunction with each other is one aspect of post-modern social arrangements that reject modernist separations of 'either/or' in favour of a more inclusive and potentially more democratic 'both/and'. In educational fields, these contemporary philosophies are articulated through new approaches to learning.

Today, 'learning' as a concept is not usually used to refer to knowledge or scholarship; 'learning' is used to refer to learning processes, and implicit in the more recent interpretations of 'learning' is the idea that learning processes can occur in many different kinds of locations, and can be very diverse in character and in outcome. 'Learning' is understood as multi-dimensional and lifelong.

Contemporary ways of thinking about learning

A range of ideas have been found useful within educational practice in museums. These include the concept of multiple intelligences[11] and of differentiated learning styles.[12] Learners were conceptualised by LIRP as highly variable in their abilities and preferred modes of learning.

Contemporary educational theorists may vary in the detail of their explanations of learning, but all agree on the basic breadth of learning:

> We learn many different kinds of things. We accumulate facts and information and digest this knowledge into opinions. We continue throughout life to develop know-how: how to use new technology, how to tell a good story. We learn to make new discriminations and learn new preferences. We develop new dispositions, learn new roles and new aspects of character, and broaden our emotional range.[13]

Learning is often described as encompassing the acquisition of new knowledge but, as the passage above indicates, it is actually much broader than that. It includes the acquisition of skills, the development of judgement, and the formation of attitudes and values. It includes the emergence of new forms of behaviour, the playing of new roles, and the consolidation of new elements of personal identity. In addition, even when concerned with knowledge, learning does not always mean the acquisition of *new* facts; much of what we would recognise as learning involves the use of what we already know, or half-know, in new combinations or relationships or in new situations. Seeing things in new relationships gives old facts new meanings.[14]

Learning is viewed as a complex set of processes in which everyone is involved in different ways and to different degrees throughout life. As learners, we are active in seeking out what we want to know, whether this is something in the everyday world (such as the way to the market) or something more rarefied (such as a theory of post-structuralism). Learners do not always agree to act as the passive receivers of information from experts, unless this suits their own intentions. Learning always involves the use of what is known already, and this prior knowledge is used to make sense of new knowledge and to interpret new experiences. Thus the world outside school affects how and what we learn inside school. Attitudes, values and self-confidence affect learning processes. Cognitive knowledge (information, facts) cannot be separated from affective knowledge (emotions, feelings, values).

The understanding of learning as a series of complex and lifelong processes entails an emphasis on the experience of learners and on both what they learn and how they learn it. The active meaning-making work that learners do in order to make knowledge their own is recognised. It is acknowledged that:

> Learners construct meaning on their own terms no matter what teachers do.[15]

As a result, knowledge is no longer seen as a body of facts that may be transmitted without change from one person to the next. Knowledge is understood as that which is known by people. Facts are interpreted, or made meaningful in different ways by different people. As Gallagher describes, learning involves meaning – things are only learnt when put into a context of meaning.[16] People build up different perspectives on the world and inflect facts and information in different ways – they pick out different parts of bodies of knowledge to remember and to adopt. The brain never merely absorbs new information, it processes it to make it personally meaningful. This processing is done on the basis of prior knowledge, individual biographies, cultural positioning, gender and other matters. Because people are all different, each person will process knowledge and produce meaning in a different way.[17]

Contemporary understandings of learning describe it as being as crucial and fundamental as breathing[18] or as being alive.[19] Learning is seen to play an integral part of our everyday lives.[20] This raises the issue of what is not learning, and indeed it is very difficult to draw the line between 'learning' and 'not learning'. We can say with confidence that we are natural problem-solvers throughout life, and have to learn in order to solve problems:

> Learning is what you do when you don't know what to do.[21]

Learning includes learning new things, using prior knowledge in new situations, and reinforcing that which is already known. Learning may relate to formal education, or may be focused in the everyday. For many people who still think about learning in traditional ways, learning is not happening unless effort is involved. But for educational theorists, learning does not necessarily have to be hard work. Enjoyment is an integral part of learning – we learn better and remember more if we are motivated through enjoyment. In addition, learning is not always positive – we can learn to be afraid, or to undervalue ourselves, or to misunderstand facts and their implications. Learning can be irregular and patchy, with ideas which were implanted when very young remaining to guide opinions much later in life.[22] And, learning can sometimes happen without us being aware of it.

Tacit/experiential learning

Learning can occur through a range of different encounters, and arguably the most important is a real encounter in a real space with real things. Learning through experience has long been recognised as of enormous significance, and this is a major component of the value of learning in museums.

To begin to understand the power of learning through experience, we need to distinguish between verbal knowledge and tacit knowledge. Verbal knowledge is that which can be verbalised – that is, spoken about, brought into articulation with existing ideas or written down. Tacit knowledge is everything we know minus everything we can say.

Clearly language is essential to learning and it is only through language that thoughts can be developed and articulated. However, being able to talk about things does not necessarily imply understanding. For true understanding, and the most powerful learning, experience is also needed. Many educational theorists would assert that a great deal of knowledge cannot be learnt simply through being told, but that experience, that results in 'tacit' knowledge, is absolutely essential to learning.[23]

> It is generally agreed that there are various levels of knowing. The strongest form of knowing comes about when we have had a suitable experience of something. That kind of knowing is coded inside us in a felt, compacted, living, tacit form and is part of our total mental structure. With some effort, we can sometimes make this kind of knowledge conscious and think about it verbally. That can help us to do things like rehearse it, modify it, extend it, plan ahead or communicate it. We can do these things because, through language, we are able to link events, or objects, that may be far apart in space and time.[24]

Experiential or tacit learning is very powerful. When we have an experience our feelings become engaged and we respond directly, apprehending the experience and the related knowledge in an immediate and sensory way. We can respond to many things at once, and the medium of language is not required.[25] Experiences result in feelings of 'really knowing' something. Compare the feeling of reading about a foreign country and then the feeling of visiting it: the learning is qualitatively different.

Real knowing occurs through experience; and much of what we learn through experience cannot be conveyed in words.[26] This tacit knowledge is the well-spring of our being, what constitutes our sense of self, and what forms our personal identities.

> Experiential learning is the process of creating and transforming experience into knowledge, skills, attitudes, values, emotions, beliefs and senses. It is the process through which individuals become themselves.[27]

The acknowledgement of the power of learning through experience is of vital importance to museums. This is one area where cultural organisations have more to offer than organisations whose sole concern is formal education. A visit to a museum offers an object-based experience; objects encode histories, memories and cultures and can be made meaningful in multiple ways. These are rich and powerful sources of learning with both short- and long-term impact. The use of museums may have specific and immediate learning outcomes, but it is equally likely that visits provide the experience and lay down the tacit knowledge that will form the prior knowledge of the future. Tacit or experiential knowledge may be used quickly, but it also remains as latent knowledge, ready to be activated when it is appropriate.

Learning through experience is learning as 'performance'. The concept of 'performativity' is complex. We have already used references to the measurement of performance, and frequently, especially in the educational (schooling) context, it is used to refer to the maximisation of efficiency and effectiveness, demonstrated through measurement and evaluation.[28] But 'performativity' as a term can be used in a second way. In a cultural studies context, 'performativity' is often used to refer to performance, in the sense of action and behaviour. Kershaw, for example, explains the use of costumed interpreters at heritage sites as one example of the 'performative frames' within which human transactions are conducted, referring here to the contemporary pervasiveness of spectacle, or being on show.[29] Hassan, in another example, points out how the verbal or non-verbal post-modern text (by which he means artwork, theatre, music, dance, etc.) invites performance and participation. Because cultural works in post-modernity are incomplete and in flux, he suggests they invite participation through the desire to complete them.[30]

'Performativity' in this sense refers to enactment, intervention, participation, involvement and response. Audiences are characterised as active, using their emotions and imagination to participate and engage with experiences as they encounter them. Bagnall explains how this is part of a new direction in the sociology of audiences which suggests that in contemporary Western societies people act both as cultural consumers (in, for example, visiting museums) but also as cultural producers (in making sense on their own terms of what they see there).[31] This sense of 'performance' is important to counteract an older view of audiences as passive.[32]

To describe learning as 'performative' is to refer to learning as participative, where bodies, minds and emotions are actively engaged, and where the multiple processes of meaning-making occur almost without conscious will.

Depths and levels of learning

In considering the scope and character of learning in cultural organisations, the concept of differentiated modes of attention is useful. Claxton suggests that attention runs along a continuum from a tight focus, such as a spotlight, to a low focus, such as a floodlight. He discusses how both are essential to learning. The 'spotlight' mode segments and analyses. It makes a sharp distinction between that which is relevant and that which is not, and focuses tightly on those elements of a situation that will enable the solving of the current problem. The floodlight mode is open and receptive and while it illuminates less brightly, may detect wider patterns and connections. Claxton describes this floodlight mode as the default mode of the brain – broad and unselective, it is essential for the generation of new ideas, and for coping with unfamiliar environments.[33] The floodlight mode describes the open-ended and unfocused way in which users sometimes cruise through museums waiting for something to attract their attention and spark off a personal response or association. The spotlight mode describes the way in which users of museums identify and 'home in' to study a group of objects, and/or when they have clearly identified objectives in mind.

Those who hold a traditional view of learning would recognise the spotlight mode as part of learning, but they would probably not recognise the floodlight mode of attention as a form of learning. And yet it is this open-ended way of being – the soft-brain mode – that is now known to be crucial to creativity, to innovation and to the generation of new solutions to problems.[34] And museums are excellent sites for exactly this kind of open-ended learning.

Teachers and educational theorists now understand learning processes much more deeply and recognise that the acquisition of facts and information cannot be separated from the feelings, values, actions and situations associated with those facts. In addition, motivation and self-awareness are now known to be basic tools for learning; learning is understood to continue throughout life with one key outcome being the construction of personal identity. Both tacit learning and verbal learning are essential; and learning can occur during times of intense focus, but also during periods when the brain is unfocused and therefore open to new ideas. Contemporary theories explain learning as multi-dimensional. It is not only multi-dimensional in scope, it occurs through multi-dimensional processes, and it will result in a diverse and multi-faceted range of outcomes. Understanding learning in a mono-dimensional way, limited to the transfer by experts of facts and information, is unhelpful for museums. Much, if not most, of the potential for learning is ignored and the potentially most significant elements of museum-based learning are negated. A different way of thinking about learning makes visible the special contribution that museums may have the potential to make to the learning society.

A critical approach to theories of learning in museums

In the past, as Falk and Dierking suggest, the approach to understanding learning in museums has focused on what has been learnt as a consequence of a visit to a museum or exhibition or attendance at a lecture.[35] With this approach to research, learning is conceptualised as intentional and purposeful, and directly linked to the content of the gallery or event that has taken place, which is expected to have resulted in changed perceptions. However, learning is frequently a more haphazard or subtle affair than this, taking the form of the reinforcement or reiteration of that which is already familiar. Much research into museum learning has focused on identifying and measuring relatively major changes in knowledge structures, which has left more subtle changes invisible and undocumented.

Falk and Dierking point out that a better research question would be: 'How does this museum, exhibition or lecture contribute to what someone knows, believes, feels, or is capable of doing?'[36] This is seen as a more appropriate approach, as 'today learning is seen as the expansion and consolidation of what is already known' and 'learning processes consist of pulling together previously unconnected facts and experience, such that a new and meaningful pattern is constructed.'[37] The comprehensive overview of research into museum-based learning presented by *Learning from museums*[38] suggests that, when an open-ended approach to research is used, visits to exhibitions and museums strengthen visitors' prior knowledge and understanding and rarely produce significant new understanding.[39]

This way of thinking about learning in museums, as the construction of meaning on the basis of prior knowledge, aligns well with the approach adopted by LIRP; and the insistence on a broader-based research question about learning is important. The work of John Falk and Lyn Dierking has been very useful in theorising museum learning and it has been widely influential. However, some internal inconsistencies in their writing are worrying. One strand of their thinking that can be regarded as problematic is their ecological approach to the concept of culture; a second problematic element is their emphasis on linking learning to functionalism. Together, these aspects point to behaviourist roots to their work, which is strengthened by a continued use of the term 'variable' to describe the diverse characteristics of learning.[40] While Falk and Dierking aim to present a view of learning that is an alternative to what they call 'traditional models of learning, such as the transmission-absorption model',[41] these inconsistencies indicate that while a great deal of their work is useful, it needs to be considered critically in the construction of a consistent approach to understanding learning.

Falk and Dierking adopt what they call an 'ecological' approach to culture, with culture defined as 'an adaptation, a social mechanism enabling individuals to survive'.[42] On the basis of this understanding of culture, they propose that the purpose of learning is accommodation to society: 'Learning results in societal members who can keep society functional and a society that defines for its members what it means to be a functional human being.'[43]

The 'ecological' approach to understanding culture and learning stems from a particular form of anthropological theory, where learning is seen as the process through which culture 'shapes the mind' of children to create the kinds of persons who will as adults be able to 'meet the imperatives of the culture'.[44] Falk and Dierking here are using the work of Ogbu, whose own references stem from Cohen, who was writing in 1971. Thinking about culture as an 'adaptation' has long been challenged, and while conceptualising learning as 'shaping the mind' initially seems unproblematic, further reading raises problems. Ogbu states: 'Learning is behaviour.'[45] He goes on to explain how anthropologists who work from this perspective have not usually researched 'what goes on inside the head of the learner'. The 'cultural frame of reference' used by Ogbu in the presentation of issues of learning related to cultural difference is overly reliant on biological and genetic factors in explaining learning.

The ecological explanation of learning is a form of behaviourist theory. Behaviourism focuses on how learning produces measurable changes in the behaviour exhibited by the learner, as opposed to focusing on how learning transforms experiences into more broadly based human attributes.[46] Behaviourism is characteristic of modernity and positivist science when it was generally believed that the only useful information about people was that which could be measured. It defines learning as: 'any more or less permanent change in behaviour which is the result of experience'.[47] As such, it is very limited.[48] It was explicitly rejected as a way of understanding or explaining learning by the LIRP team, and rejected as a way of measuring the outcomes or impact of learning. In many ways, the task of the LIRP team was to find a way of 'measuring learning' that stood in opposition to the behaviourist position.

The idea of people and society as 'functional', which forms a major part of Falk and Dierking's definition of learning,[49] raised further worries. Functionalism was the dominant paradigm in sociology and cultural anthropology in the first half of the twentieth century.[50] Functionalism assumes a society that is harmonious and where institutions work together to maintain and reproduce stable social arrangements. Society is frequently understood as though it were a biological organism, with the various parts sustaining the whole in an organic way. The definition outlined by Falk and Dierking suggests that the purpose of learning is to enable individuals to fit into pre-existing social arrangements. In this functionalist view, individuals are seen as cogs in the wheel of society, taking their place within the social machine in order to keep it operational. Functionalism has been criticised as unable to deal with social conflict and social change; consensual norms are proposed, and deviance is positioned as 'dysfunctional'.[51] How then can this approach encompass the multiple cultural perspectives that can be found in any school classroom or museum today?

A second major weakness of functionalism as a social theory is its inability to deal with meaning, and its lack of recognition of the capacity of people to create meaningful worlds.[52] If learning is characterised as 'meaning-making', and this is a key concept in the explanation of learning in museums, not least in the work of Falk and Dierking,[53] this characterisation sits uneasily within a functionalist framework.

The work of Falk and Dierking is underpinned by a lack of discussion of the specificities of learning in relation to class, gender or ethnicity. While they acknowledge that learning is 'situated', they fail to develop the significance of this for different perspectives on learning and culture. While Falk and Dierking accept that 'stories and artefacts play a critical role in transmitting culture',[54] and that objects and artefacts shape views about the self,[55] they do not consider the issue of contested artefact-based narratives that are one of the major tensions in museums today. In a post-colonial world, functionalism is not a helpful social model, and it does not offer appropriate ways to think about learning. There is a distinctly North American flavour to this approach; social analysis in North America has until recently been dominated by functionalist approaches, including the assumptions of behaviourism.[56] In Europe, the influence of French thinkers such as Bourdieu and Foucault has been strong, especially in the development of cultural studies[57] and of museum studies, and this has offered alternative ways of thinking.

LIRP and learning

LIRP was based on an understanding of culture as 'the social production and reproduction of sense, meaning and consciousness'.[58] Raymond Williams has analysed four ways of conceptualising 'culture', which include: 'culture' as 'cultivation', a training in discrimination and appreciation; 'culture' as 'high culture', the best (in terms of works of art) a society can produce; 'culture' as a whole way of life; and 'culture' as a 'realised signifying system', a dimension of all institutions. The anthropological approach to culture as a whole way of life is open to Giroux's critique, in that it ignores the histories of social struggle inherent in the locations of culture. The conceptualisation of culture that under-pinned the definition of learning used in LIRP acknowledged power relations in society, was fully aware of the existence of historical inequalities and injustices, and regarded culture as constitutive rather than reflective. That is, the displays of artefacts and the visual and textual narratives produced and reproduced in museums have the power to produce meanings that work towards constructing specific social formations.[59]

LIRP reviewed the definition of learning that was already being used by MLA and decided to use it, not least because it was already in place within *Inspiring Learning for All*. But it is also a broad open-ended way of thinking about learning that goes well beyond equating learning with the acquisition of information. It acknowledges that the cognitive and the affective are integrally linked, and it encompasses experience as a key element. However, this definition does not explicitly recognise the power relations that are inherent in social arrangements.

LIRP summarised learning as a set of complex interrelated processes that:

- are idiosyncratic and unpredictable
- are both individual and collective
- relate and shape individual learning through interactions with other people, with social spaces and with specific tools for learning
- involve personal and collective identity and the search for personal and group relevance
- are 'situated' – linked to a physical or subject-related context
- generally build upon what learners already know to make prior knowledge deeper, more explicit, and more finely developed

- more rarely involve learning things that are completely new
- result in explanations and knowledge which appear meaningful to learners but which are provisional (that is, last as long as they are useful or until they become superseded by new meanings).

Learning is circular, developing over time. Human beings strive after meaning[60] and this is what provokes learning. Information and experience is used as and when it becomes personally useful and may be ignored, forgotten, or remain at a tacit level unless needed. Knowledge, in this formulation, is knowledge *in use*, in a social situation, or as part of a community of practice. This explanation of learning accepts the active role of the individual mind in making meaning. Prior knowledge is a vital part of making meaning. Sotto puts it this way:

> If I have a working model of what is being talked about already inside my head, I am able to follow what is being said. But if I do not have such a working model, . . . I may understand the individual *words* being said to me but I do not really understand their full *meaning*. The result is I begin to lose track of what is being said to me.[61]

It also recognises that individual meaning is mediated among and between communities of interpretation,[62] and communities of practice.[63] That is, the making of meaning (which is one way of describing learning) is a social or collective endeavour, even though meaning is produced by individuals, with interpretations of experience being tested and validated through the communities that shape our lives (school, family, workplace or leisure communities).

The emphasis in this way of thinking about learning is on learners rather than teachers. This is a broad way of thinking about learning that includes everyday problem-solving as well as formal teaching. The emphasis on the facilitation of learning means that appropriate teaching methods will be selected, so that where a formal didactic approach is the most suitable for learners (as in many formal educational organisations), this will be chosen. Equally, however, it is acknowledged that formal teaching does not suit all learners and all forms or spaces of knowledge, and so other methods that emphasise active, sensory and experienced-based learning will also be deployed.

The approach taken by LIRP to understanding learning was one of the first steps in the development of a cultural theory of learning, one that acknowledges that museum meanings shape social and individual identities, that they may be contested, and that learning in museums takes place in a contested arena. This is a dynamic approach to learning, one that is fully aware that not all cultural narratives, or cultural arrangements, empower all people. The approach to measuring learning taken by LIRP was premised on the belief that world views are produced within specific gendered, class-based, cultural contexts, that these world views are therefore perspectival, stemming from different perspectives or judgements about how the world works, and that sometimes these world views are incommensurate – that is, they are not reconcilable. This does make opposing views intrinsically 'wrong'. Indeed, it is in the struggle to sustain and represent our own views and values in a context of opposition, that self-awareness, and thus learning, is grounded.[64] Critical pedagogy enables an engagement with this through encouraging an analysis of norms, which opens up rather than closes down the possibility of challenge and change.

Conclusion

The understanding of learning that underpinned LIRP acknowledged social and cultural difference and the resulting perspectival character of knowledge. It understood culture as a system of producing meaning, and, from a basis in social constructivism, it perceived 'reality' as multiple.[65] It saw learning as integral to everyday life, rather than limited to specific educational moments; as such it adopted a lifelong learning position. Learning was understood as constructivist and experiential/performative, involving active minds and bodies. Learning was perceived as one way in which individual identities were produced.

The explanation of learning developed by LIRP was discussed and accepted by the stakeholders of the research by March 2002. It made possible the identification of learning outcomes that could be found in museums, archives and libraries and it underpinned the evolution of the five generic learning outcomes that formed the framework for the measuring of learning in museums that would later follow. The approach to learning used by LIRP was, as presented earlier, informed by contemporary learning and cultural theory and fully acknowledged the complex, unpredictable and multiple character of learning. But at the same time, MLA needed a method of 'measuring learning' that produced data which could be quantified. MLA wanted to be able to produce a composite picture of learning across their sector. Evidence needed to be comparable across museums, archives and libraries, and able to be aggregated from evidence from individual institutions. The concept of *generic* learning outcomes offered a method of combining data from different sources in order to produce a large-scale picture of cultural learning, and it is to an examination of these generic learning outcomes that we will now proceed.

4

The Generic Learning Outcomes: a conceptual and interpretive framework

The last two chapters have discussed the conceptualisation of 'measurement', 'outcomes' and 'learning' that shaped the LIRP approach to evaluating educational performance in cultural organisations. This chapter discusses how these ideas were used to identify a suite of learning outcomes that were agreed by the research stakeholders as appropriate for museums, archives and libraries. Five Generic Learning Outcomes were identified and these are described here. The GLOs, as they came to be known, were tested in 15 cultural sites through small-scale research projects carried out by the staff of the various organisations. Once the pilot projects were complete, and after considerable collective discussion and some small modifications, the GLOs were accepted. They were perceived as sufficiently diverse to encompass all potential learning outcomes, easy to understand and as providing a language with which to talk about the multiple dimensions and outcomes of learning.

The pilot projects exposed a range of levels of research expertise which the devising of a research framework could not be expected to address. The original idea when LIRP was commissioned was that a 'Toolkit' could be devised that would (magically) enable staff in museums, archives and libraries to draw up a picture of the learning that occurred in their organisations. What had not been sufficiently considered was that carrying out research and evaluation demands high-level expertise, knowledge and experience; the identification of a research methodology could not provide the staff development that was required. It was perhaps thought that a single research tool, such as a short questionnaire, could be devised that would be able to be used in all organisations across the cultural field; in the event, what LIRP proposed was an interpretive framework, a conceptual structure that could be used in common by diverse researchers.

The gradual realisation that this was the best way forward emerged because of a number of factors, including the close working relationship between the commissioners of the research and the research team; the length of time taken to develop the conceptual framework; the discussions with an unusually large and differentiated group of professional staff from across the three domains (libraries, archives, museums); and the desire to gain the trust of these professionals so that the approach eventually devised would actually be used. There was perhaps also a collective feeling of hope that, after decades of embattled effort to move cultural education forward, the need to 'measure' its 'outcomes' would actually achieve this.

Learning and its strategies

As described in Chapter 3, contemporary educational research suggests that people are born learners, that learning is a natural and lifelong process, and that the most basic outcome of learning is personal meaning. This way of thinking about learning is appropriate and useful when thinking about learning in the open, rich, diverse and informal environments for learning that are offered by museums, archives and libraries, and it was accepted as a basis for further work by the research stakeholders. It was also agreed that individual learning is highly diverse and unpredictable; that learning involves a range of modes of attention, from open and diffuse to tightly focused, all of which are equally valuable; that users in museums, archives and libraries will vary in the depth and level of their immersion in learning; and that learning in the different cultural organisations is differentiated.[1] Having achieved this collective understanding, the next task was to identify appropriate learning outcomes. This was not straightforward.

Where formal curricula are in place with specific subjects defined and established, specific learning outcomes can be set out in advance which can be linked to appropriate levels and standards. In museums, archives and libraries, specific learning outcomes cannot be established in advance in the same way. Often, these outcomes in the formal education sector are the result of a review of what learners should be able to achieve by the end of a specific set period of instruction. The classic behaviourist approach describes a 'needs assessment' and the identification of the gap between an 'existing condition' (in the learners) and the 'desired condition'. The learning outcomes should be structured around the learner's behaviour that should be changed to achieve this desired condition.[2] Such a 'needs assessment' is not appropriate for casual users of museums, archives and libraries, and would be impossible to carry out anyway. It would also be extremely unethical to identify a 'desired condition' for cultural learners 'to achieve' and to try to move visitors towards this position. While the expression 'baseline' was used more than once in discussions with the research stakeholders, and it is still in use in discussions about impact studies,[3] it was agreed that this could not take the form of a measurement of what people knew prior to entering a museum, archive or library. It was also accepted that it would not be appropriate for cultural organisations to 'set standards' that their users had to attain.

The formal educational systems that societies establish enable the acquisition of knowledge, skills, attitudes and values designed to enable individuals to create meaningful lives. Formal qualifications and induction into recognised cognitive, subject-based and professional structures are important as individuals establish their own life-ways and identities. Equally, the cultural sector can enable learning that deepens the knowledge and experience of individuals. Learning within cultural organisations is more open-ended than learning in formal learning. It offers greater opportunity for creativity and increased motivation. There is no curriculum and it is not examined. A different range of skills, attitudes and behaviours are required from learners. Learning frequently occurs within groups, which may be family or friendship groups, but equally it might be structured in relation to the needs of groups within formal educational systems, such as school groups. Much of the learning is collaborative and exploratory.

The idea of generic as opposed to individual learning outcomes had already been identified as potentially fruitful as this approach offered the possibility of producing a large-scale picture of learning across a number of different learners and institutions. In beginning to identify appropriate generic learning outcomes, Claxton's 'learning toolkit' was useful. Claxton's definition of learning had already proved relevant; it was sufficiently broad to be able to accommodate what was already known about learning in museums. Claxton was clear that learning encompassed many different sorts of things, including knowledge, which develop into opinions; know-how (practical skills such as riding a bike or making a cake); discriminations and judgements; preferences; dispositions; aspects of character; emotional range. Learning, he says, 'changes not just our knowing and our doing, but our being too'.[4] Claxton was also clear that learning happens in a great variety of ways, and that learning power can be developed. Much of his book is concerned with the development of this power to learn. Defining learning as 'what you do when you don't know what to do', Claxton suggests that a personal learning toolkit is used in learning. He identifies four main parts to his learning toolkit:

- Immersion in experience – exploration, investigation, experimentation, social interaction and imitation
- Imagination – fantasy, visualisation, story-telling to create and explore hypothetical worlds
- Intellectual skills – language, reasoning, analysis, communication
- Intuition – creativity, germination of ideas.[5]

The learning toolkit takes the form of generic learning strategies which are used selectively as they are found to be appropriate and useful. These are:

- Experience-based strategies – exploration, investigation, experimentation, use of space and resources
- Creative strategies – imagination, intuition, fantasy, visualisation, story-telling, play, role-play, making something, germination of ideas
- Intellectual strategies – language, reasoning, analysis, communication
- Social interaction strategies – discussion, show and tell, share with friends or family, modify ideas after discussion, imitation, modelling, demonstrating.

These generic strategies for learning are familiar strategies used in museum-based learning. The four strategies – experience-based, creative, intellectual and socially interactive strategies – do in fact describe well what people do in libraries, archives and museums. These four strategies result in variable, unpredictable and personalised individual learning experiences. The strategies and the learning toolkit demonstrated that it was possible to devise a generic scheme that could, in a simple but complex way, encompass myriad individualised learning experiences. If the limited number of strategies could be linked to a limited number of outcomes, then it might be possible to devise a similarly simple-but-complex approach that focused on the outcomes rather than the strategies of learning.

Developing an appropriate set of generic learning outcomes for the cultural sector

Learning in cultural organisations can take myriad forms. In all cases, except perhaps those of formal group visits (schools, colleges), learners have their own individual reasons for visiting a museum or using a library or archive; they set their own agendas for the visit, which may be more or less (and probably less) focused on learning something specific. In these instances, the idea of setting learning outcomes in advance was problematic. Who would set them? The staff of the organisation? Clearly not. The learners themselves? This was also doubtful; people are rarely so clearly focused when visiting cultural organisations.

It became clear that a new way of thinking about learning outcomes was needed. This approach would need to be broader and looser than the classic behaviourist approach, relevant to the ways in which museums, archives and libraries were actually used, and one which fitted the cultural approach to learning that had been developed as part of the work of LIRP.

If the concept of establishing learning outcomes in advance was tricky, the idea of mapping what actually occurred had potential. It was known that while people generally did not set themselves specific aims to achieve when, for example, visiting a museum, something generally did happen. And given the very wide and open definition of learning that had been agreed, combined with the concept of *generic* learning outcomes, a scheme began to emerge. It began to seem possible to gather data from people who had used museums, archives and libraries, and to then gather up the data into specific categories. If the categories could be sufficiently broad, and if there were enough of them to encompass every kind of potential outcome across all types of museum, archive or library, then a general picture could be developed, as the data from individual research sites was combined.

Claxton's learning toolkit presented a basis from which the idea of generic learning outcomes could be developed. A draft set of learning strategies and outcomes was developed by May 2002 (see Table 4.1). A distinction was made between the generic learning strategies that would form the basis of research and enquiry and the generic learning outcomes that presented categories for analysis and interpretation of the research data.

As LIRP formed part of the development of *Inspiring Learning for All*, MLA was rightly concerned to test the ideas of the LIRP team against the perceptions of cultural practitioners, staff working in libraries, archives and museums. The embryonic generic learning outcomes were fully discussed and analysed as they developed, and were modified through collective discussion. Each of the generic

Table 4.1 The first attempt at developing a set of generic learning outcomes for the cultural sector

Claxton's generic learning strategies
(Processes to be researched)

Experience-based strategies
Creative strategies
Intellectual strategies
Social interaction strategies

First draft of generic learning outcomes
(Categories for analysis and interpretation of data within each organisation and across the three domains and the sector as a whole)

Knowledge
Skills for use in the cultural sector
Other skills
Inspiration/enjoyment
Personal identity
Critical thinking
Values for diversity
Progression

learning outcomes could be supported by evidence from earlier RCMG evaluations, or other research. In addition, towards the beginning of LIRP in November and December 2001, the research team had interviewed people leaving archives, museums and libraries in a number of venues across England to see what they said about their experience. These conversations also produced evidence of the multiple dimensions of the learning that had taken place immediately beforehand (see Table 4.2).

Each generic outcome was intended to be commodious and to capture the richness and complexity of multiple learning experiences. Some (by no means all, of course) of the possible 'contents' of each outcome are indicated in Table 4.3.

Discussions continued as the concept of 'generic learning outcomes' was thoroughly reviewed and assessed by members of the LIRP team, members of MLA, the consultants developing the *Inspiring Learning for All* framework,[6] the Thinktank for *Inspiring*, and the cultural organisations who were working to develop and pilot the *Inspiring* framework.[7] As the concept became more familiar and seemed to have the potential to do what was needed, 15 libraries, museums and archives were selected which would be involved in piloting the use of the generic learning outcomes in their own research.

The review of the use of generic learning outcomes in other educational fields had produced examples of how generic learning outcomes could be expressed, and this was helpful up to a point. Where examples could be found that were already being

Table 4.2 The draft generic learning outcomes with supporting evidence from earlier evaluations and LIRP interviews (excerpt from draft report dated 26 May 2002)

First draft of generic learning outcomes (with a selection of the supporting evidence)	
Knowledge	'I visited the archive because I am doing research for a book and I managed to do that.' (LIRP/01/CP)
Skills/knowledge for use in the cultural sector	'Anne taught me a lot about ways of using artefacts.' (Clarke et al., 2002: 23)
Specific and transferable skills	'We've done real research skills.' (Clarke et al., 2002: 15)
Inspiration/excitement/ enjoyment/curiosity	'I'm retired and I read for pleasure, as a hobby.' (LIRP/01/JV)
Positive personal identity	'I've created the most unbelievable piece of work I've ever done.' (Hooper-Greenhill and Nicol, 2001: 62)
Critical and ethical thinking	'It has confirmed my conviction that literacy is a skill that runs through people's learning.' (Clarke et al., 2002: 14)
Values appropriate to a culturally diverse society	'This is done by an Indian man . . . and it shows that not only the West can draw.' (Hooper-Greenhill and Moussouri, 2001: 15)
Progression	'*Represent* gave me a job and the chance to prove it could work, and I feel differently to how I used to.' (Hooper-Greenhill and Dodd, 2002: 21)

used by government-sponsored bodies, this was regarded as useful. In a challenging political environment, if the expression 'positive learner identity' was being used by a research project already being funded by a government research council such as the Economic and Social Research Council, this was all to the good.[8] It was interesting to note, however, that the emphasis for appropriate learning outcomes in the context of formal education, such as those suggested in the guidelines produced for the development of learning outcomes for university-level study,[9] concentrated on the development of knowledge and skills, with less attention paid to the development of attitudes, and barely a mention of enjoyment or creativity.

It was decided that the generic learning outcomes for the cultural sector would be explicit about enjoyment and inspiration as a possible learning outcome. It had been marked in earlier studies that this was of great significance when people discussed their cultural experiences. This decision was to be very important as the research based on the GLOs later produced consistent findings of the importance of enjoyment and inspiration to teachers and their pupils using museums.

By the end of June 2002, the number and range of generic learning outcomes had been considerably simplified. While the commodious capacity of each outcome was always insisted upon, it was felt that there were confusing overlaps in the categorisation of statements made by learners. During seminars with project participants, statements made by museum, library and archive users were discussed and categorised by project participants, and it gradually became clear that the broadest and most abstract categories would be the most useful. A simplified set of categories of generic learning outcomes was devised (see Table 4.4).

The five categories of outcome were fleshed out with suggested 'content' to indicate how they could be used to group up certain kinds of statements (Table 4.5).

Table 4.3 The draft generic learning outcomes under development (excerpt from draft report dated 26 May 2002)

Knowledge/understanding
 Specific objects, books, documents – e.g. Chinese scrolls, sculpture
 Local or personal matters – e.g. my family, my neighbourhood
 Specific subjects – e.g. history, science, art
 Connections within and across subjects

Skills/knowledge in using cultural organisations
 About the site (history, geography, use)
 About processes/products (reading objects, using a document)

Specific and transferable skills
 Practical (craft-based, manipulative)
 Cognitive, emotional
 Numeracy, communication, ICT
 Subject-related skills (mapping, estimating)

Inspiration/excitement/enjoyment/curiosity
 Creativity and personal enrichment
 Fun
 Making new connections, lateral thinking
 Increased motivation

Positive personal identity
 Self-esteem, self-respect
 Confidence, independence
 Sense of self in community
 Understanding and relating to others, team-working
 Sense of personal achievement/capacity

Critical and ethical thinking
 Moral issues
 Differing values and perspectives, alternative histories
 Developing questions, analyses, hypotheses, linking far and near

Values appropriate to a culturally diverse society
 Understanding and relating to others, respect for others
 Accepting and valuing difference, tolerance
 Individual or social cultural action, social responsibility

Progression
 To employment
 To further use of this/other cultural site
 To further learning/involvement

Table 4.4 The categories of generic learning outcomes as agreed by summer 2002
(excerpt from report dated 12 July 2002)

Knowledge and understanding
Skills: intellectual, practical, professional
Values and attitudes
Creativity, inspiration and enjoyment
Activity and behaviour

Table 4.5 The generic learning outcomes as agreed with suggested detailed content
(excerpt from report dated 12 July 2002)

Knowledge and understanding
    Subject-specific (e.g. history, science)
    Between and across subjects
    Specific artefacts, books, documents (Chinese scroll, vase)
    Site-specific (history, geography, use of site)
    Locality, neighbourhood, region, country
    Self, personal matters (my family)
    Others (my neighbours past and present)

Skills
    Subject-specific (mapping, estimating, painting)
    Site-specific (how to use a library, archive, museum)
    Practical (craft-based, manipulative, bodily–kinesthetic)
    Transferable (working in teams, using a computer)
    Key (numeracy, literacy, communication)
    Critical and ethical thinking
    Other cognitive skills
    Emotional skills (managing anger, or powerful feelings)

Values, attitudes, feelings
    Motivation (to learn more, become interested, feel confident)
    About oneself (positive personal identity, self-esteem, self-respect, confidence,
    independence, sense of personal achievement, sense of self in the community)
    About others (tolerance of difference)
    About museums, archives, libraries

Creativity, inspiration, enjoyment
    Personal enrichment
    Fun
    Making new connections, lateral thinking
    Generation of new ideas or actions
    Making and producing things
    Invention
    Experimentation

Behaviour (now and in the future/looking back)
    Doing more of something (reading, visiting an archive, learning)
    Doing something different (visiting a museum for the first time, going to college)
    Bringing others (family, friends)
    Working in teams
    Employment, work placement

51

These five dimensions represent broad generic categories or classes of learning. The use of these categories enables the identification of the outcomes of learning along each of these dimensions. The Generic Learning Outcomes, which have become known as the GLOs, were to remain largely in this form, although one or two small changes were made following the pilot research projects. They were presented in diagrammatic form on the MLA website (Figure 4.1).

Each GLO was now presented to indicate a degree of progression, where this was thought to be relevant; thus Understanding is placed *after* Knowledge in Knowledge and Understanding, and Enjoyment was moved to *precede* Inspiration. The indication of depth of outcome reminds us that learning may be both slight and profound and may proceed from the one to the other. Thus learners may experience enjoyment, which leads on to inspiration and then to the creation of something new. 'Progression' was added to the Activity and Behaviour outcome; this refers to purposeful action, such as joining a library, which leads to change.

The next section of this chapter discusses each of the five outcome categories in turn, and gives examples of each from some of the pilot (and earlier) research projects.[10]

Figure 4.1 The GLOs as presented on the MLA website

The five Generic Learning Outcomes

Knowledge and understanding

Knowledge and understanding includes learning facts or information (knowing 'what' or knowing 'about') and developing a deeper understanding, or grasping meaning more firmly, in relation to diverse specific fields. Well-known information may take on a new relevance or be understood in a new way during a museum, archive or library visit. Knowledge can be acquired in a range of ways, through reading, listening, talking, looking and trying things out in a practical way. Learners will have preferred ways of acquiring knowledge. Knowledge itself (facts and information) does not result in understanding until it has been linked by the learner to what he or she already knows and understands. Understanding is personal, individual and developed by learners to explain to themselves how things work. Understanding is always on the learner's terms. Again, learners will have their own preferred ways of developing their understanding, which may be reflective or physically active.

Knowledge and understanding might be subject-specific, or might result in making connections between or across subject areas. Disciplinary divisions, while not entirely arbitrary, are often fluid and conventional. Working from cultural artefacts these conventional distinctions can often be exposed and lead to new perspectives on knowing and learning. Is a historical portrait art or history? Is a historical diary history or English? Does it matter and who decides, for what reason? Knowledge and understanding can also include the discovery of new information about oneself, one's family, neighbourhood, or personal world.

> *I gained an insight into life in major cities and how it is different to my life.*
>
> Teenage Library User in Poole

Learning outcomes in relation to knowledge and understanding can relate to specific cultural organisations.

> *We thoroughly enjoyed our visit and learnt a lot of what you do and how we can benefit if we want to research anything ourselves.*
>
> Somerset Record Office group visit

Increased knowledge can be indicated by the ability to give specific information; to name things, people and places; and to give details. For example, a child's thank-you letter to Warwickshire Museums included the statement:

> *when you went to sketch, that rock did look very like a sandwich. I can remember their names, they are Hook Norton limestone and Clypeus grit.*

Increased understanding can be indicated by showing connections or links, clarifying, describing in detail, making relationships and offering assessments.

Skills: intellectual, practical, professional

Skills refer to knowing how to do something. Skills outcomes result from the experience of doing something. Skills can be broadly divided into cognitive/ intellectual, social, emotional and physical dimensions. Using the imagination can also be seen as a skill, especially in relation to empathy and creativity. Each of these can also be further subdivided, and there may well be some skills that overlap two or more dimensions.

Different formal learning programmes list different skills according to their objectives. These can include 'key skills' such as numeracy, communication, use of ICT, and learning how to learn. Each of these might also be further subdivided; for example, communication skills can include writing, speaking, listening, giving a presentation, making a TV programme. Cognitive or intellectual skills fall into these kinds of areas. The information management skills that can be strongly developed in libraries and archives can be placed in this field.

Following Essex Libraries Big Summer Read programme a parent wrote:

> *It does have an effect on reading, certainly with my son, it maintains his fluency and familiarity with words.*

A 13- to 14-year-old wrote after a visit to the Imperial War Museum:

> *I have learnt to look at the exhibits and reflect on why they are there and their importance.*

Social skills are frequently developed during cultural visits. These include communication with others, team-working and developing relationships. Emotional skills such as managing anger or frustration will perhaps be observed more rarely in museums, archives or libraries, but the study of many books, documents or artefacts can result in strong emotional responses. Physical skills might be bodily skills such as running or dancing, or manipulative skills such as making a corn-dolly. These could be found after practical workshops.

Attitudes and values

Attitudes and values are developed by learners as an integral part of their learning in both formal and informal environments. As new information is absorbed, attitudes to that information are developed, and these attitudes contribute to the formation of the values that inform the decisions people make about how to live their lives. Visits to museums, archives and libraries can result in shifts or change in attitudes, and can sometimes be seen to alter the values that people hold. With young learners, where attitudes can change frequently and values are still to be firmly established, there are considerable opportunities to influence their development. It is highly possible that the effects on values and attitudes will not be apparent in the short term; and they may be forming without the learner's conscious awareness.

Attitudes to oneself affect personal decisions and levels of achievement. Visits to cultural organisations can result in more positive personal attitudes, increased confidence and greater comfort with new ideas and risk-taking. For example, following an information skills training session at the University of Leicester library, one student said:

I feel much happier about requesting and getting hold of information.

On the other hand, where the visit has not been a positive experience, more negative attitudes may prevail. People may feel less self-confident, less secure, and less determined.

Attitudes to other people are part of basic values. Positive visits to museums, archives and libraries may result in increased tolerance for diversity and difference, perhaps based on new information about different ways to worship, learn or think. On the other hand, sometimes cultural visits may be used to confirm negative views about people and things. It is not always possible to change long-held views.

Empathy is an important component of this dimension of learning. Empathy is the ability to share, understand and feel another person's feelings, or to enter into the spirit of something such as a book or piece of music or art. Using the imagination to aid learning is an important skill. Empathy may relate to the present or the past. A child said after a visit to a Victorian classroom reconstruction at St John's Museum in Warwick:

It was really scary and it felt like you were in a real Victorian classroom.

Developing an appreciation of multiple perspectives, understanding cultural difference and tolerating complexity are some potential outcomes in this dimension of learning.

Attitudes to cultural organisations are very often an outcome of the experience of using a museum, archive or library. Good experiences lead to positive learning outcomes. Someone wrote in the Somerset Record Office website guest-book:

It is so fantastic to be able to search and then get information right from source. . . . The staff at the SRO have been so supportive.

Poor experiences will result in more negative outcomes where someone has learnt that the organisation does not suit them.

Museums are not welcoming to us. I get the feeling you have to look round silently and it is difficult with children, they want to talk and ask questions. You have the staff walking round and following you, feel constantly observed.[11]

Enjoyment, inspiration, creativity

Enjoyment as an outcome of learning is likely to lead to the development of positive learner identities and to the desire to repeat the experience. When learning is enjoyable, it is easier, and may sometimes take people by surprise. One young visitor to the Woman's Library wrote:

I love the Dewey numbers and I learnt a lot.

Creativity, invention and innovative ways of thinking and doing can result from visits to museums, archives and libraries. These are open-ended learning environments, where learners can control the pace, direction and focus of their own learning and can remain open to new insights, connections and relationships. The unselective and un-focused mode of attention that sometimes characterises the way people use museums and libraries – browsing through the shelves and the displays, waiting for something to stand out – is an essential component of the generation of new ideas.

Where exploration and experimentation can be offered, creativity, inspiration and enjoyment may result. Visiting a museum, archive or library may result in feeling inspired about the way someone behaved. A young teenager visiting the Holocaust exhibition at the Imperial War Museum, London was inspired by:

> *Martin Luther King and how he was brave enough to stand up to America.*

A visitor to Wolverhampton Museum and Art Gallery used the gallery to lift her out of her everyday routine:

> *I think you spend most of your life living from one day to the next, thinking about bills, thinking about going to work, driving up and down the motorway or something – you go to an art gallery and you are living and experiencing art. It's a higher form of living. It's a higher form of living in your head and it's challenging. It's what keeps the human race evolving I think.*[12]

Visits to cultural organisations can also result in the production of new things. A six-year-old gallery user said:

> *I think it was great with all the sculptures and paintings and the building was new and called SCVA and when we was at the gallery we made our own sketch book and we got into teams and we wrote all the feelings we could think about.*[13]

Activity,[14] behaviour, progression

Activity and behaviour may be observed, remembered, or intended. Activity and behaviour refers to actions – what people do. It does not refer to manners, which is one dictionary definition for behaviour.[15] The things that people do, their actions and activities, are the result of their learning. Activity and behaviour as learning outcomes include the way people balance and manage their lives, including their work, study or family contexts. Some activities may be innovative and creative, some less so.

It may be possible to observe certain kinds of activity or behaviour during use of museums, archives and libraries; or people may report what they did during a visit. For example, a visitor to an exhibition at Leeds Art Gallery which experimented with using sound as part of the experience of the exhibition wrote on a label that acted as a comment card:

> *I think the sound makes the viewer use all the senses. I found myself more involved in actually stopping and looking.*

This visitor is reporting on the way their use of the exhibition changed as a result of responding to the experience of the sound. This can be seen as a short-term learning outcome.

Activity or behaviour may indicate longer-term learning outcomes. For example, repeat visitors to the Australian Museum in Sydney told the museum researcher Lynda Kelly that several different kinds of activity had resulted from a former visit to the exhibition *Indigenous Australians*. This included buying a book related to the exhibition, buying Aboriginal artworks, bringing others to see the exhibition, and returning to the exhibition themselves.[16] While these activities and behaviour do not tell us what knowledge, attitudes or values led to the actions taken, the fact that they were taken does indicate that learning has occurred. Behaviour can suggest that learning has happened, but only further investigation with the learner (through interviews and discussions) will reveal what that learning was.

One outcome of learning may be the intention to do something for the first time, do something more frequently, or do it in a different way. Comments about the intention to act in a certain way can be interpreted as a learning outcome. For example, an email to Essex Record Office stated:

> *Thank you for your excellent reply. I am thoroughly impressed by the speed, depth and clarity of your response. The information is wonderful and I will be following up on all your suggestions.*

This statement indicates strongly that the information given has been assimilated and certain actions are planned on the basis of that information.

Sometimes learning outcomes in relation to behaviour can be very profound. Increased skills can change the way lives are lived. A comment card in Leamington Library read as follows:

> *I come here to practise. I am just learning to use the computers. The computer is now an accessory for living.*

Use of the library over a period of time has resulted in managing daily life in a new way. Progression can be seen as the result of action that has achieved a change, such as is indicated in the example above.

Piloting the GLOs and the issues arising

The GLOs were piloted in 15 museums, archives and libraries between September 2002 and February 2003. These organisations were chosen to give the best possible coverage of the diversity of museums, archives and libraries with reference to size and mission of the organisation, governing body and geographical location. Experience of working in educational delivery, or of impact research was not part of the selection criteria for the LIRP pilot organisations as the capacity to measure learning was intended to be available to all and any organisation, not just those with specialist staff. The pilot organisations were chosen from those already involved in piloting *Inspiring Learning for All*. Training was given prior to the LIRP pilot phase, and LIRP team members supported the pilot organisations through site visits, telephone and email contact, and group meetings during their work.

The aim of the pilot phase was to test the GLO conceptual framework in relation to its value across the diversity of organisations. The 15 organisations developed individual plans for generating, analysing and interpreting evidence of learning. These included using the GLOs to analyse existing data, to improve tools for data generation, and to drive the development of new projects for measuring learning outcome. While these three approaches were designed as part of the pilot phase, in addition, the GLOs were used in a number of other ways, including staff training, briefing designers, and future planning for the institution through incorporation into a business plan.

Data was gathered, coded according to the GLOs, analysed in either a quantitative way (counting the occurrence of each GLO and producing tables of comparative statistics) or in a qualitative way (describing the range and depth of evidence in relation to each GLO). The findings were interpreted in various ways and reports were produced by all pilot sites according to a given proforma. All the 15 organisations produced a project report. All completed the work more or less within the time-frame. The piloting process was absolutely vital in both testing the conceptual framework and in revealing the issues that would arise as museums, libraries and archives set about 'measuring learning' through using the eventual intended outcome, an instructive website that would form part of the *Inspiring Learning for All* website.

The pilot phase revealed that many of the participants were unused to thinking about or talking about learning. Learning was discussed in different ways across the sectors, with a range of views about delivering and facilitating learning in libraries, archives and museums. Developing a way of generating, analysing and interpreting evidence of the outcomes of learning represented a steep learning curve for many. One way in which this was demonstrated was in the reports of the pilot projects; in the majority of reports no claims were made on the basis of the evidence of learning that was collected. While evidence for learning outcome was found in all institutions and was presented in the appendices, many participants lacked the experience to interpret the evidence and to make confident claims based on it. Increasing the understanding of learning across museums, archives and libraries emerged as a big issue that demanded capacity-building across the sector.

It quickly became clear that organisations were not asking their users about learning very much at all. Even where educational programmes were being evaluated, the focus was on satisfaction with the organisation's provision rather than on the learning outcomes of this provision. Once the focus of evaluation was shifted, more useful evidence of the outcome of learning began to emerge. The participants in the pilot studies did not always distinguish between statements that gave evidence of learning outcome, and statements that made more general comments. Coding in relation to each GLO was also a problem for some. There were instances of multiple coding and mis-coding. Some people were worried about bias and subjectivity.

A further issue to arise from the pilot phase was the lack of experience of many (but not all) participants in carrying out evaluation research. In addition, where participants had experience of research, this was highly variable. Some, especially in the library domain, were very familiar with working with quantitative data, but were much less comfortable with the qualitative approaches that are necessary to gather in-depth evidence of the outcome of learning. Some, on the other hand, were more comfortable and confident in working with qualitative evidence but were not familiar with research design, basic quantification or clear reporting techniques. Subsequently, advice on these procedures was built into the website.

The pilot phase confirmed that the proposed GLOs could be used as generic categories for measuring the range of learning outcomes that emerged. Evidence was found for each GLO and no additional GLOs were thought to be required. While there was some initial scepticism about their value, this proved to be unfounded.

> The outcome of the data analysis did not justify initial scepticism. Although standard comment and complaint forms, and user surveys, yielded very little, other more focused sources were surprisingly fruitful. The exercise repaid the work that it demanded and yielded valuable insights both in respect of the most effective ways of collecting rich data and the most effective ways of facilitating learning.[17]

Finding the time to carry out the work during the pilot period was a major issue for many, especially those who had not carried out evaluation research before. However, those who were familiar with this way of working used their normal methods of integrating evaluation into their daily practices without difficulty.

The generic learning outcomes were welcomed by the pilot organisations as they offered a way in which demands to demonstrate performativity could be met. Many organisations could see ways in which reporting on learning outcomes could link to their existing evidence-delivery requirements, and listed these in their reports. In addition, some of the participants pointed out how working with the GLOs had begun to build a stronger professional community within their organisation:

> Working on the pilot has enabled the formation of a learning culture within Culture and Community by bringing staff at all levels together. The Generic Learning Outcomes have given us a language and a framework to demonstrate to more traditional learning providers the unique contribution that museums, archives and libraries make to the learning agenda. This will help us to develop local learning partnerships to deliver community learning based on individual learners' needs. It will also help us to make more effective bids for external funding as we can now demonstrate learning outcomes.[18]

However, the general lack of experience in understanding and researching learning and its outcomes suggested that considerable support would be needed in building capacity. The GLO approach formed a strong basis on which to build, but could not be sufficient in itself to produce professionals who were experienced and confident in researching and presenting evidence of the impact of learning in museums, archives and libraries. The research reports pointed out that this was the beginning of a long-term process, and that while pilot participants were very enthusiastic about the GLOs and the potential of this approach, the skills required to use it well would need time to develop.

The value of the GLOs to the cultural sector

The interpretive framework offered by the GLOs was based on constructivist and socio-cultural learning theory[19] and also the adoption of the definition of learning used by the Campaign for Learning in the UK. Taking critical account of diverse approaches to learning outcomes (including those in the US), the GLOs go beyond earlier, frequently behaviourist, approaches to this idea. They consist of a conceptual framework for developing research questions, designing research tools and analysing and interpreting research findings that is particularly appropriate to the multi-dimensional, creative and open-ended learning environment of the museum and other cultural organisations.

Holmes describes how 'outcomes' are used as a shorthand for pre-determined competences and skills, for specific proscribed requirements which are set out in advance.[20] This is not how the GLOs work. They provide a language for the description of individual experience, but there are no external measures to be achieved. While teachers and museum educators may have directions in which they want experience to go, and they can use the GLOs to talk about this, the learning outcomes are open-ended rather than set in advance. The GLOs are not targets to be met.

Following a learning experience or event, individuals frequently talk about what has happened to them and what they feel about things in personal ways. These results of learning might be short term or long term; they might be intense or shallow; they may be deeply experienced such that awareness increases, attitudes and perceptions changed, or, and this is more frequent, they may confirm learners in what they already know (however mistaken others might feel this knowledge to be[21]). Records of these personal accounts (individual learning outcomes) are susceptible to categorisation into more generic outcomes. The GLOs can be seen as a way of capturing and encoding ineffable qualities such as experience, pleasure or creativity.

The GLOs can be deployed using a range of research methods. Based on an interpretivist ontology,[22] which recognises multiple standpoints for making meaning and for constructing both generalised world views and interpretations of specific events, the GLOs can be used to shape both quantitative and qualitative research. In researching the deep outcomes of learning, qualitative methods are needed, and this poses particular problems when the research is conducted within a policy climate that demands quantification, and where policy makers have a particular view of what counts as 'science'. Ethnographic approaches, including case studies and flexible research instruments, need to be considered in the development of research into the outcomes of museum-based learning, but equally, for the findings to be taken seriously by policy makers, these findings need some level of quantification. The GLOs offer a method for conceptual linking of quantitative and qualitative evidence. The GLOs open up the highly variable activities and experiences of museum education to a systematic analysis; and in categorising and classifying things that could not be discussed before they begin to create a discourse.[23]

Post-modern educational theorists Usher, Bryant and Johnston point out that it is through language and practice that discourses are 'domained' into being.[24] The GLOs provide a shared language for museum education, one which is recognised by those educational fields with which it overlaps; for example, schooling and adult education.

> We expect the use of the GLOs to become common practice, embedded into our project planning and evaluation. It is a vocabulary through which we can describe what we achieve. The fact that it is being done across the country gives it great weight and credibility.[25]

This shared language begins to constitute a more tangible discursive field, bound together through shared ways of talking about the intangible processes of learning from culture.[26] The use of a shared language enables the recognition of a distinct field of practice, a 'surfacing' or 'bringing to visibility' of museum education. As Bourdieu shows, talking about something and using the specialist language constitutes it as valuable. The discourse constitutes the field.[27]

The GLOs enable engagement with current government agendas and the demand for performativity and accountability. This can be described as one element of governmentalism; the measurement of educational performance brings museums more centrally into the management of education and culture. While the increased emphasis on performativity may be experienced as burdensome by those who feel too exposed, for those who wish to increase that exposure it offers strategies to achieve increased visibility. The GLOs enable museums to demonstrate and give evidence of effective and efficient educational performance. The GLOs can be seen as one example of the double-edged, paradoxical character of power in post-modernity, where they enable museum educators to provide the evidence for government of efficient performance, but at the same time, they require subjection to those activities of measurement that are burdensome and disliked.[28] The GLOs can also be seen as a form of institutional reflexivity.[29]

Conclusions

The demand for evidence of effective performance is a major characteristic of post-modern society. With the recent prioritisation of educational purpose and provision, cultural organisations have been subject to a demand for evidence of the impact of learning. The approach to measuring the outcomes and impact of learning in museums, archives and libraries that was devised by RCMG for LIRP is based on a conceptual and interpretive framework that can be used to shape all aspects of research design, analysis and interpretation.

Once the approach had been developed, RCMG was commissioned by the Department for Culture, Media and Sport and the Department for Education and Skills, and MLA, to carry out two large national studies.[30] These research programmes took place from July 2003 to early 2004. MLA commissioned research into the outcomes of school visits to regional museums in order to explore the impact of *Renaissance in the Regions* funding; DCMS commissioned research into the outcomes of their *Museum Education Strategic Commissioning* programme. It was hoped that these two large studies, running concurrently and using the interpretive framework of the GLOs, would produce a picture of museum education in the regional and national museums across England. In 2005, these pieces of research were followed by a second commission from MLA to repeat the 2003 study.

Together, these three national studies have produced a great deal of evidence of the outcomes and impact of learning in museums. The next chapters describe the evaluation research studies, discuss the research methods used, and present the data that was gathered. Treating the three studies as a collective databank, a detailed and dynamic view of learning in museums can be produced. We begin by reviewing the background to the research into learning in English museums between 2003 and 2006 and the research methods used.

5

The research programmes:
background and method

The development of a way to 'measure the impact and outcomes of learning' was carried out at a time of upheaval in the cultural field in England, with the grouping together of museums, archives and libraries and the prioritisation by central government of education and social inclusion as the main purpose of these organisations. Resource/MLA drew up plans to enable museums, libraries and archives to move towards this shift in purpose and introduced a staff development initiative *Inspiring Learning for All*. This was presented on a dedicated website which was available by 2003; the Generic Learning Outcomes, along with suggestions and examples of how they could be used drawn from the pilot studies, formed one part of this.

At the same time that *Inspiring Learning for All* and the GLOs were being developed and piloted, Resource/MLA was also working on another front. The museum community had been worried for some time about the condition of regional museums in England, and government was persuaded that in light of the new policy demands, a strategic review of this section of the museum community would be beneficial. Following this review, and the publication of the report *Renaissance in the Regions*, central government funding was offered to regional museums for the first time. The circumstances were complicated and will be explained later in the chapter, but at this point we should note that the allocation of government funding, much of which was intended to be spent on the develop- ment of very specific educational services, led directly to an opportunity to use the new GLO framework.

With the prioritisation of education and social inclusion being funded by govern- ment in regional museums, the position of the national museums arose. In 2003, the Department for Culture, Media and Sport (DCMS), together with the Department for Education and Skills (DfES), introduced a funded programme of educational partnerships between the national and regional museums. The evaluation of this initiative presented a further opportunity to use the new GLO framework. MLA and DCMS were of the view that if the same research methods could be used for these two national evaluation research programmes, then a national picture of the impact of learning in English museums could be produced. Very shortly afterwards (in 2005), a third national evaluation study based on the earlier *Renaissance* study was commissioned. RCMG carried out all three linked studies.

In a policy environment that claimed to be evidence-based, the lack of evidence that learning could happen in museums prevented the presentation of a strong case for funding. However, with the instigation of funding streams to support the growth of the educational capacity of museums, evaluation studies emerged very rapidly, largely because of the need to clearly demonstrate the impact and value of these investments. Museums carried out their own evaluations and also commissioned freelance staff (many of them experienced museum educators) to evaluate specific projects. But as educational evaluations and impact studies began to emerge, charges were heard that many of the evaluations were virtually useless because of methodological inadequacy, rudimentary analysis and interpretation, failure to describe research methods and claims that could not be backed up by the evidence.[1] It was also pointed out that lack of robust research hampered the analysis and understanding of the potential of museums and of the success or failure of museum policy.[2]

Museum education evaluation is a field that is developing rapidly, and at the end of 2006, it is possible to identify a considerable number of reliable, thorough and useful evaluation studies, carried out by a mix of university-based researchers, freelance museum evaluation professionals, and research-based consultancies. The credibility of any research cannot be assessed unless researchers set out clearly what they have done and why. There are always decisions to be made about how to choose appropriate methods that will deliver the data that is needed to answer the research question, and how this data will be analysed and interpreted.[3] The ontological and conceptual framework for the RCMG evaluation research has been described in Chapters 2–4. Chapters 6–9 will present the evidence of learning generated by these research studies, but Chapter 5 will first set out the research methods, and attempt to explain how certain decisions were made and why.[4]

The three large recent RCMG studies, supported by two other national research studies, form the basis for the discussion to follow, and they will be introduced at the beginning of this chapter. The rest of this chapter will be taken up with a discussion of the research methods that were used in the three linked RCMG studies. The early thoughts of Resource/MLA were that a single questionnaire sheet could be developed that, used in all instances across all museums, would gather a picture of learning; in the event, the process of developing the research methods has been a great deal more complex and took a great deal longer than had been initially expected.[5] LIRP involved the development, articulation and agreement among all stakeholders of a theory of museum-based learning; during the research studies which followed, the fears, anxieties and misunderstandings of those museum practitioners who were enrolled randomly in the research pro-esses through the allocation of special funding had to be addressed. Appropriate research methods that would enable the production of a national picture of museum-based learning but that would not, at the same time, compromise the complexity of what was known about museum-based learning had to be identified. In addition, one of the main reasons for RCMG to engage in these projects was the desire to understand more deeply how learning occurred in museums; the desire on the part of the research team to be able to use the research in theory-building also needed to be accommodated.

The evaluation research studies were commissioned by government (DCMS, DfES) and its agent (MLA). The research had overt objectives: first, to assess the effectiveness of the use of the special funding; and second (especially in the case of MLA and DCMS), to provide evidence that might convince the Treasury that museums were worthy of increased funding. The research team, however, were adamant that these advocacy-linked purposes for the research would not compromise the robustness or independence of the research. While the research team worked closely with MLA and (to a lesser extent) with DCMS/DfES and other research stakeholders such as museum education staff, a very clear distinction was drawn between the research, and the uses to which the findings might be put by the research commissioners. The research team balanced the needs of the policy-focused commissioners of the research with their own theory-focused intentions. This was aided by the fact that all involved accepted that research that was not robust, internally consistent and informed by an appropriate intellectual framework would be a waste of time.

Given the lack, in Britain, of robust evidence that museums could be used as sites for learning, the underpinning multi-part research question was: Does learning happen in museums, and if so, in what way and to what purpose? What is the character of learning in museums and what are the outcomes and impact of this learning?

The research background

The early years of the twenty-first century in England saw considerable change in the internal landscape of cultural institutions. Museums were charged with modernising their attitudes and practices. Government's emphasis on education and learning demanded a new way of thinking in museums; and targeted funding was used to bring about the focus on audiences, especially on school-based learners. Two funding streams were of particular importance. *Renaissance in the Regions* is a very large modernisation programme which has involved, in one way and another, the whole museum community, although the funds have only been received by some of the larger regional museums. The initial analysis of the culture of museums embraced the whole museum field, with senior and influential individuals being involved in its production. The second funding stream, the *DCMS/DfES Strategic Commissioning Programme* has been more self-contained, focusing on partnerships between national and regional museums in the development of innovative and exploratory education projects. Both funding programmes are on-going at the time of writing.

Following a detailed presentation by MLA and senior members of the museum community of the potential, strengths and weaknesses of regional museums, central government funds were for the first time systematically channelled to regional museums in England in what has become known as the *Renaissance in the Regions* programme. The educational potential of museums formed one of the strongest planks on which the initial argument for *Renaissance* was made, and, with governmental attitudes to culture and its social utility becoming more strongly developed, educational work has remained very high on the agenda.

One of the first tasks that Resource/MLA undertook at the request of the Secretary of State for Culture was to review the condition of regional museums in England. The specific objectives were to see how museums might be more fully involved in educational work and in combating social exclusion; to propose a strategic and operational framework; and to push forward the modernisation agenda.[6] The resulting report *Renaissance in the Regions: a new vision for England's museums*[7] is a detailed account of a group of museums that had been largely neglected by central government and that were subject to the vagaries of local government policies which had on the whole resulted in limited funding and development. But it was also more than that. *Renaissance* was the result of work of a powerful task force which included a number of national museum directors and others of influence in the cultural sector.[8] The report took a hard and realistic look at the non-national museums, and also took the opportunity to set out some basic concepts and principles in relation to the transformation of museums as a whole.

The report was hampered by the lack of definitive and reliable information.[9] Some estimations of the total number of museums in Great Britain have suggested between 2,000 and 2,500 depending on which definition of a museum is used. *Renaissance in the Regions*, however, based its estimation on a narrower geographical focus (England) and took the Museums and Galleries Registration Scheme[10] as evidence for the statement that there are 1,432 museums in England that meet basic standards.[11] These break down into groups as is shown in Table 5.1.

These museums are governed and funded through local and central government, universities, admissions charges and commercial operations.[12] The Heritage Lottery Fund has provided a considerable level of funding for capital projects.[13] Government funding, whether by local authorities or through the structures of

Table 5.1 Number of museums in England according to their governing body (from Resource, 2001: 25)

	Number	*% of total*
Independent	565	39
Local authority	527	37
National Trust	134	9
Armed services	87	6
University	57	4
National	32	2
English Heritage	30	2
Total	1432	100

central government,[14] makes up a large part of the funding of museums in England, unlike museums in, for example, the United States, where the patronage of wealthy individuals underpins museum development and continuity.[15] There is considerable imbalance in level of funding between London and the regions of England, with government, lottery and business sector funding all favouring the capital. As *Renaissance* put it: 'The regions are culturally rich but financially impoverished.'[16] This disadvantage for regional museums in England is compounded by the fact that unlike the library service, which is mandatory, museums are a discretionary service.

Renaissance identified the culture of the museum field as one of the main barriers to change and called on museums to change, adapt and transform themselves;[17] structural weaknesses included fragmentation across the field, a leadership vacuum and a lack of capacity. The report suggested that in order to move forward it would be necessary to 'change the professional culture within museums and galleries'.[18] In addition to developing their provision for learning, social inclusion and cultural diversity are described as the two biggest challenges for museums as they plan for the future.[19] *Renaissance* stated firmly that museums should be prepared to 'place social inclusion and learning as a mainstream policy priority and redirect resources accordingly' and to 'change the content and presentational style of what is displayed to make collections more interesting and accessible to a wider range of people'.[20]

Renaissance placed education firmly at the forefront of the purpose of museums, stating as the first of five aims:

> To be an important resource and champion for learning and education.[21]

It also described what museums could deliver. In setting out the value of museums to society, the report focused on the potential for museums for learning. It also outlined the potential breadth of the impact of learning in museums, which it suggested included the building of confidence and self-esteem in addition to the acquisition of skills and knowledge.[22] The report gave a short account of the competitive funds for educational projects that had been introduced to help take forward the agendas of the Labour government.[23] In 1999 a two-year £500,000 Education Challenge Fund (ECF) was established by DCMS (managed first by the Museums and Galleries Commission and later by Resource/MLA, its successor body) to fund educational projects which would increase capacity to implement the MGC guidelines. In 2000, the Department for Education and Employment (DfEE, later to be called DfES) established the Museums and Galleries Education Programme (MGEP) with £2.5m project funding over a two-year period. A second programme (MGEP2) followed shortly afterwards. Other organisations such as the Heritage Lottery Fund and the Clore Foundation have also provided project funding for educational projects and events in museums and galleries.

In spite of the desires of government and the additional funding that had been provided to enable these desires to be realised, the *Renaissance in the Regions* report was very clear that there was considerable resistance to cultural change:

> Museum and gallery governing bodies and managements have proved
> unwilling or unable to use the opportunity afforded by the project-
> /challenge-funding schemes to bring public services such as learning,
> education and inclusion from the periphery to the core of institutions'
> activities.[24]

In order to change those aspects of museum culture that were inhibiting
modernisation, *Renaissance* proposed a radical restructuring of those museums
within the remit of the report, the English regional museums. The establishment
of a clear framework for regional museums and galleries was suggested, based
on the concept of 'regional hubs'. These 'regional hubs' would consist of one key
museum service[25] with a small number of regional partners which could act
together in a strategic way, 'responding to new agendas which put people and
communities first'.[26] Each of the nine regions of England would contain one of
these hubs which would act as a centre of excellence and expertise in the region.[27]

The *Renaissance* report identified £267.2m as necessary to undertake the work
required to modernise England's regional museums. A complex programme of
development was set out, spread over the years 2002–07.[28] In the event, central
government accepted the argument that regional museums were open to change
and could offer valuable social benefits if they were able to do so. A funding
programme was instigated. The funds allocated for 2003–06 by DCMS (£70m)
fell short of the £267m by a long way,[29] and it was decided by Resource/MLA to
divide the *Renaissance* programme into two phases. Although all museums in the
programme received additional funds, three phase 1 hubs ('pathfinder hubs'[30])
were chosen to receive a larger tranche of funding and were charged with
demonstrating what all regional museum hubs would be able to achieve with
additional central government funding.[31] Eventually, and due in part to the success
of demonstrating the value of museums through the research reported in this
volume, £147m was allocated for the *Renaissance* programme in the period up
to 2007/08, an unprecedented investment in regional museums.[32]

The first priority for the use of the additional funding was the establishment of
a comprehensive museum school service, with over £12m ring-fenced for this
purpose,[33] £10m from DCMS and a further £2.2m from the Ministry for Education, the Department for Education and Skills (DfES). A specific target of
increasing the number of contacts between schools and regional museums by 25
per cent by 2005/06 was set by DCMS.

The museums in all nine regional hubs immediately began to research and develop
Education Programme Delivery Plans (EPDPs) which would guide their work
with schools from April 2004.[34] The EPDPs involved considerable consultation
with local teachers, and set out how museums could offer support for the delivery
of the curriculum, and for gifted and talented children, children with special
educational needs and children at risk of exclusion. These specific areas for focus
were directly related to contemporary government policies. The museums in each
region also began to develop strategic links with each other in order to achieve
their collective hub goals. Staff began to be recruited in the autumn of 2003;
there was a strong emphasis on staff working with education and the public, and

some of these were employed to work across and between the museums in the regional hub. In the North East, for example, 10 assistant Education Officers were appointed, working with the Hub Education Manager. In the East of England, appointments included a Community History Curator, a Disability Officer, and an Outreach Officer.[35]

Area Museum Councils (AMCs), regional policy and advisory bodies working with local museums, had been abolished as part of the reorganisation of the museum field.[36] New regional agencies were now created from the remains of the AMC structure. In contrast to the more dispersed and localised work of the AMCs, these regional agencies had a strong remit to take forward national cultural policy. Where the AMCs had focused on aiding museums in their region primarily in relation to curation and conservation, often with a view to securing Registration status, the new regional agencies emphasised education from the start. And very importantly, they also had a much broader cultural remit, encompassing libraries and archives in addition to museums. These agencies became Museums, Libraries and Archives Councils in the regions; at the time of writing a further restructuring has taken place as MLA and the regional agencies have been formally brought together as the MLA Partnership under a single corporate plan.[37]

At the same time as the *Renaissance* programme, DCMS and DfES together had, with the purpose of furthering government policies, established an educational programme based on partnerships between national and regional museums – the *DCMS/DfES Strategic Commissioning: National/Regional Museum Education Partnerships*. It was significant that the two ministries were working together to promote the use of museums. The focus of this programme was specifically on museum education projects.

What can now be seen as a systematic national research programme arose from these two funding strands. Special funding for educational work had been offered prior to the two funding programmes,[38] but it was with the instigation of central government funding for regional museums through the *Renaissance* programme that educational funds began to be disbursed in a systematic manner, accompanied by specific objectives and targets. The *DCMS/DfES Strategic Commissioning Programme* also led to a demand for evaluation, though its aims were more open-ended and less tightly defined.

Collecting evidence of learning in museums: five national evaluation research studies

The first of the three linked RCMG studies was carried out from July 2003 to February 2004. It used the LIRP approach to measuring learning to evaluate the first tranche of *Renaissance* funding in the three phase 1 hubs, which involved 36 museums in the West Midlands, the North East and the South West of England (see Figure 5.1).

There were several outputs from the research;[39] the full research report, *What did you learn at the museum today? (2003)*,[40] was accompanied by a 24-page summary with the same name[41] that was widely distributed within the museum field. A small-scale spiral-bound booklet, entitled *What amazed me most at the museum today . . . the impact of museum visits on pupils at Key Stage 2,*[42] with examples of children's drawing and writing was also produced.[43]

A second study of the impact and learning outcomes resulting from *Renaissance* funding was carried out by RCMG from July 2005 to February 2006. This time

Figure 5.1 Museum services in the three phase 1 hubs involved in the *Renaissance in the Regions* museum education programme, RR1: 2003 (Copyright Resource/MLA. Design Tom Partridge)

the research involved 69 museums in the nine regional hubs (the three phase 1 hubs and the six phase 2 hubs) (see Figure 5.2) and was charged with, as far as possible, using the same research methods as the earlier study so that comparisons over time could be made.

The research outputs took the same form as for the first study: a full research report *What did you learn at the museum today? Second study (2005)*,[44] and an

Figure 5.2 Museum services in the nine regional hubs involved in the *Renaissance in the Regions* museum education programme, RR2: 2005 (Copyright Resource/MLA. Design Tom Partridge)

accompanying 23-page summary with the same name.[45] This time two spiral-bound flip-books were produced with pupils' work. The first contained examples of the work of the younger pupils aged 7–11 (Key Stage 2), and was given the same title as the earlier version,[46] and the second contained the work of older pupils aged 11–18, and was entitled *The most interesting thing at the museum today was . . . the impact of museum visits on pupils aged 11–18 years*.[47] Both of the two research studies commissioned by MLA were concerned with the impact of the *Renaissance in the Regions* funding. The research team referred to these research projects as RR1 and RR2, and this is how they will be referred to here too, with the dates added for clarity.

RR1: 2003 and RR2: 2005 were concerned solely with museums in the English regions, and mainly with museum school services, although where museums had chosen to use the *Renaissance* funding to work with communities rather than schools (which was rare, because of the rather specific terms of the funding), this was included where possible in the research. At the same time as the first study RR1: 2003, RCMG was commissioned by DCMS and DfES to carry out an evaluation of their *Strategic Commissioning Museum Education Programme*. As part of the encouragement of educational capacity-building, DCMS and DfES had invited the national museums to bid for grants to fund educational partnerships between themselves and a small number of non-national museums in England.

This third national study involved 12 theme-based partnerships comprising 12 national museums and 35 museums across London and the English regions (see Figure 5.3).

There were two outputs from this research. The full research report was entitled *Inspiration, identity, learning: the value of museums: the evaluation of the impact of DCMS/DfES Strategic Commissioning 2003–2004: National/Regional Museum Education Partnerships. June 2004*.[48] This report was accompanied by a 38-page summary[49] with the same title as the research report. At the time of writing, a second study has been commissioned by DCMS/DfES to be carried out between July 2006 and June 2007. The first DCMS/DfES programme will be referred to as DCMS/DfES1: 2004. As DCMS/DfES: 2 will not be completed until after this book has been finished, it will not be discussed here, but the final report will be available on the RCMG website in the same way as the other RCMG reports.

The three museum education programmes, RR1: 2003, RR2: 2005 and DCMS/DfES1: 2004, were linked in complex ways. The *Renaissance* programme was based in museums in the English regions and was focused specifically on the growth of museum school services, with a specific numerical target to meet. Thus the museums involved in both of the *Renaissance* evaluation research projects concentrated on developing their existing school provision. In many of the hub museums, especially in the phase 1 hubs, these services had been established for a considerable time and staff were experienced and confident. With additional resources, capacity could be quickly increased, mainly through increasing the number of single visits from primary schools to museums. The second *Renaissance* study, RR2: 2005, compared the 2005 findings with the earlier 2003 findings.

Laing Art Gallery, Newcastle

Sunderland Museum & Winter Gardens

National Museum of Photography,
Film & Television

Bradford Museums, Galleries & Heritage

Beningbrough Hall

York Museums Trust

Leeds Museums & Galleries

Sheffield Galleries & Museums Trust

Leicester City Museums Service

Norfolk Museums Service

Dove Cottage

Abbot Hall Art Gallery, Kendal

Harris Museum & Art Gallery, Preston

Imperial War Museum North

Manchester Art Gallery

Manchester Museum

Salford Museum & Art Gallery

National Museums Liverpool

New Art Gallery Walsall

Birmingham Museums & Art Gallery

Bristol Museums & Art Gallery

British Empire & Commonwealth Museum

Roman Baths Museum

Montacute House

Philpot Museum, Lyme Regis

Dorset County Museum

Imperial War Museum
Duxford

Luton Museums Service

Ragged School Museum

London Canal Museum

National Museums, London

British Library
British Museum
National Gallery
National Portrait Gallery
National Maritime Museum
Science Museum
Tate Gallery
Victoria and Albert Museum

Royal Pavilion Libraries and Museums

Figure 5.3 Museums and museum services involved in the DCMS/DfES1: 2004 programme
(Copyright DCMS. Design Tom Partridge)

The DCMS/DfES1: 2004 programme involved both national and regional
museums and was intended to develop best practice in museum education and to
strengthen links across the museum field. The partnerships involved in the
DCMS/DfES1: 2004 programme were ambitious in scale and complexity. They
were based on themes that were of interest to the partners, were often multi-
stranded, involved several mini-projects, and took the form of extended relationships between museums and community organisations. Acknowledging

governmental policy aims relating to social inclusion, these projects frequently engaged vulnerable groups and individuals such as refugees and asylum-seekers, teenage mothers and fathers, young people who were not at school because of illness, and children who were at risk because of environmental and behavioural difficulties.[50] The museums involved took the opportunity to experiment and innovate, with no specific numerical target to meet. While the number of schools involved in this programme was lower, the statistical findings were directly comparable to the findings of the first *Renaissance* study, RR1: 2003.

Several regional museums were involved in both the *Renaissance* and the DCMS/DfES1: 2004 programmes. Bristol City Museum, for example, was one of the partners in the *Understanding Slavery* project that was led by the National Maritime Museum, and at the same time Bristol City Museum was the lead partner in the South West phase 1 hub. Tyne and Wear Museums were the lead partner in the North East phase 1 hub and one of the Tyne and Wear museums, the Laing Art Gallery, was one of the partners in the DCMS/DfES1: 2004 project *Take one Picture* led by the National Gallery in London.[51] The same members of the museum education staff worked on both programmes in some cases.

All three evaluation research studies used research methods structured around the concept of the Generic Learning Outcomes. As far as possible, RCMG was expected to use the same research tools in order to link the results across the studies. Multiple methods were used in all studies, including quantitative and qualitative methods. In total, the three research studies have produced an enormous amount of data which will be used to build up a picture of learning in museums.

National studies such as these are unusual, but in England, they can be related to two earlier evaluations of a large-scale government-funded museum education programme, the DfES *Museums and Galleries Education Programme* Phases 1 and 2. MGEP ran from 1999 to 2004, with £4 million invested in museum/school projects. The first phase of the programme (MGEP1) took place between 1999 and 2002 and involved 65 separate projects, with £3m funding.[52] RCMG evaluated the first MGEP1 and produced an 84-page research report entitled *The impact of the DfES Museum and Gallery Education Programme: a summative evaluation*.[53] This was accompanied by a 56-page good practice guide, *Learning from culture: the DfES Museums and Galleries Education Programme: a guide to good practice*, commissioned by the DfES.[54] It was also reported in *Curator*.[55]

The second phase of the DfES *Museums and Galleries Education Programme* (MGEP2) involved 118 projects in 130 museums and galleries and £1m funding. MGEP2 was evaluated by the Centre for Education and Industry (CEI) at the University of Warwick, under the direction of Julian Stanley. An interim report was produced entitled *Learning from culture is working!*[56] This was followed by the full research report entitled *The impact of Phase 2 of the Museums and Galleries Education Programme*, Volumes 1 and 2[57] and a summary of the final research report entitled *Final Report on the impact of Phase 2 of the Museums and Galleries Education Programme*.[58] The project was also reported in *Museum and Society*.[59]

The research carried out for MGEP1 was prior to the development of the Generic Learning Outcomes, but was based on the same broad conceptual framework as that which underpinned LIRP. Research methods included visits, observations, and interviews with teachers and children, but questionnaires were not used. A considerable amount of qualitative evidence was collected from teachers and children, which presented a broad-brush picture of learning in museums.

The evaluation of MGEP2 carried out by CEI can be used to compare and contrast with the RCMG research. It focused on directly comparable projects but took a conceptual approach that was not grounded in the GLOs. Research methods included project descriptions and monitoring reports submitted by the museums, exit and entry questionnaires for teachers and children, and individual evaluations of 53 of the projects using a range of methods including interviews, observations and examination of work and resources.[60]

Research methods in the three linked RCMG studies

The three linked RCMG studies used the same research tools, with only minor modifications. It is possible, therefore, to treat the three bodies of evidence as one large data set. The five GLOs were used to structure the research tools and to shape the analysis and interpretation of the data. The intellectual framework that has underpinned much of the work of RCMG underpinned the research.[61]

The three linked RCMG studies, RR1:2003, RR2:2005 and DCMS/DfES1:2004, consisted of both fixed and flexible research processes.[62] With 'fixed processes', the research plan and the research tools are not subject to change during the research process, whereas with 'flexible processes' the research tools and plans need to be used in a fluid way and may change as the research moves on. Where research is being carried out that requires people to reflect on their views and experience, a fixed research tool such as a questionnaire is not appropriate and more useful results can be gained through 'conversations with a purpose'.[63] These are loosely structured interviews which respond to the situation in which they are held, but which have very clear objectives based on the information needed by the researcher.

The fixed processes included surveys of teachers and pupils which examined their views about the outcomes of learning immediately following a museum visit. The flexible elements of the research plans involved observational visits, focus groups of teachers, school case studies and seminars with the museum research participants. The fixed elements of the research were managed through a series of questionnaires. The flexible elements did not have specific research tools, but the objectives for visits and discussions were very carefully identified, discussed and recorded before the activity took place to enable focused observation and questioning.

In the three research studies, the various research methods are used in a complementary way, to enhance understanding of the research puzzle.[64] Thus the large-scale surveys of the views of teachers and pupils provide an overview of their attitudes of the extent to which each of the five GLOs is achieved following a museum visit, while a more in-depth understanding, and examples of the occurrence and character of these outcomes, has been gained through the school case studies. Discussions in focus groups with teachers facilitated a deeper understanding of these outcomes from the perspective of the teachers. The flexible elements of the research (the focus groups and case studies) produced qualitative data which allowed detailed analysis of the contexts and character of the learning in museums which was mapped through the large-scale quantitative study. The diverse methods used in the research were carefully chosen because they were judged to be appropriate to generate the kind of information that was needed for the research questions being asked.[65]

Questionnaires for teachers and their pupils

One of the main reasons for commissioning the research was MLA's desire to develop a national picture of learning in museums. It was very important that the research was able to produce statistical evidence, based on large samples, which would provide a convincing account of the impact of museums on learning across England. This demanded the use of questionnaires that could be used in each participating museum, and a recognition that the research would not focus on evaluating individual museum projects.

In all three studies, one teachers' questionnaire (Form A) and 40 pupils' questionnaires (Form B) were put together into an envelope (an 'Evaluation Pack') which was given to all teachers at the end of their visit to any of the museums in the study during the research period. Once the staff in the participating museums understood their role in the evaluation research, and accepted that this rather burdensome task would contribute to a national picture of learning that could be used to show the value of museums, they worked hard to give out and retrieve questionnaires from teachers and pupils, and the return rates were extremely high. The response rate in RR1: 2003 was 78 per cent across all museums; in RR2: 2005 it was 67 per cent in the Phase 1 museums and 82 per cent in the Phase 2 museums; in the DCMS/DfES1: 2004 study the response rate was 88 per cent across all participating museums. The overall return rate of the Evaluation Packs is extremely respectable for large-scale surveys of this kind. Harvey and MacDonald suggest that the response rate for postal questionnaires can be as low as between 10 per cent and 40 per cent, while the response rate for questionnaires administered by interviewers is generally higher, between 40 per cent and 80 per cent.[66] Barnett, on the other hand, suggests that the response rate for postal questionnaires may be as high as 50 per cent.[67] The Evaluation Packs were not postal surveys, but neither were they administered by interviewers. They were given to teachers at the end of a school visit to a museum. Arguably, this is a very difficult time to complete a fairly complex questionnaire, and museums were given advice at the beginning of the research process during the briefing seminars as to how best to aid teachers in completing the questionnaire at a time when the bus might be arriving to take the pupils back to school, the space might be needed by an in-coming group, there might be no level surface on which to lean, and innumerable other calls on the teacher's time might be made.

To some extent, the high return rate reflects the successful establishment of research communities, which was the approach that RCMG tried to develop in the various studies. The senior members of the RCMG research team were largely made up of researchers who were familiar to the research participants in the museums, having been deeply embedded in museum education work for a considerable length of time. This meant that researchers and research participants shared values, experience, language and references, and it was easier to build a shared sense of the importance of the research. Key senior museum education staff proved essential in mediating between the researchers and the museums; they were also called on by the research team when their expertise could help with research processes. This building of a research community was more successful in the first *Renaissance* study, RR1: 2003, where numbers of museums were somewhat less than in the other two studies, and there was a shared sense of experimentation. The research team had to negotiate carefully the maintenance of a stance that was sufficiently close to the museum participants to inspire their confidence and commitment, and sufficiently distant to assure the research commissioners of the impartiality of the research.

The quantitative evidence on which the picture of the outcomes of museum learning to be presented is drawn from the three linked RCMG studies (RR1: 2003,[68] RR2: 2005[69] and DCMS/DfES1: 2004[70]). There were 3,172 teachers and 56,810 pupils of all ages participating in the three linked RCMG research studies through completing questionnaires and participating in discussions (see Table 5.2).

A teacher's questionnaire (Form A) was devised which asked general questions about the school and the teacher's use of museums, before focusing on a number of very detailed questions which asked specific questions about each of the GLOs. A pupil's questionnaire (Form B) was also devised, which asked questions designed to generate information relating to each of the GLOs. These questionnaires were completed by a large proportion of the teachers and their pupils who visited the museums in each of the *Renaissance* projects in September and October of 2003 and 2005; teachers and pupils participating in the DCMS/DfES1: 2004 programme completed questionnaires between September 2003 and March 2004. The questionnaires were handed out by museum staff in each of the

Table 5.2 Numbers of teachers and pupils participating in the three evaluation research studies

	Numbers of teachers completing questionnaires and participating in focus groups	Numbers of pupils completing questionnaires and participating in discussion groups
RR1: 2003	1,004	20,604
RR2: 2005	1,665	26,791
DCMS/DfES1: 2004	503	9,415
Total	3,172	56,810

participating museums; in some museums, imaginative strategies were put in place to help teachers allow time and space for the completion of the questionnaires.

There were two versions of Form B, the questionnaire for pupils: Form B Key Stage 2 (KS2) and below was for pupils aged 5–11 years, and Form B Key Stage 3 (KS3) and above was for pupils aged 11–18 years.[71] Both Form Bs asked the same questions about each of the GLOs, but in slightly different ways, with the exception of the omission of a question on Skills for the younger pupils, as it was judged that children of that age would not be able to respond sensibly to such a question. The questionnaires were piloted prior to the first study (RR1: 2003) and their purpose and design discussed with education staff from the participating museums; following this some modifications took place.[72]

In the first two studies where these forms were used (RR1: 2003 and DCMS/DfES1: 2004) the questionnaire for the younger pupils (Form B KS2 and below) had included a space which took up most of the bottom half of the page, for writing or drawing, stimulated by the statement: 'What amazed me most at the museum today . . .' This produced some unexpectedly powerful results and for the second *Renaissance* study (RR2: 2005) it was decided that the questionnaire for the older pupils would also contain a space for open-ended comments or drawings, stimulated by: 'The most interesting thing about today was . . .' This entailed a slight modification in the questions to allow for the space needed.

RR2: 2005 included a questionnaire for museum staff which asked about the impact of *Renaissance* funding on their museum education provision (Form D). Other forms collected numerical data on contacts with schools and communities and descriptive detail of projects.

Gathering evidence from interviews, focus groups and school case studies

Throughout the three RCMG studies, a range of qualitative methods were used. Where depth information about learning is needed, questionnaires are of limited use. While the teachers' and pupils' questionnaires could produce a broad-brush overview of their attitudes to learning in museums, restricting the questions to those that could be asked in such a large number of museums with such large numbers of participants meant that much of the detail could not be researched. The questions in the questionnaires were constructed on the basis of each of the GLOs, and were couched in general terms – 'Do you think your pupils will have learnt subject-specific facts?' In talking face-to-face with teachers and pupils, it was possible to probe on specifics – 'Tell me more about what facts your pupils learnt about the people who lived in the workhouse.'

Qualitative data, generated through discussions, can work in at least two ways in relation to quantitative data. Face-to-face discussion can be used to gather more detail of something where the outlines are already known. For example, from the questionnaires, it seemed that teachers were less interested in their pupils increasing their skills in the museum; discussions with teachers confirmed this, but the situation became more complicated and interesting.[73] People's words, which encapsulate their ideas and feelings, can also be used to generate new ideas which can then lead to new questions in questionnaires; for example, it was clear after the first *Renaissance* study, RR1: 2003, that the pupils' enjoyment was a very significant factor for teachers, but the questionnaire had not asked a direct question about this. The teachers' questionnaire in the second *Renaissance* study, RR2: 2005, therefore included a specific question, which proved the point convincingly, with 99 per cent of the 1,632 teachers completing questionnaires agreeing it was likely or very likely that their pupils had enjoyed the experience. This is important information to feed into policy-related analyses and also into theory-building which could have been missed.

Interviews with individual or pairs of teachers enabled close discussion about specific projects, including the aims of teachers, the learning outcomes for individual children, and the gathering of details of particular schools and communities. They also enabled researchers to check and, if necessary, to modify their interpretation and understanding of particular matters. These interviews mainly took place during the school case studies. Focus groups, in comparison, tended to result in teachers using examples of their experience in a more abstract manner to illustrate general issues or points. Where the focus groups consisted of more than about ten members, they proved very difficult to manage, especially

Plate 5.1 Talking to teachers in their classrooms with the pupils' work on the walls was fruitful

in trying to pin down details about learning outcomes. Teachers were more interested in discussing more general matters.

Case studies were used in the RR2: 2005 and DCMS/DfES1: 2004 studies.[74] In the preparation for the evaluation research for RR2: 2005, the case studies were carefully planned, but these plans could not be achieved. It had been hoped to take an approach to the case studies that would enable a comparison of the potential differences in outcomes of learning based on a single museum visit with learning which resulted from a number of museum sessions; it was also hoped to review any issues concerning learning outcomes for pupils in schools which were first-time museum users compared to those in schools that were frequent museum users. However, the rapid time-frame for the research confounded these rather sophisticated plans. A more pragmatic approach was adopted which resulted in two primary and one secondary case study schools. Each school case study focused on one school class group, and the classes included a multi-ethnic primary-level class from a deprived urban area visiting a museum for a single visit; a second primary-level class from a deprived white working-class urban area using an art gallery over a six-week period; and a secondary-level (KS3) class from a rural area visiting a museum for a single visit.

Each case study in RR2: 2005 involved a number of research processes. The class concerned was observed during at least one teaching session in school and also while on a museum visit. Pupils who represented a mix of gender, ability level, experience of museums and potential to benefit from the museum visit were interviewed, as was the class teacher and the head or deputy headteacher and other teachers as appropriate. Pupils were asked to fill out the pupils' questionnaire immediately after their museum visit and then again on the subsequent visit to the school (a week or up to four weeks later). The school postcodes were analysed and relevant data in relation to deprivation and child poverty was reviewed. Ofsted Reports, DfES and other available data about the school and its context were collected, and information about the museum was gathered.[75]

The first case study involved a primary school with 200 pupils aged 7 to 11 years on roll, located in a deprived white working-class area in the English Midlands where one class, aged between 7 and 8 years, visited the local art gallery, which was part of the city museum service. The school was located in a ward which was the second most deprived area in its city and in the top 10 per cent of the most deprived areas in England according to the Indices of Multiple Deprivation (IMD) 2004.[76] In 2004, 15.8 per cent of pupils on roll had Special Educational Needs and in 2005 no pupils in the school had English as an additional language. The school had above-average figures for pupils receiving free school meals (47 per cent), attendance was erratic and children's levels of attainment frequently poor. The art gallery was part of a phase 1 hub in the *Renaissance* programme, with funds made available to allow a member of the gallery's staff to go into school for five half days over a number of weeks following a gallery visit. This was planned to support the school's art scheme of work and was mainly focused on the teacher's professional development.

The visit observed at the art gallery involved two classes who were introduced to portraiture and the use of composition to portray relationships as part of the Art

National Curriculum. In the museum the pupils were introduced to sculpture and paintings of people; in the follow-up sessions at the school the pupils were taught a number of art and craft skills such as graffito, press printing and collage, chosen in consultation with the class teacher.

The second case study involved a very large primary school with a nursery, catering for pupils aged from 3 to 11 years in the English Midlands. In 2005 this school had 690 pupils drawn mainly from its local neighbourhood which was in the top 10 per cent of most deprived areas in England.[77] The area had changed in recent years from being a primarily white working-class neighbourhood to being multi-ethnic, with large Asian and Black communities. Fifty-five per cent of the pupils were receiving free school meals and the school was in receipt of special funding because of the high incidence of drug abuse and teenage pregnancies in the area. About 25 per cent of the pupils in the school had Special Educational Needs and the deputy headteacher estimated that a further 15 per cent had learning difficulties arising from having English as an additional language. Pupils' level of attainment on entry to school was generally well below average especially in language and literacy; however, pupils achieved high levels of attainment over the course of their attendance at this school.

The class observed visited a large Tudor timber-framed farmhouse with a substantial kitchen garden, located in the middle of a 1930s housing estate, which was part of a large city museum service where education programmes were very well established. These took the form of a tour of the house followed by site- and object-based small group workshops. The school group was very multi-ethnic with a mixture of pupils from Asian, Middle Eastern and Black heritages and with a range of ability levels. The class was at the end of a study block on the everyday life of the Tudors.

The third case study was a popular, larger-than-average comprehensive school catering for 11- to 18-year-olds in Eastern England. In 2004 it had 1,557 pupils drawn from the surrounding rural area. The socio-economic and attainment profile of pupils was about average with a below-average proportion of pupils with Special Educational Needs. The school and the area were very ethnically homogeneous, with the ward where the school was located being 98.48 per cent White, in comparison to 91.31 per cent for England and Wales.

The museum this school visited was part of a larger county-wide service housed in a large former workhouse built in 1777. In 2001, after a major refurbishment, it was re-opened as the first museum to tell the story of the nineteenth-century workhouse and its everyday life. At the same time, the education service was re-launched; based on theatre-in-education, it used actors playing a number of characters associated with the workhouse who presented conflicting viewpoints. *Renaissance* funding had enabled an extra half-time staff post which had been used to target new groups and extend the subject areas covered at the museum. At the time of the research, in addition to a large number of primary school pupils, the museum also worked with secondary-age groups doing history, geography and psychology. The museum and the school had worked in a very close partnership to develop the session that was observed. It was part of a four-week focus on the nineteenth-century workhouse and poor laws and was assessed through a written assignment entitled 'Was the Workhouse So Bad?'

The depth research of the case studies was linked to the statistical overview through a number of strategies. First, the schools that were selected as case studies were typical of the schools that were using museums in the English regions. Through analysing the postcodes of the case study schools and the proportion of pupils eligible for free school meals, it is possible to see how these case study schools fit into the general picture of schools using regional museums. Second, the school visit to the museum concerned was in no way different from the visit that any school visiting during the research period could have experienced. Third, the same research tools were used, with the pupils completing the same questionnaire that they would have completed had they not been selected as a case study. In this way, the comments of pupils and their teachers, while specific to the school site and the particular museum experience, can be seen to go beyond the anecdotal through being embedded in the research as a whole.

Using the free drawing and writing to interpret pupils' learning

The space at the bottom of the pupils' questionnaires encouraged an open response through either writing or drawing. This was used with the younger pupils in the first *Renaissance* study (RR1: 2003) and in the research for DCMS/DfES1: 2004 in 2004, and because the results were so interesting, it was decided to invite the older pupils to write or draw something on their questionnaire in the second *Renaissance* study (RR2: 2005). The majority of the pupils took up the opportunity. There is, therefore, an enormous quantity of evidence that can be used to support the statistical data discussed previously. There are more responses from the younger pupils, who both wrote and drew with gusto; the older pupils had less opportunity, as this method was only used in one study, and therefore there are fewer responses from them; older pupils tended to write rather than draw.

In the discussions in the next chapters, it has only been possible to use a few of the responses. However, the ones that have been chosen are typical of the most interesting responses and many others could have been selected to illustrate the points made.[78] Not all of the pupils produced comments that were highly detailed or thoughtful; clearly the amount of time at the end of a museum session influenced how much could be done. Many of the pupils reveal themselves as poor writers, but sometimes the need to communicate overrides a lack of skill; sometimes the responses are visual – lively and exuberant drawings. The verbal and visual statements are highly variable in terms of depth of response, quantity of material and ability to write or draw.

Reviewing a complete set of responses from any one class sometimes reveals a considerable degree of agreement about what was most exciting. In a workshop at the Usher Gallery, Lincoln, for example, 28 7-year-old children participated, making jewellery in role as slaves; 15 of the children drew the jewellery, with some stating that they liked it or enjoyed making it; ten children drew themselves as slaves and wrote comments such as: 'I wore the slave clothes'; three children enjoyed both activities, with Kayleigh, aged 7, writing in response to the question 'What amazed me most on my visit was . . .': 'Being head slave and making jerwelly.'[79] It is not possible, of course, with these questionnaires, to know how they were introduced or what prompts could have been given to the children when the sheets were given out.

The pupils' thoughts, expressed in both words and pictures, provide powerful evidence of the power of learning in museums. The pupils are fired up as their visits draw to a close, and the strong impact of their experiences is very clear in their responses. The words and pictures have a spontaneity and immediacy because they were produced as the visit was drawing to a close and before succeeding events could overlay the museum experience. It seems likely from the verve and enthusiasm with which the pupils responded that they enjoyed the opportunity to express themselves. The questionnaires looked like museum worksheets, and although some museum participants were very anxious about asking pupils to complete survey questionnaires, it is possible that the act of writing or drawing may have aided in embedding students' learning. It is quite clear from the written and drawn impressions that a powerful tacit learning resource has been laid down, for later activation. The responses show how pupils called on what they knew already, used this knowledge in new contexts and learnt new things that could be used later. The responses also show how strongly pupils responded to the activities and the events they experienced as part of their visit.

The qualitative data represented by the open writing and drawing demands specific modes of interpretation in relation to learning. The questions asked in the top half of the pupils' questionnaires were each structured to focus on one specific GLO; thus in the younger pupils' questionnaire, for the Generic Learning Outcome 'Knowledge and Understanding', the statement 'I learnt some interesting new things' was presented for a 'yes'/'no'/'don't know' answer. In the older pupils' questionnaire, in relation to the gain or development of new Skills, a similarly direct statement was made: 'A museum visit is a good place to pick up new skills.' The responses tell us to what extent the respondents thought they had learnt new information and could or did pick up new skills. These statements focused on a single GLO and thus evidence emerged about a single GLO. The words and pictures are not like that. The pupils could write or draw what they wished, and the results generally relate to more than one GLO. For example, Stacey, a 15-year-old visiting Manchester Art Gallery, wrote:

> Taking photographs, and making pictures from tape, it was using a new method to express creativity. The whole trip was inspirational.

This text contains statements about Skills and also about Enjoyment, Inspiration, Creativity. It seems clear that Stacey has enjoyed using the specific art skills and techniques (taking photographs, making pictures) to express her ideas and feelings (creativity). She has enjoyed it all so much that she actually found the practical workshop and the whole experience 'inspirational'. This statement, and many thousands of others, shows how learning outcomes are interrelated. The integrated character of learning is revealed, as is the power of museums to stimulate the imagination through interesting and unusual activities.

Conclusions

Since the millennium, one outcome of the turbulent and fast-moving cultural field, with its insistent demands for the modernisation of museums and the demonstration of effective educational performance, has been a flurry of large-scale museum education evaluation research studies. A close analysis of three of these studies which are linked through purpose and methodology will enable a unique overview of the relationship between museums and schools, and, in a more limited way, a view of what museums can achieve with diverse groups in communities. Mixed methods were used in the three linked RCMG studies. The teachers' and pupils' questionnaires provide statistical data about the views of teachers and school pupils across England on the value of learning in museums. This is deepened by qualitative data gathered through interviews, focus groups and case studies, and from the free writing and drawing of pupils. This evidence, in combination, offers an excellent overview of the outcomes and impact of museum-based learning in England.

Government policies stress the need for museums to act in an inclusive manner, and one way in which this may happen, as the next chapter will show, is through working with schools where the pupils may be at risk of social and cultural deprivation because of a range of mixed factors including poverty, low parental expectations, lack of parental employment and poor family health. Chapter 6 reviews the use of English museums by schools, analysing which schools visit museums, focusing in particular on their geographical locations. Chapter 7 looks closely at teachers' motivations in using museums, as their expectations are likely to influence how museums are used and valued. In the two chapters which will follow (Chapters 8 and 9) we will examine the evidence of the outcomes of museum-based learning from the perspective of teachers and the pupils themselves.

6

The pattern of school use of museums

Learning opportunities for schools form a highly significant part of the educational provision of museums in England. The RCMG research produced an analysis of which schools used museums and what form this use took. While primary schools make the most actual visits, both primary and secondary schools are represented in proportion to their distribution across England. Special schools, where pupils may have specific learning difficulties, are, however, over-represented in relation to their numbers, reflecting high levels of use by this group of schools. Approximately one-third of the schools using museums are located in areas classified as deprived, and many of these schools have very high numbers of pupils who are entitled to free school meals because they are at risk.

The plans for educational delivery made by the museums which were in receipt of special funding were drawn up to address government agendas, especially those that focused on the relationship of education to social inclusion. The early policy statements from DCMS made it clear that museums, archives and libraries should recognise their potential in this respect:

> Combating social exclusion is one of the Government's highest priorities, and I believe that museums, galleries and archives have a significant role to play in helping us to do this.[1]

Education was positioned as vital to the effort to empower individuals to avoid social exclusion through developing their self-identities:

> Learning can be a powerful agent in combating social exclusion by giving people the abilities, skills and confidence to engage with society.[2]

Considered in relation to use by schools, the RCMG evidence shows that museums play a powerful role in working towards an inclusive society. In analyses of museum visitors, children and school use are rarely included; the continuing evidence is of use by highly educated middle- and upper-class White groups.[3] The evidence from the use by schools paints a very much more diverse picture, where children from all ethnic groups, children with physical and learning disabilities, and children of all ages, both genders and from across the social spectrum, find museums enjoyable, exciting and interesting places where they can shape their own meanings from richly kaleidoscopic experiences.

This chapter begins to set out the evidence on which this claim is based by describing the schools' use of museums.

Meeting government targets

One of the conditions of the funding for the *Renaissance in the Regions* programme was the establishment by DCMS of specific targets for museums to meet, focusing on the development of a 'comprehensive service to schools'. Those museums in the phase 1 hubs were charged with increasing their contacts with schools by 25 per cent by 2005/06.[4]

The first *Renaissance* evaluation study, RR1:2003, was carried out during September and October 2003, which was at a very early point of the *Renaissance* funding as this only became available in April 2003. However, even by then, the museums in the phase 1 hubs as a whole had increased their pupil contacts by 28 per cent. 'Contacts' included pupil visits to museums, and pupils who were visited through museum outreach visit to schools. Each contact with each pupil was counted once on the basis of education diaries and the figures for 2002 were compared with the figures for 2003 to ascertain any increase or decrease. The relationship between the two years varied tremendously between museums according to local circumstances. Wolverhampton Museum, for example, had been closed for renovation in 2002, and only 446 pupils could be counted during this year. The numbers for September and October 2003 (1,809) represented a 307 per cent increase. Other museums, such as Ironbridge Gorge Museum, an open-air museum on several sites which has long been popular for large-scale visits from school parties which frequently bring several coaches, were already running to capacity and could not report much increase.[5]

The target remained in place after 2003 and increase in pupil contacts was again measured in 2005, where the museums which formed part of the phase 1 hubs were measured for a second time, along with a further group of museums[6] from the six phase 2 hubs. By this time, the notion of 'contacts' had been refined by MLA; 'contacts' now referred to 'school-aged children' in a number of categories, including organised school visits, visits by after-school clubs and outreach activities.[7] The concept 'school-aged' allowed museums to count all children and young people up to the age of 18 years. The numbers of school-aged children using museums increased between September and October 2003 and the same period in 2005 by 40 per cent. The phase 1 museums increased their contacts with school-aged children by 47 per cent and in the phase 2 museums, the increase was 29 per cent. As before, there were considerable variations in the uplift achieved by each museum service. These figures showed that museums in the *Renaissance* programme were making great efforts to increase their use by schools and families, and that these efforts could be both sustained and improved over time with continued funding.

A manifesto published in 2004 by the National Museums Directors' Conference (NMDC) on behalf of a consortium of museum stakeholders and agencies claimed that visitors to regional museums in the three phase 1 hubs increased by 7 per cent in 2003/04 following investment in the *Renaissance* programme.[8] If this is the case, the increase in pupil contacts has been at a much higher level, at 28 per cent, than the increase in general visitors.

There is not a great deal of research into the numerical use of museums by schools and it is not easy to know what percentage of pupils visit museums in England or in its various regions. Some few clues can be identified, but these figures need to be interpreted carefully to ascertain what population is being discussed. A complete picture cannot at present be found. Statistics from the DfES show that in January 2006 there were 8.2 million pupils in 25,200 maintained and independent schools in England.[9] The NMDC manifesto suggested that 50 per cent of school-age children visit museums and galleries at least once a year and that a quarter of all museum visits are made by children, though no further detail was presented to support these claims.[10] A more detailed study also published by the NMDC reported that a total of at least 6.1 million children visited a national museum in 2002 outside of specific educational trips.[11] Later, the same report on national museums states that three million people participated in formal learning activities on-site and a further 5.6 million off-site learners in 2002, the equivalent of one-tenth of the UK population.[12]

Which schools use museums?

The three linked RCMG studies can be used to produce a picture of the ways in which schools use both regional and national museums. The picture is not a static and unchanging one. Although some constant trends can be identified, the funding streams and their characteristics and requirements act to shift and modify the ways that museums attract schools and the kinds of schools that take up the educational provision that is available. In reviewing the evidence below, the data from all three RCMG studies are discussed together, but it is important to remember that the bulk of the material is drawn from teachers who were using regional museums in England. All three studies asked the teachers visiting museums during the period of the research to complete questionnaires; in the first *Renaissance* study, RR1: 2003, the number of teachers who completed them was 936;[13] in the second *Renaissance* study, RR2: 2005, the number of teachers was 1,643;[14] and in the DCMS/DfES1: 2004 study the number of teachers was 503.[15] The *Strategic Commissioning Programme* involved national museums in partnership with regional museums, and in this study, Evaluation Packs were given out in both national and regional museums (and some other types of museums as well). More than five-sixths of the 3,082 teachers whose questionnaire responses we will be discussing over the next few chapters were visiting regional museums.

The teachers' questionnaires used in all three studies asked for the name and address of the school, followed by a question about the type of school it was. The aim of this was to map the pattern of use by primary, secondary or tertiary institutions.[16] The results for the two *Renaissance* studies (RR1: 2003 and RR2: 2005) are remarkably consistent. The highest percentages of school visits (RR1 – 78 per cent; RR2 – 81 per cent) were made by primary schools where the pupils are aged 4 to 11 years (this category included nursery, infant and junior schools), with far fewer visits made by secondary schools where the pupils are aged 11 to 18 years (RR1 – 13 per cent; RR2 – 10 per cent). 'Special' schools[17] were included in the 'primary' or 'secondary' category unless this was not specified; the 'special' category therefore includes only those special schools for which there was no other category in which to place them. The 'other' category includes, for instance, home schoolers and Brownies. 'Private' schools, which are also sometimes called Independent schools, are non-state-funded schools. The pattern can be illustrated by the data from the second study, where there were 1,594 valid responses from teachers (see Figure 6.1).

Primary schools are perceived by museum education staff as their core bread-and-butter users, and clearly from the *Renaissance* studies, primary schools make up the highest number of school visits. A comparison of the figures from the *Renaissance* studies to one of the earlier studies shows a strong degree of consistency, with 84 per cent of school pupils involved in MGEP1 coming from primary (including nursery) schools.[18]

Interestingly, the DCMS/DfES1: 2004 study shows a slightly different pattern, where primary schools (of all types) make up 71 per cent of the schools visiting museums, secondary schools 18 per cent and middle schools 5 per cent. As funding for the *Strategic Commissioning Programme* did not entail numerical targets, museums were able to work with those groups that were harder to reach, which include groups from secondary schools and colleges, and community-based groups. In a similar manner, during the MGEP2 programme, a number of museums reported that they were using the funding to work with older and younger pupils rather than what they perceived as the easiest group to target – pupils aged 7 to 11 years (Key Stage 2).[19]

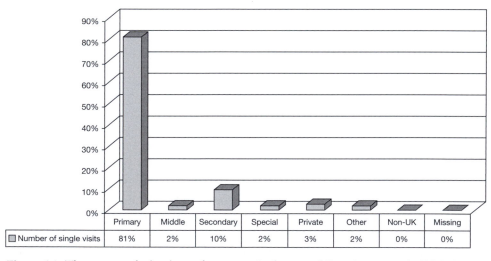

	Primary	Middle	Secondary	Special	Private	Other	Non-UK	Missing
Number of single visits	81%	2%	10%	2%	3%	2%	0%	0%

Figure 6.1 The pattern of school use of museums in the second *Renaissance* study (RR2: 2005). Form A, Q.5: 'Type of school'

Table 6.1 Total number of schools in England according to *School and Pupils in England January 2005*, DfES

	Primary	Secondary including City Technology Colleges & Academies	Special	Independent	Total
2005	17,642	3,416	1,122	2,250	24,430[1]
%	72%	14%	5%	9%	100%

[1] Figures exclude nursery schools and pupil referral units.

The school data from the second RCMG study, RR2: 2005, can be compared to a national breakdown of school types. From the DfES data, *School and Pupils in England January 2005*,[20] actual numbers of the different types of schools in England can be ascertained. This also gives the proportions of the various different types of school in England as percentages of the total number of establishments as set out in Table 6.1.

The schools in the RR2: 2005 study were coded in a slightly different way to the DfES data.[21] Nevertheless, it is possible to use the DfES data to consider in broad terms the proportions of primary and secondary schools that museums reached during the research period and to compare these to the overall breakdown of school types in England. Figure 6.2 compares the distribution of school visits to the 69 museums with the distribution of types of schools in England.

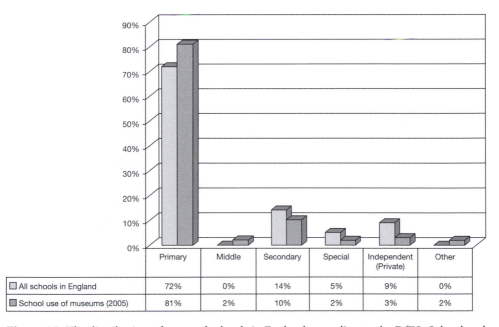

	Primary	Middle	Secondary	Special	Independent (Private)	Other
All schools in England	72%	0%	14%	5%	9%	0%
School use of museums (2005)	81%	2%	10%	2%	3%	2%

Figure 6.2 The distribution of types of schools in England according to the DfES, *School and Pupils in England January 2005*, compared to the pattern of school visits to the 69 museums in RR2: 2005

Another way to consider this issue is to compare the actual schools visiting the 69 museums in the RR2: 2005 study, looking at schools rather than school visits (as some schools visited more than once during the research period). In order to do this, the schools in the RCMG research were recoded to match the coding used by the DfES more closely. Middle schools were split 50/50 into the primary and secondary categories, and special schools were considered as a separate category, where previously in the RCMG study they had been added to either the 'primary' or 'secondary' categories when this was known. Non-UK schools and any entries in the 'other' category were removed. Figure 6.3 shows the comparison.

In both comparisons, primary schools emerge as the largest category of school users of museums. However, secondary schools are very well represented as users of these 69 museums in relation to their numbers in England, possibly rather better than is customarily believed. While both primary and secondary schools are well represented as museum users in relation to numbers of schools, these statistics say nothing about how many pupils from each school were brought to the museum or what proportion these pupils would make up in relation to the total numbers of pupils at each school. Primary schools are frequently very small, sometimes consisting of only 30 to 50 pupils, spread over the age range. Secondary schools, however, are much larger, typically having quite a number of feeder primary schools whose pupils come together at secondary level. If the ages of the 26,791 pupils who completed the pupils' questionnaires during this study are considered (see Figure 6.4), then it becomes clear that while pupils at primary

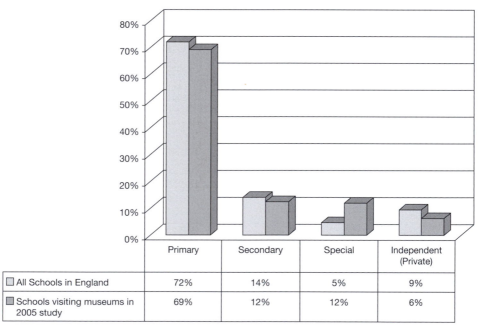

	Primary	Secondary	Special	Independent (Private)
All Schools in England	72%	14%	5%	9%
Schools visiting museums in 2005 study	69%	12%	12%	6%

Figure 6.3 The distribution of types of schools in England according to the DfES, *School and Pupils in England January 2005*, data matched against the schools visiting the 69 museums in RR2: 2005

level might frequently have the opportunity to be taken on a museum visit, pupils are much less likely to have this opportunity when they reach secondary school and, indeed, the older they get, the less likely they are to use museums as part of formal schooling. In other words, while the proportions of both primary and secondary schools using museums match closely their distribution within all schools in England, large numbers of pupils from many small primary schools are visiting museums, while smaller numbers from fewer large secondary schools are doing so.

Findings from a well-conducted study of teacher and parent attitudes to museum school visits carried out for the Tower of London in 1990 also suggest that as pupils move through their school careers, they are less likely to use museums and heritage organisations. In focus group discussions with mothers of school-age children, 'there was fairly general agreement that as they got older the children went on fewer outings'.[22] The CEI evaluation of MGEP2 also found that older pupils were less well represented as museum users.[23] Robins and Woollard found in their study of 68 secondary schools in London that the majority of visits to museums by teachers of art and design were made with their older examination pupils, with those secondary students who did not elect to follow art and design courses in danger of not visiting museums once they had left primary school.[24]

Special schools figure much more highly in the RR2: 2005 museum sample than they do in the national figures, reflecting a very high level of use by schools in this category. The focus group research suggested some of the reasons why teachers of children with learning difficulties and Special Educational Needs value museums. A teacher from a special school in Birmingham for children on the autistic spectrum said in one of the RR2: 2005 focus group discussions: 'Our sort of children need hands-on activities.' She explained that her pupils really enjoyed

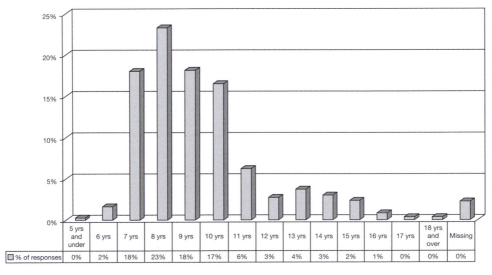

	5 yrs and under	6 yrs	7 yrs	8 yrs	9 yrs	10 yrs	11 yrs	12 yrs	13 yrs	14 yrs	15 yrs	16 yrs	17 yrs	18 yrs and over	Missing
% of responses	0%	2%	18%	23%	18%	17%	6%	3%	4%	3%	2%	1%	0%	0%	0%

Figure 6.4 Breakdown of all KS2 and below and KS3 and above pupils completing the pupils' questionnaire, Form B, by age (RR2: 2005)

going to the museum. As the school history co-ordinator, she had found that because they have seen historical things in the museum and 'have held it in their hands', they were more enthusiastic and able to remember more. A second primary teacher described how museum visits gave opportunities for those children who are not academically bright to shine. She described how one boy responded so well during a museum visit that one of the staff said: 'He's bright, isn't he.' He had never been told that he was clever before, as, on paper, he didn't perform well, but being able to respond orally to what he experienced around him by talking and questioning had enabled him to show his intelligence.[25]

To summarise the material above: the evidence shows that museums in the three RCMG studies were working with high numbers of younger pupils and much lower numbers of older pupils, although in both cases, the pattern of school use appeared to match the pattern of school provision across England. The pattern of use of museums by special schools, on the other hand, shows a much higher use than would be expected, suggesting that special schools find museums very helpful and that museums are able to provide appropriate educational experiences for these particular pupils.

The geographical locations of the schools using museums

The teachers completing questionnaires in all three studies were asked to give the names and addresses of their schools and these were reviewed using two strategies. First, the school postcodes[26] were coded against government indices of deprivation. And second, the names and addresses of the schools visiting the museums were graded according to the percentage of pupils eligible for free school meals.[27] Eligibility for free school meals is the measure used by the DfES and other government departments when considering issues of social inclusion. These two strategies were made possible through the use of a database of schools compiled by the DfES which shows the number of pupils on roll, the number and percentage of pupils known to be eligible for free school meals, and the IMD 2004 rank.[28]

The first *Renaissance* study, RR1: 2003, carried out an analysis of the school postcodes using the DETR Indices of Multiple Deprivation (IMD) 2000, which were publicly available via *National Statistics Online* and discovered that a surprisingly high percentage of the schools visiting museums were located in wards classified as highly deprived. Just over 28 per cent of the visits were from schools located in wards which were classified as among the 10 per cent most deprived wards in England, and 46 per cent of the visits were made by schools which fell into the 20 per cent most deprived. Analysing the postcodes in relation to the Child Poverty Index confirmed these results.[29] The DCMS/DfES1: 2004 study also used this strategy and discovered very similar results in relation to the schools using the national and regional museums in the 12 partnership projects. In this study, 22 per cent of recorded visits come from schools located in wards classified as being among the 10 per cent most deprived wards in England, and just under 43 per cent of the visits were made by schools located in wards which fell into the 20 per cent most deprived. Again, the analysis using the Child Poverty Index confirmed these findings.[30]

By the time of the second study (RR2: 2005), new indices of multiple deprivation had been compiled by the Social Disadvantage Research Centre at the University of Oxford for the Office of the Deputy Prime Minister. Unlike the IMD 2000, which measured deprivation at ward level, the IMD 2004 measures multiple deprivation at Super Output Area level (SOA). SOAs are aggregates of census output areas with units of, on average, 1,500 individuals. The intent is to identify smaller pockets of deprivation that might otherwise be hidden at ward level, which vary considerably in size, area, extent and population size.[31] For the IMD 2004, the more deprived a ward, the lower its ranking; the most deprived ward in England is given a rank of 1 and the least deprived ward a rank of 32,482. However, the representation of social exclusion and deprivation is complex[32] and even this more detailed approach may still fail to show a complete picture. In addition, in relation to schools, the levels of deprivation indicated by the school's postcode may not necessarily represent the levels of deprivation experienced by the pupils themselves. Schools do not always draw their pupils in from the immediate area and their catchment area may in fact extend over multiple SOAs. This is particularly problematic for independent schools, secondary schools, rural schools and other schools where pupils may have to travel. It was not possible in the timeframe of the research to investigate the catchment area of the schools involved so the decision was made to include all possible schools within the data. From 1,594 postcodes collected during the second study RR2: 2005, 1,584 postcodes were matched to the IMD 2004 rankings (see Figure 6.5).

From this analysis, it was found that schools visiting museums in the nine regional hubs during September and October 2005 were located in areas that experience

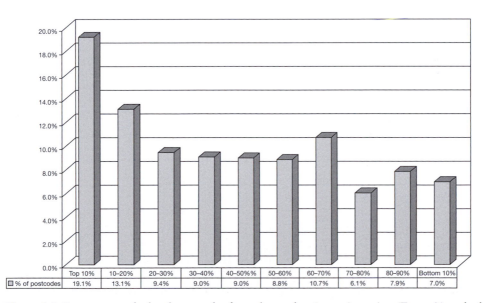

	Top 10%	10–20%	20–30%	30–40%	40–50%%	50–60%	60–70%	70–80%	80–90%	Bottom 10%
% of postcodes	19.1%	13.1%	9.4%	9.0%	9.0%	8.8%	10.7%	6.1%	7.9%	7.0%

Figure 6.5 Percentages of school postcodes from the teachers' questionnaires (Form A) ranked by IMD 2004, SOA rankings, from top 10% most deprived to bottom 10% least deprived (RR2: 2005)

a range of deprivation. There were 19 per cent of recorded single visits from SOAs classified as being among the 10 per cent most deprived in England, and 32 per cent of the visits were made by schools located in the 20 per cent most deprived SOAs in England. The most deprived SOA included in the analysis was ranked 2 out of 32,482 (in Monsall, Manchester) and the least deprived was ranked 32,458 out of 32,482 (in Saffron Walden, Essex).

The postcode data for 664 schools collected during the first study RR1: 2003 was also re-categorised using the IMD 2004 in order to enable a direct comparison to be made between the two studies[33] (Figure 6.6).

When comparing the 2003 data (Figure 6.6) with the 2005 data (Figure 6.5 above) there is a remarkable similarity in terms of proportions of schools from areas of high deprivation making visits to museums. This is particularly noticeable among schools visiting from the top 10 per cent and the 10 to 20 per cent most deprived SOAs. It is also apparent that museums are working with schools across the social spectrum.

The postcode data for 329 schools from the third study, DCMS/DfES1: 2004, was also re-analysed using IMD 2004.[34] The results mirror the *Renaissance* findings. While the museums involved in the *Strategic Commissioning Programme* can be seen to be working with schools across the social spectrum, large percentages of these schools are based in areas of deprivation. There were 19 per cent of schools in this study located in SOAs classified as among the 10 per cent most deprived in England, while 30 per cent of schools were located in SOAs which fell into the 20 per cent most deprived wards in England (Figure 6.7).

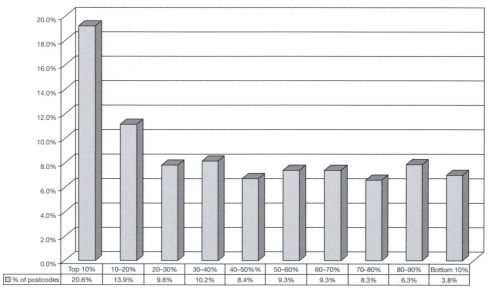

	Top 10%	10–20%	20–30%	30–40%	40–50%%	50–60%	60–70%	70–80%	80–90%	Bottom 10%
% of postcodes	20.6%	13.9%	9.8%	10.2%	8.4%	9.3%	9.3%	8.3%	6.3%	3.8%

Figure 6.6 Percentages of school postcodes from the teachers' questionnaires (Form A) ranked by IMD 2004, SOA rankings, from top 10% most deprived to bottom 10% least deprived (RR1: 2003)

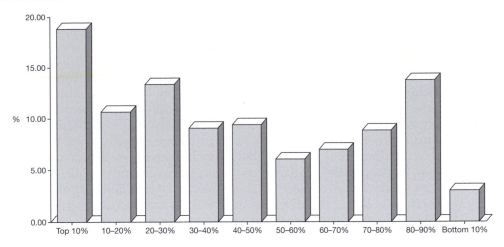

Figure 6.7 Percentages of school visits ranked by Index of Multiple Deprivation 2004, Super Output Area rankings, from top 10% most deprived to bottom 10% least deprived (DCMS/DfES1: 2004)

An assessment of the postcode data in relation to the Income Deprivation Affecting Children Index (IDACI) shows a similar picture. There were 17 per cent of the visits made by schools located in SOAs which were among the highest 10 per cent on IDACI, while 30 per cent of the visits were made by schools located as lying within the top 20 per cent of this index (Figure 6.8).

From the findings of all three studies, it can be seen that museums in England are working with schools that lie across the social spectrum, with disproportionately

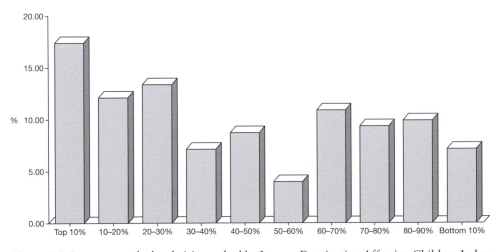

Figure 6.8 Percentage of school visits ranked by Income Deprivation Affecting Children Index 2004, Super Output Area Rankings, from top 10% most deprived to bottom 10% least deprived (DCMS/DfES1: 2004)

high numbers of schools located in areas of deprivation. However, the levels of deprivation indicated by the school's postcode may not necessarily represent the levels of deprivation experienced by the pupils themselves. In order to investigate this more deeply, a well-established pupil-centred measure, eligibility for free school meals, was used as a second strategy to further understand the relationship between school postcode and deprivation experienced by individual pupils.[35] Access to the DfES database allowed this issue to be addressed via records of the proportion of pupils eligible for free school meals. According to DfES statistics, 16 per cent of the 8.2m school pupils in England are entitled to free school meals.[36] The distribution of pupils eligible is highly skewed, with large numbers of schools in England containing very low percentages of pupils eligible for free school meals, while a small number of schools have very high numbers of eligible pupils. To take account of this distribution, it was decided to classify schools in the RR2: 2005 research according to their positions within 'quartiles' within the national distribution as calculated from the DfES database.

This classification showed that of the 1,441 schools included in this analysis, 287 schools (19.9 per cent) could be placed in the first quartile; 319 schools (22.1 per cent) could be placed in the second quartile; 287 schools (19.9 per cent) could be placed in the third quartile; and 548 schools (38.0 per cent) could be placed in the fourth quartile (Figure 6.9).

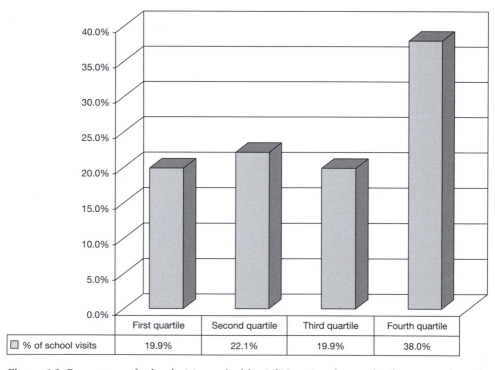

	First quartile	Second quartile	Third quartile	Fourth quartile
% of school visits	19.9%	22.1%	19.9%	38.0%

Figure 6.9 Percentage of school visits ranked by DfES national quartiles for range of pupils (%) eligible for free school meals (RR2: 2005)

Given that the boundaries of the national quartiles are set to each encompass a quarter of schools, it can be seen that disproportionately high numbers of schools (38 per cent) in the second study (RR2: 2005) were drawn from the uppermost quartile. The postcode analysis using indices of multiple deprivation for this and the other studies consistently suggested that museums are working with unexpectedly high numbers of schools located in deprived areas. The postcode analysis using eligibility for free school meals as a pupil-centred index confirms that, for the second study, the children within these schools do in fact live in circumstances that could be described as deprived.[37] As mentioned above, one of the aspects of government policy that was addressed at the time of planning for a comprehensive school service was that of inclusion. From the evidence of these three studies, museums in England are providing an inclusive service.

The analysis of postcodes and entitlement to free school meals usefully enables a tying together of the evidence from the numerical and statistical data arising from the questionnaires and the qualitative data generated by the case studies. Where the schools providing both sources of data conform to the same social patterns, as was the case with the schools in the RR2: 2005 case studies, for example, strong relationships between the qualitative and quantitative evidence can be assumed.

How do teachers use museums?

In the teachers' questionnaire (Form A) there were a number of questions asking about the ways in which teachers used museums and the responses showed that museums are visited by teachers as part of a regular pattern of use of cultural organisations as a whole. Evidence from the first *Renaissance* study, RR1: 2003, showed that 85 per cent of the teachers surveyed came from schools that made regular visits to cultural organisations. The findings were very similar for the RR2: 2005 study with 86 per cent of teachers responding that their school uses cultural organisations on a regular basis, although primary teachers seem slightly more likely than secondary teachers to do so.

The research into school visits at the Tower of London also found that schools visited museums as part of a general culture of educational visits, trips and outings. Schools visiting the Royal Armouries at the Tower of London had also visited Hampton Court, the Science Museum and the British Museum, Alton Towers and Yorvik.[38] Discussion with the mothers of school-age children revealed a different way of talking about the visits of younger and older pupils; younger children were taken on 'trips' or 'outings', while older pupils went on 'educational visits'. Outings for the younger pupils could be divided into five categories: those related in some way to animals, historic sites, museums, places of local interest, and places connected to contemporary life. The educational visits made by older pupils were linked more strongly to specific disciplines (history, geography, art).[39]

Those teachers who use museums seem to do so on a regular basis. A small-scale survey carried out for the Inner London Education Authority in 1988–89 found that 52 per cent of the 100 primary schools responding to the survey had visited between one and five museums or galleries during the year, and a further 29 per cent had visited between six and ten museums.[40] The findings of the RCMG studies also suggest this regular use. Teachers in the RCMG research studies were asked if they had visited a museum (in their role as a teacher) in the past two years other than the museum they were using at the time of the research, and 86 per cent of the total stated that this was so. In the focus groups for RR2: 2005, teachers talked about how museum visits were a joy for children, especially when this was not part of their everyday lives. Some teachers described how many of their pupils did not stray far outside their neighbourhoods, few visiting the city centre, for example, and for these children, museums offered new experiences. The more removed a visit from their normal lives, the more a child would remember it.

The second *Renaissance* study explored the ways teachers used museums in a little more depth than the two earlier studies. Overall, 64 per cent of teachers in the RR2: 2005 study had used on-line museum resources during the past two years,[41] showing that teachers are using museum resources as well as visiting museums. On-line resources were a frequent point of reference in the focus group discussions. Museums have been exploiting the possibilities of new communication technologies, and are aware of the developing DfES e-strategy.[42] This suggests that digital and interactive technologies can be used to develop a more personalised approach to teaching and learning, especially with hard-to-reach groups. Many museums in receipt of *Renaissance* funding up-graded their on-line provision, including the development of new web-based projects, curriculum links and advice on how to manage a school visit. Birmingham Museums and Art Gallery, for example, reported that usage of its web pages has risen from 52,000 user sessions in 2003 to 462,000 user sessions in 2005. As usage dips in August, they are fairly certain that it is mainly pupils and teachers using the site.[43]

Teachers who completed the questionnaire were asked if they had borrowed an object or handling box from a museum in the last two years and 40 per cent reported that they had done so. Fewer teachers used these resources than made a visit to a museum or used on-line resources, but this may reflect a lack of availability as many loan services were closed down in the 1980s and object loan services are not uniformly available across England. Primary teachers (45 per cent) were more likely to use these resources than were secondary teachers (22 per cent).

Many of the teachers in the focus groups and case studies in all studies reported using museums frequently, flexibly and competently. These teachers were able to see the benefits of a museum visit at all stages of teaching a topic: 'taking kids to the museum at the beginning generates enthusiasm and taking them at the end [is about] making connections.'[44] A comparison of these attitudes with those of teachers who were past or potential users of the Royal Armouries at the Tower of London suggests that while teachers may appreciate the value of museums at all stages in the learning process, in practice they tend to use museum school visits to support and illuminate work in progress rather than to initiate or conclude a particular project.[45] However, much more research is needed before firm conclusions can be drawn.

The observations of school visits and the discussions with teachers during the RCMG research revealed some instances of misunderstandings about what museums could provide, and some examples of less than excellent museum provision. Where museum education provision was new, struggling to find ways to develop as rapidly as required, and where communication with teachers was under-developed, some pockets of poor practice were identified.

Museums and the curriculum

Most teachers, most of the time, need to link museum visits with the curriculum their pupils are following. Without this connection, it is harder to justify a museum visit. As a result, most workshops or projects developed by museums for schools make explicit reference to the curriculum. As one museum education officer said when asked whether she had used the National Curriculum to connect to teachers: 'All the time or teachers would not want to know.'[46] However, the ways in which teachers link museums and the curriculum are highly individual and contingent, depending on what museums were offering and how teachers could use these offers for their own purposes.

In the first *Renaissance* study, RR1: 2003, 94 per cent of teachers agreed that their work at the museum was linked to the curriculum; in RR2: 2005, 90 per cent of teachers stated that they took this approach. In RR2: 2005, there was

Plate 6.1 Teachers considering how museum artefacts could be used during a museum training session at the Herbert Museum, Coventry

some difference of approach between primary and secondary teachers, with 94 per cent of primary teachers stating that the work they were doing with their pupils at the museum was linked to the curriculum compared to 87 per cent of secondary teachers. The time period during which the research was carried out may have had a bearing on the high levels of connection to the curriculum, as more visits carried out at the beginning of the school year are likely to be linked to the curriculum than at the end of the school year in June/July. Both *Renaissance* studies, RR1: 2003 and RR2: 2005, were carried out during the autumn term, in September and October, when attention in schools to covering the basic curriculum is high. In addition, this funding programme, as we saw earlier, was intended to build capacity in relation to museum school services, and so museums chose to target the audience which they found easiest to reach – that of primary schools visiting on one occasion to deliver the curriculum.

In the DCMS/DfES *Strategic Commissioning Programme*, museums took the opportunity to work in innovative and creative ways that would not perhaps normally be possible, and they also worked with higher numbers of secondary pupils. There were no numerical targets to reach. Many museums tried hard to reach community audiences they found difficult to work with, such as refugees or asylum seekers, or chose themes, such as Slavery,[47] which were controversial and difficult. The research was also able to be carried out over a greater period of time, with teachers completing questionnaires from September 2003 to March 2004. In this study, 85 per cent of teachers linked their work to the curriculum, with little difference in approach between the proportions of primary (85 per cent) and secondary (84 per cent).

Curriculum use naturally centres on specific disciplines, and in the RCMG studies history consistently played a large part. In the first *Renaissance* study, RR1: 2003, when asked: 'What theme are you studying?', 70 per cent of the 924 teachers who responded stated that they were working on history-related themes, with 15 per cent on themes focused on art and design, and very much smaller numbers in the other categories (Figure 6.10).

However, although history appears to consistently make up a large proportion of the themes teachers address in museums,[48] in any research study these themes are likely to vary according to the museums included within the research sample. This can be demonstrated by reviewing the breakdown of themes being addressed by those teachers who completed questionnaires as part of the DCMS/DfES1: 2004 research. The theme categories were based on those used for the *Renaissance* evaluation. Analysis of the 503 teachers' questionnaires shows that of teachers working on projects that emerged as part of this funding programme, while history remains the dominant category at 51 per cent there are much larger percentages of teachers studying both art (18 per cent) and science and technology (26 per cent) than in the *Renaissance* studies (see Figure 6.11).

The DCMS/DfES1: 2004 study involved a broader set of museums than the two *Renaissance* studies, including national museums, regional local authority museums and a small number of independent museums. The higher proportion of science-themed visits is likely to be because of the large number of science sessions provided by the *Partners in Time* project at the Imperial War Museum, Duxford, and *Creative Canals* at the National Museum of Science and Industry in London.

The ways in which museums and the curriculum are linked vary according to the ways teachers are working, and to a large extent this is determined by government policy, which can change frequently and rapidly. In 2000/01, the government

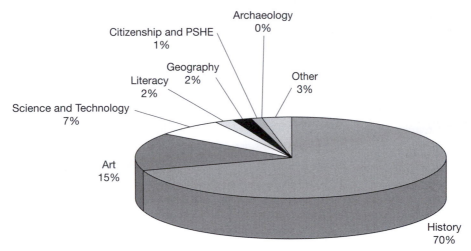

Figure 6.10 Responses to the teacher's questionnaire: Form A, Q.4: 'What theme are you studying?' (RR1: 2003)

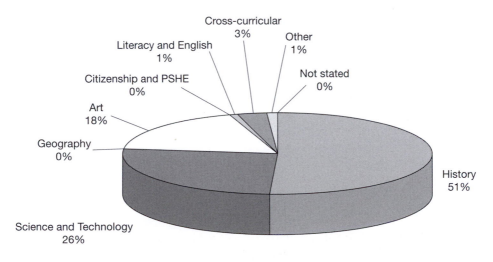

Figure 6.11 Responses to the teacher's questionnaire: Form A, Q.4: 'What theme are you studying?' (DCMS/DfES: 2004)

was placing a great deal of emphasis on improving literacy in primary schools through the National Literacy Strategy, which set specific word, sentence and text level targets for all pupils to achieve. Responding to this initiative, one-third of the projects of the MGEP1 contained literacy components,[49] as did 45 per cent of the projects funded through MGEP2.[50] In 2003, a new strategy for primary schools was published which encouraged schools to manage their teaching content in more flexible and creative ways, focusing on the individual needs of pupils.[51] One teacher in focus groups during the RR2:2005 study stated that

> The culture of teaching is changing again after the literacy and reading strategy, everything went into boxes and now it is changing again because it didn't work.[52]

The second *Renaissance* study, RR2: 2005, found that teachers did seem to be using museums more flexibly than in the earlier *Renaissance* study. In the 1,525 responses to the specific question in this study, a large and surprising increase was found in teachers using museums in an interdisciplinary way. There were 27 per cent of teachers who indicated that their visit was 'Interdisciplinary'; examples were history and literacy, history and science, citizenship and maths (Figure 6.12).

There are one or two methodological issues to consider here. The question concerning the theme being studied was phrased more broadly in 2005, as the research team feared that references to 'themes' might encourage narrow responses and that this might render any interdisciplinarity invisible. The broader question using the phrase 'curriculum areas' did indeed result in a large number of entries that could be coded 'interdisciplinary'. In order to check the significance of the emergence of this large 'interdisciplinary' category, the data from the first study, RR1: 2003, was reviewed and recoded to identify those themes that could

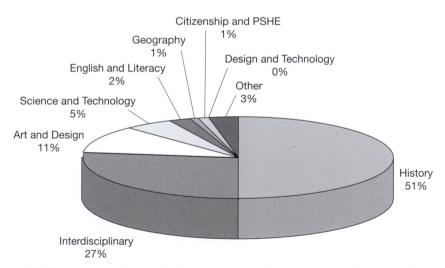

Figure 6.12 Responses to the teachers' questionnaire: Form A, Q.23: 'What curriculum areas are you covering in your visit today?' (RR2: 2005)

be understood as interdisciplinary. It was found that this category did exist in 2003, but was very small at 4 per cent.[53] It may be the case that the rephrasing of the question in the plural encouraged teachers to refer to more than one discipline, but it does not seem very likely that this would account for such a large rise in the interdisciplinary category. It seems more likely that teachers are indeed using museums more flexibly. Teachers in the focus groups in 2005 seemed to find the curriculum less constraining than in 2003, and this is in line with government intentions. The focus group discussions seemed to indicate that it was those teachers who were the more experienced users of museums who were more likely to use them in a cross-curricular way and who were the most articulate about this approach.

The 'Interdisciplinary' theme was further investigated in order to explore the disciplinary basis of the increase from 4 per cent to 27 per cent. Where history or specific periods were mentioned, responses were coded as 'History'; where humanities were mentioned with no reference to history, responses were coded 'Humanities' and other responses were coded 'Other'. There were 78 per cent of the 'Interdisciplinary' responses that could be coded as 'History', with only 1 per cent coded as 'Humanities', and 21 per cent in the 'Other' category. History can thus be seen to be playing a large part in structuring these interdisciplinary themes. When the 409 responses that had been coded 'Interdisciplinary' were analysed in relation to the age of the pupils, it became clear that it was the primary school teachers who were mainly working in this way. There were 90 per cent of the responses coded 'Interdisciplinary' made by primary teachers. From this analysis, it would seem that primary teachers are taking advantage of the opportunity to work in creative ways, as encouraged by the new primary strategy.[54]

Multiple objectives for visiting museums

Most of the teachers in the RCMG studies, most of the time, linked their visits to the curriculum. An interesting paper by Anderson and his colleagues suggests that this is an international approach; three studies reported would seem to show that teachers in Canada, America and Germany also link museum visits to curriculum-based themes.[55] But Anderson's work suggests that this is not as straightforward as it seems. In one of the studies discussed in this paper, which was carried out in Los Angeles with a class visiting the Natural History Museum of Los Angeles County, 90 per cent of participating teachers reported that a connection to the curriculum was an important reason for the visit. However, multiple other reasons were also cited, including exposing students to new experiences (39 per cent) and fostering interest and motivation (18 per cent). When asked when they knew that a visit had been successful, 61 per cent of teachers stated that this was judged by whether or not their students had had a positive experience. In the Vancouver study reported in this paper, strong evidence emerged from survey and focus group data that a close fit to the curriculum was the most important issue for most teachers, but this study and other evidence suggested that teachers did not integrate the field trip or visit into their curriculum-based teaching, focusing instead on the motivational aspects of the visit. In all three of the studies reported in this paper, the teachers talked about the link to the curriculum, but actually judged the success of the school visit by student enjoyment and other emotional and attitudinal criteria.

The RCMG studies suggest that for most teachers, most of the time, the link to the curriculum is essential, but while it has to be in place for the visit to take place at all, this may not be the most important aspect of the visit. Teachers in the RR2: 2005 focus group discussions pointed out that visits enhance the curriculum, but they also suggested that visits go much further than this. Some teachers were of the view that by coming out of school they were doing much more than just looking at the curriculum. And indeed, as Griffiths points out, where the curriculum is limited, and museums have strong moral convictions about what young people need to know, as is the case with colonialism, post-colonialism and slavery, museums may be offering ways to supplement the curriculum in important ways that are used positively by teachers.[56]

The research study of school visits to the Tower of London that was carried out in 1990 reported that the main reason which teachers have for taking their children on school visits was to 'stimulate their pupils' interest in the subject under study'.[57] Increasing subject knowledge was also of considerable importance, as was the development of study and social skills, but to a lesser degree. Interestingly but not very surprisingly, very few teachers used school visits as a reward for good work. This study provides useful comparative data for the RCMG studies and confirms that teachers value museums because of their power to switch on learning. The Tower study also reported that most teachers used school visits to support work in progress, rather than to initiate or conclude a particular project.[58]

Conclusions

The three linked RCMG studies have produced a national picture of which schools use museums that has a high degree of generalisability. In these studies, museums worked with schools across the social spectrum, and of those primary, secondary and special schools that used regional and national museums in England, very high numbers were located in areas at risk of deprivation, and many of the pupils in these schools were at risk of social exclusion. This approach reflects the wish of museums to address government policies, but also reflects to some extent the wishes of the education staff involved.

Primary schools were more likely to use museums than secondary schools, and museums hosted a disproportionately large number of special schools. While museums found it more difficult to attract secondary schools, partly because the culture of taking pupils out is much weaker with older pupils, where opportunities permitted, museum staff were keen to expand on their customary primary audience and did so with some success.

Many teachers used museums to help deliver the history curriculum, with use in other disciplines more limited in these particular research studies. But teachers also used museums more broadly than in the delivery of the curriculum, and a more creative and flexible approach to the curriculum, especially by those teachers who were experienced in visiting museums, was noted in the second *Renaissance* programme, with a large increase in interdisciplinary projects between 2003 and 2005.

The research showed that museum staff involved with education are proactive and energetic; they responded rapidly and efficiently to new funding programmes and, where increased numerical targets were set, they reached and exceeded them. The challenge of increasing the contacts between museums and schools was achieved by many (though not all) of those regional museums funded through the *Renaissance* programme. The postcode and free school meals analysis shows that this increase includes a disproportionate percentage of schools located in areas with high levels of deprivation, where children may be at risk of social exclusion. Regional museums in England, as a whole, have a deep reservoir of skills and expertise in museum education and have frequently been pioneers in developing an understanding and engaging with new and non-traditional audiences.[59] Evidence of this capacity of museums, to work with schools where deprivation may be experienced by children, is strong and consistent.

7

The value of museums to teachers

What is it about museums that teachers value? Why do they take the trouble to take their classes to museums? How do they feel about what museums can offer and what is it that affects their attitudes to museums? Teachers expect their pupils to learn during their museum visits, but which learning outcomes were the most important?

There were 3,113 teachers and 56,810 pupils who completed questionnaires during the three linked RCMG studies. The level of enthusiasm for museums was very high in these responses, and for both teachers and pupils, it was the pleasure and inspiration that they experienced during their visits that was most highly valued. It is important to realise that for these school visits, the museums offered workshops and active learning sessions. The young people were engaged in handling objects, drama and role-play, problem solving, dressing up, drawing, writing and making artwork and so on. These school visits did not take the form of gallery tours, as museum staff know that in 'museums where you just walk around and have a look (and) you can't really ask questions' pupils can soon become bored. Being actively involved in workshops, or, for example, discussion with costumed interpreters, 'it makes you remember things more than just looking at it'.[1]

Teachers' attitudes to the Generic Learning Outcomes

The teachers' questionnaires asked a number of questions about how teachers valued the five Generic Learning Outcomes. One question presented the five GLOs and asked teachers to rate each one on a five-point scale running from 'very important' to 'not at all important'. The idea was not to place the five GLOs on one scale, rating them against each other, but to assess the importance of each independently. The same question was asked in each of the three linked studies.

Figure 7.1 presents the results of the question from the second *Renaissance* study, RR2: 2005. Teachers were enthusiastic about all the GLOs; there were very high levels of positive responses, with very few responses in the other categories. The most important learning outcome in teachers' eyes is that of enjoyment and inspiration. As we shall see, nearly all pupils enjoy and are inspired by their museum experience, and this is of tremendous importance to teachers as it increases pupils' curiosity and thus motivation to learn. Over three-quarters of the teachers (76 per cent) rated Enjoyment, Inspiration, Creativity 'very important', with a further 18 per cent rating it 'important'.

Before exploring this very important finding further, a small issue of methodology needs to be pointed out. In the second *Renaissance* study, RR2: 2005, it was decided to add a 'Don't know' option in addition to the various degrees of importance that teachers could choose in order to make a clearer distinction between those teachers who did not complete this question (and were therefore classified as 'Missing') and those teachers who did not understand the question or were not sure about the answer. In the event, the 'Don't know' category was rarely used by teachers. A very few teachers failed to complete some or all of this question, leaving it blank; as can be seen, the missing values stand at 5 per cent or 6 per cent for most of the categories. However, for Action, Behaviour, Progression, the

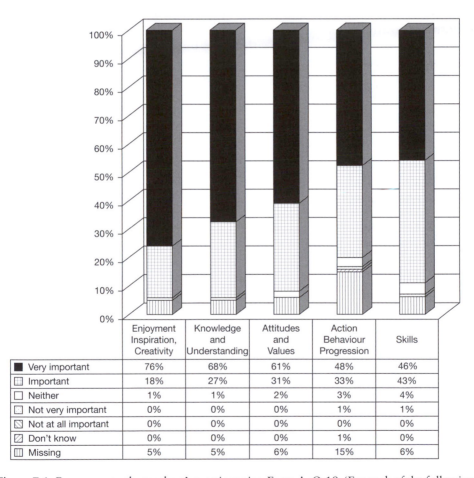

	Enjoyment Inspiration, Creativity	Knowledge and Understanding	Attitudes and Values	Action Behaviour Progression	Skills
■ Very important	76%	68%	61%	48%	46%
▦ Important	18%	27%	31%	33%	43%
☐ Neither	1%	1%	2%	3%	4%
☐ Not very important	0%	0%	0%	1%	1%
◩ Not at all important	0%	0%	0%	0%	0%
▨ Don't know	0%	0%	0%	1%	0%
▥ Missing	5%	5%	6%	15%	6%

Figure 7.1 Responses to the teachers' questionnaire: Form A, Q.19: 'For each of the following potential outcomes from the use of the museum, please could you rate the importance of each one in your view?' (RR2: 2005)

107

missing category suddenly jumps to 15 per cent. It is unclear whether this means that teachers did not understand the category, did not value this category, or perhaps, as one teacher suggested in a focus group discussion, teachers saw change in Action, Behaviour, Progression as longer-term occurrences which would not be expected to happen immediately after a museum visit. Another teacher pointed out that it was hard to identify progress over time following a museum visit. The impact at the time of the visit could be observed, but a permanent change would need to be sustained over time, and this was hard to map in individual children.[2] The large percentage of missing responses needs to be remembered in the interpretation of results for this GLO.

A striking thing to note about the responses to the question about the importance of each of the GLOs in RR2: 2005 is that, looking at the 'very important' responses, there is a clear scale of relative importance. Enjoyment, Inspiration, Creativity is the GLO that was most frequently valued as 'very important' and there is a clear scale of value in the ratings of the other outcomes (Table 7.1).

If both the positive values are taken together, this scale is not quite as clear. The percentages of teachers who ticked either 'very important' or 'important' are very high, and particularly so for Enjoyment, Inspiration, Creativity; Knowledge and Understanding; and Attitudes and Values. All learning outcomes were highly valued by those teachers who used the museums in the second *Renaissance* study, RR2: 2005, even Skills and Action, Behaviour, Progression that seemed to be less significant when only the most positive values were counted (Table 7.2).

Table 7.1 Responses to the teachers' questionnaire: Form A, Q.19: 'For each of the following potential outcomes from the use of the museum, please could you rate the importance of each one in your view?' Teachers ticking 'very important' (RR2: 2005)

	RR2: 2005
Enjoyment, Inspiration, Creativity	76%
Knowledge and Understanding	68%
Attitudes and Values	61%
Action, Behaviour, Progression	48%
Skills	46%

Table 7.2 Responses to the teachers' questionnaire: Form A, Q.19: 'For each of the following potential outcomes from the use of the museum, please could you rate the importance of each one in your view?' Teachers ticking 'important' and 'very important' (RR2: 2005)

	RR2: 2005
Enjoyment, Inspiration, Creativity	94%
Knowledge and Understanding	95%
Attitudes and Values	92%
Skills	89%
Action, Behaviour, Progression	81%

These responses were further analysed to compare the attitudes to the five Generic Learning Outcomes of primary and secondary teachers; teachers whose work was linked to the curriculum with those whose work was not linked to the curriculum; and teachers who were on their first visit to the museum with teachers who had visited previously. While this last category did not seem to affect to any great degree the ways in which teachers felt about the importance of learning outcomes, considerable variation was found between teachers of primary-aged and secondary-aged pupils, and teachers who were and who were not using the museum for curriculum-related purposes (Table 7.3 and Table 7.4).

It is very clear that primary teachers consistently regard the five potential types of outcome as more important than do the secondary teachers, and this is particularly so in the case of Enjoyment, Inspiration, Creativity, and Attitudes and Values, where there are differences of 13 per cent and 11 per cent respectively in the numbers of teachers regarding these as 'very important'. While primary teachers appear to value the activities that their pupils may engage in and the progression that may result slightly more highly than secondary teachers, once the missing and don't know categories are excluded this difference is not statistically significant.[3]

While these results suggest that teachers working with younger pupils are more likely to use museums because they anticipate powerful learning outcomes, the purposes for which museums are used also have an effect on how important the learning outcomes are to teachers. Table 7.4 shows the percentages of teachers who were and who were not using the museum to deliver the curriculum who ticked the option 'very important' when asked how they felt about each of the generic learning outcomes.

The relationship of the work done in the museum to the curriculum has a considerable impact on teachers' attitudes to all the GLOs. In all cases, it is the teachers who are using the museum to deliver the curriculum who feel that the learning outcomes are most important. The most marked difference is that accorded to Knowledge and Understanding; 73 per cent of those teachers whose work was linked to the curriculum said that the knowledge that their pupils would gain was 'very important', compared to 45 per cent of those whose work was not linked to the curriculum, a difference of 28 per cent. There is an 18 per cent difference in relation to Skills and a 12 per cent difference in relation both to

Table 7.3 Responses to the teachers' questionnaire: Form A, Q.19: 'For each of the following potential outcomes from the use of the museum, please could you rate the importance of each one in your view?' Primary and secondary teachers ticking 'very important' (RR2: 2005)

	Primary teachers	*Secondary teachers*
Enjoyment, Inspiration, Creativity	81%	68%
Knowledge and Understanding	72%	65%
Attitudes and Values	66%	55%
Action, Behaviour, Progression	58%	49%
Skills	49%	44%

Table 7.4 Responses to the teachers' questionnaire: Form A, Q.19: 'For each of the following potential outcomes from the use of the museum, please could you rate the importance of each one in your view?' Teachers using museums for curriculum-related and non-curriculum-related purposes ticking 'very important' (RR2: 2005)

	Curriculum-related	*Non-curriculum-related*
Enjoyment, Inspiration, Creativity	80%	75%
Knowledge and Understanding	73%	45%
Attitudes and Values	65%	53%
Action, Behaviour, Progression	57%	45%
Skills	50%	32%

Attitudes and Values, and to Action, Behaviour, Progression. Interestingly, there is a much smaller differentiation at 5 per cent in relation to Enjoyment, Inspiration, Creativity, and this was found not to be statistically significant.[4]

The enjoyment factor remains a very important outcome regardless of the purpose in using the museum. Although the differences are smaller in relation to the other GLOs, the purpose of the visit has a strong impact on how teachers value the outcomes of the visit. While maintaining a strong positive view about the learning outcomes, teachers regard learning outcomes as less important when work is not curriculum-related.

The analysis above shows that, in considering how teachers value museums and the learning that may result from their use, it is vital to differentiate between primary and secondary teachers, and also between the purposes for which those teachers are using museums. Primary teachers as a whole are much more likely to find the museum-based learning outcomes 'very important' than secondary teachers, and more of those teachers who are using museums for curriculum-related work think that the five GLOs are 'very important' than those who are not linking the museum work to the curriculum.

When the levels of importance accorded to each of the GLOs by teachers in the second *Renaissance* study, RR2: 2005 were compared with those from the first study, RR1: 2003, some interesting results emerged (Table 7.5). The percentages of teachers ticking 'important' and 'very important' are extremely consistent across the two studies. The major difference is in relation to Action, Behaviour, Progression, where the large percentage of missing has had an impact. There were some variations in the numbers of teachers agreeing that the GLOs were 'very important' across the two studies, but an in-depth analysis showed that this was probably accounted for by a slight drop of 4 per cent in those teachers stating that they were using the museum for curriculum-related purposes.

During the three linked RCMG studies, 3,172 teachers' questionnaires (Form A) were completed, with remarkably consistent results in relation to the importance accorded the five GLOs (see Table 7.6). While the teachers' ratings of the individual GLOs vary a little across the three studies, the levels of comparative importance accorded to each do not. It is extremely interesting to see that across the quantita-

Table 7.5 Responses to the teachers' questionnaire: Form A, Q.19: 'For each of the following potential outcomes from the use of the museum, please could you rate the importance of each one in your view?' Teachers ticking both 'important' and 'very important', comparing RR2: 2005 and RR2: 2003

	RR2: 2005	*RR1: 2003*
Enjoyment, Inspiration, Creativity	94%	96%
Knowledge and Understanding	95%	96%
Attitudes and Values	92%	93%
Skills	89%	88%
Action, Behaviour, Progression	81%	92%

tive data from the three studies, while the Knowledge and Understanding that pupils might gain from museum visits take a strong second place, it is not the cognitive aspects of learning in museums that teachers think the most important. Rather, teachers value Enjoyment, Inspiration, Creativity most highly (Table 7.6).

The statistical data shows conclusively that what teachers value most about museums is the opportunity for their pupils to have an experience that is enjoyable and inspirational and which might lead to creativity. However, the statistical data cannot tell us why this might be so, or give examples of how this might work. Quantitative approaches are useful in gaining a broad overview, but to explore the depth of a phenomenon, other methods which yield more qualitative data are necessary. In order to fully understand the character of learning in museums, this statistical data needs to be fleshed out by listening to teachers and pupils as they talk about their experiences and describe their feelings. In the case studies and focus groups, teachers discussed the learning outcomes stimulated by museum visits in a general way, calling on their memories of a number of visits on a number of different occasions.

Pupils' attitudes to their own learning

Pupils visiting the museums were asked to complete their own questionnaires and the numbers doing so were very high. In the second *Renaissance* study

Table 7.6 Responses to the teachers' questionnaire: Form A, Q.19: 'For each of the following potential outcomes from the use of the museum, please could you rate the importance of each one in your view?' Teachers ticking 'very important', comparing across the three studies: RR2: 2005; RR1: 2003; DCMS/DfES1: 2004

	RR2: 2005	*RR1: 2003*	*DCMS/DfES1: 2004*
Enjoyment, Inspiration, Creativity	76%	81%	79%
Knowledge and Understanding	68%	72%	63%
Attitudes and Values	61%	58%	55%
Action, Behaviour, Progression	48%	57%	50%
Skills	46%	44%	46%

(RR2: 2005), for example, 26,791 pupils completed Form Bs. An analysis of these returns shows that 82 per cent of these (21,845) were from younger pupils aged 7 to 11 years (KS2 or below) and 18 per cent (4,946) were completed by older pupils aged 12 to 18 years (KS3 and above). In terms of gender there was a fairly even division for pupils completing Form B KS2 and below (48 per cent female and 49 per cent male), while at KS3 and above there were more girls (55 per cent) than boys (42 per cent). These breakdowns were virtually identical to the first *Renaissance* study (RR1: 2003). The age range of pupils completing the questionnaires in 2005 was also very similar to the earlier study, with most pupils concentrated in the 8 to 12 age range, as we saw in Chapter 6 (Figure 7.2).

Reviewing the responses from the DCMS/DfES1: 2004 research, it can be seen that altogether 9,415 pupils completed questionnaires; primary school-age pupils made up 78 per cent of the total, with 22 per cent of the pupils at the older age range. There were higher numbers of older pupils, and more girls, taking part in these projects that involved partnerships between national and regional museums than in those projects based in the regional museums.[5] The lack of numerical targets to be met and the focus in the programme on developing partnerships based on good practice encouraged museums to be more adventurous and to attempt to reach secondary groups that did not always use museums.

The questions for the pupils were designed to elicit their views in relation to the five GLOs. Tables 7.7 and 7.8 compare the results from the three linked RCMG studies. The younger pupils are very enthusiastic about their museum experiences, and confident about their own learning (see Table 7.7).

In the second *Renaissance* study, RR2: 2005, 93 per cent of the younger pupils enjoyed their visit and 86 per cent thought museums were exciting places. There were 90 per cent who learnt some interesting new things and 80 per cent could

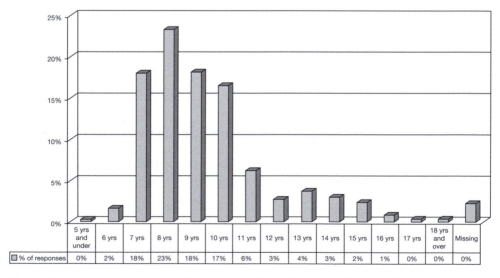

	5 yrs and under	6 yrs	7 yrs	8 yrs	9 yrs	10 yrs	11 yrs	12 yrs	13 yrs	14 yrs	15 yrs	16 yrs	17 yrs	18 yrs and over	Missing
% of responses	0%	2%	18%	23%	18%	17%	6%	3%	4%	3%	2%	1%	0%	0%	0%

Figure 7.2 Breakdown of all pupils completing Form B, by age (RR2: 2005)

Table 7.7 What younger pupils said about their learning in RR2: 2005; comparing percentages that ticked 'yes' in RR1: 2003 and DCMS/DfES1: 2004

Younger pupils (KS2 and below)	Yes, RR2: 2005	No	Don't know	Missing	Yes, RR1: 2003	Yes, DCMS/ DfES1: 2004
I enjoyed today's visit	93%	2%	5%	1%	94%	91%
I learnt some interesting new things	90%	3%	6%	1%	90%	90%
I could understand most of the things we saw and did	80%	6%	13%	1%	81%	79%
This is an exciting place	86%	4%	8%	2%	87%	83%
Visiting has given me lots of ideas for things I could do	72%	11%	15%	2%	73%	71%
A visit is useful for school work	86%	4%	8%	2%	87%	83%
The visit has made me want to find out more	76%	9%	13%	2%	77%	73%

understand most of the things they saw and did. Some 86 per cent of these younger pupils thought the museum visit was useful for school work, which is surprisingly high, but is maintained at this high level across the three studies, as is the idea that the visit has motivated curiosity to find out more.

While the figures vary a little across the three studies, altogether there is a remarkable consistency between the different studies and across the different time periods. The findings suggest very strongly that children between 7 and 11 years have found museums enjoyable and exciting, places where they have learnt about interesting things, felt stimulated to go further with their learning, and found ideas and experiences that have helped with what they were doing in the classroom.

Younger pupils find it easier to be enthusiastic. Older pupils find this less easy, but the results of their questionnaires are also very positive (see Table 7.8). The first question in the older pupils' questionnaire in RR2: 2005 was a new one which asked whether they had enjoyed their visit. This was asked in order to probe pupils' views of Enjoyment, Inspiration, Creativity following the results of the teachers' questionnaires in RR1: 2003 and DCMS/DfES1: 2004, where this GLO was found to be the most important one from the teachers' perspectives. Some 86 per cent of the older pupils agreed that the visit had been enjoyable.

In RR2: 2005, 85 per cent of the older pupils agreed they had discovered some interesting new things; this was a slightly lower percentage than in the first *Renaissance* study (RR1: 2003) or the DCMS/DfES1: 2004 study, where 87 per cent and 89 per cent respectively agreed. These are very high figures for pupils

Table 7.8 What older pupils said about their learning in RR2: 2005; comparing percentages that ticked 'yes' in RR1: 2003 and DCMS/DfES1: 2004

Older pupils (Key Stage 3 and above)	Yes, RR2: 2005	No	Don't know	Missing	Yes, RR1: 2003	Yes, DCMS/DfES1: 2004
I enjoyed today's visit (a)	86%	4%	9%	1%	n/a	n/a
Today's visit has given me lots to think about (b)	n/a	n/a	n/a	n/a	73%	77%
I discovered some interesting things from the visit today	85%	6%	8%	1%	87%	89%
A museum/gallery visit makes school work more inspiring	68%	12%	19%	1%	58%	64%
The visit has given me a better understanding of the subject	71%	12%	16%	1%	72%	77%
A museum visit is a good place to pick up new skills	68%	11%	20%	1%	62%	70%
The museum is a good place to learn in a different way to school	83%	6%	10%	1%	82%	86%
I could make sense of most of the things we saw and did at the museum	73%	8%	18%	1%	70%	74%
I would come again	54%	14%	31%	2%	55%	55%
I've left the museum more interested in the subject than when I came	58%	17%	23%	2%	59%	63%

Note (a) This question was asked in RR2: 2005 only.
Note (b) This question was asked in RR1: 2003 and DCMS/DfES1: 2004 only.

aged 11 to 18 years. It would be interesting to see if a change in the wording to 'learnt' from 'discovered' would produce different results. However, the first question in the RR1: 2003 and DCMS/DfES1: 2004 studies was: 'Today's visit has given me lots to think about', which elicited rather less positive responses, although it seems to cover much the same ground. Possibly the more concrete question, 'I discovered some interesting things', enabled pupils to think about specific activities, objects or images that they had done or seen during their visit and that they could immediately recall, whereas the less specific and more abstract reference to 'lots to think about' with its future projection demanded an intention to do something (think) in the future. There was a fairly high percentage of responses in the 'don't know' boxes (14 per cent and 15 per cent) in both studies.

It is very encouraging to find that quite a high percentage (58–68 per cent) of older pupils find that museums make school work more inspiring, but even more encouraging and surprising to see the very large percentages (82–86 per cent) of these older pupils who have really enjoyed learning in museums in a different way to school. The numbers of pupils who found that museums inspired them increased between the first and second *Renaissance* studies by 10 per cent. About three-quarters of the older pupils felt that they left the museum with a better understanding of their subject, and more than half thought they left with a greater interest in the subject. Both their understanding and their interest increased in many pupils. About two-thirds of pupils thought museums were good places to pick up new skills. Over half of the older pupils thought they might come again.

The most noticeable change between the three studies in Table 7.8 concerns the attitudes of older pupils to museums. Some 10 per cent more of the older pupils in 2005 considered visits to museums and galleries can make school work more inspiring than in 2003. This is an interesting finding, which can be illustrated by some of the responses to the open question on Form B completed by older pupils. Stacey, aged 15, visiting Manchester Art Gallery, wrote:

> *Taking photographs, and making pictures from tape, it was using a new method to express creativity. The whole trip was inspirational.*

Vicky, aged 15, who was visiting Birmingham Museums and Art Gallery, wrote in response to the stimulus 'The most interesting thing about today was':

> *To be able to look at various artist work, and explore different styles of painting and to be more inspired by other peoples work.*

The statistical evidence from the pupils' questionnaires shows clearly that pupils of all ages in all three studies in both national and regional museums in England find museums diverting and stimulating sites for learning. These pupils are also to a very large degree confident that learning has occurred.

The importance of museums in teaching

It can perhaps be assumed that if teachers are using museums, then they think they are useful and important. However, prior to the recent RCMG and CEI research there was no clear research-based evidence of this in England. The teachers' questionnaire (Form A) that was used for the three linked RCMG evaluation studies included an explicit question 'How important are museums to your teaching?' The answers to this turned out to be very positive, but the importance of museums to teachers is embedded in their reasons for using the museums in the first place.

In the first study, RR1: 2003, the total percentage of teachers feeling positive about museums and finding them either 'very important' or 'important' for teaching was 95 per cent. Two years later, however, there seemed to be a significant change in how teachers rated the importance of museums to their teaching. While the overall positive value was much the same (95 per cent in 2003, 94 per cent in 2005), the balance had shifted significantly, so that fewer teachers in 2005 stated that museums were 'very important' than in 2003 (46 per cent compared with 58 per cent), and more stated 'important' (48 per cent compared with 37 per cent). Probing for the reasons why teachers' attitudes might vary as part of the second *Renaissance* study showed that while the age of pupil did not affect teachers' views, the purpose of the visit in relation to the delivery of the curriculum did have an impact. As Figure 7.3 shows, teachers were more likely to rate museums as important to their teaching if their work with pupils at the museum was linked to the curriculum.

Some 97 per cent of teachers who were using the museum for curriculum-related work in RR2: 2005 stated that museums were either 'very important' or 'important.' However, 89 per cent of those who were not using the museum for curriculum-related work also expressed positive attitudes. But there was a difference of 15 per cent between the 'very important' ratings; 15 per cent more of those teachers using the museum for curriculum-related work rated museums as 'very important' to their teaching than those using the museums for work which is not focused on the curriculum. Some 90 per cent of teachers responding to the survey in 2005 stated that their work was linked to the curriculum. Comparing the two *Renaissance* studies, the percentage of teachers rating museums 'very important' appears to have dropped from 58 per cent in 2003 to 46 per cent in 2005. But the percentage of teachers whose work was linked to the curriculum

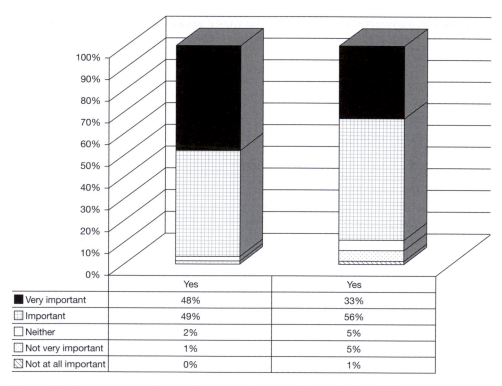

	Yes	Yes
■ Very important	48%	33%
▦ Important	49%	56%
☐ Neither	2%	5%
☐ Not very important	1%	5%
◪ Not at all important	0%	1%

Figure 7.3 Responses to the teachers' questionnaire: Form A, Q.26: 'How important to teaching?' by Q.22: 'Is today's work linked to the curriculum?' (RR2: 2005)

116

in 2003 was higher at 95 per cent than in 2005, and this drop in direct relationship to the curriculum between 2003 and 2005 may explain the apparent drop in the ratings of the importance of museums to teachers.

Comparing the importance accorded to museums by teachers across the three most recent RCMG studies shows that although the degree of enthusiasm as measured by ticking 'important' or 'very important' might vary a little, the overall enthusiasm for museums exhibited by the teachers who are using them is consistent and at a very high level (Table 7.9).

The drop in linkage with the curriculum between the two *Renaissance* studies is itself of interest. Although it is not very large at 4 per cent of teachers involved in the two studies, it does chime with government policy for the use of museums. But there is perhaps a contradiction in this; if it is teachers who are using the museum for curriculum-related purposes who value the learning that museums can stimulate most highly, a drop in these teachers may result in lower numbers of teachers valuing museums. Are teachers as utilitarian in their view as government, only valuing museums because they can help with the basic work they have to do in delivering the curriculum? Are personal and identity-related issues not important? It seems very likely that for those teachers working in schools where their pupils are at risk, any method that can be found to enable these young people to feel more positive about their capacities for learning would be welcomed, and there were indeed statements made to this effect by teachers in the face-to-face discussions. However, this is one of the many areas thrown up by the RCMG studies that would benefit from further research.

Conclusions

This chapter has begun to explore the value of museums to schools, focusing on teachers' and pupils' attitudes to the five Generic Learning Outcomes. While attitudes are in general extremely positive to museums, there are subtle variations in attitude according to how museums are used.

Primary teachers as a whole are more likely to find the museum-based learning outcomes 'very important' than are secondary teachers. Considering the GLOs in relation to teachers' purposes in using museums shows that these differences in purpose have a considerable impact on how teachers value the potential

Table 7.9 Responses to the teachers' questionnaire: Form A, Q.26: 'How important to teaching'. Percentages of teachers stating that museums were 'very important' and 'important', comparing RR1: 2003, RR2: 2005 and DCMS/DfES1: 2004

	RR2: 2005	*RR1: 2003*	*DCMS/DfES1: 2004*
Very important	46%	58%	47%
Important	48%	37%	47%
Totals	94%	95%	94%

learning outcomes. More of those teachers using museums for curriculum-related work think that the five GLOs are 'very important' than those who are not linking the museum work to the curriculum.

An overview of the pupils' responses to the GLO-related questionnaire shows a largely positive response. This is particularly strong for the younger pupils, but even the older pupils, who might be expected to find museums less than cool, are enthusiastic.

It is the enthusiasm and pleasure that young people experience in museums that teachers value most. The next two chapters will analyse the five learning outcomes in more detail, and in probing these outcomes, the dimensions of museum-based learning begins to emerge. The character of the learning experiences of the pupils has immensely powerful effects, and a consideration of this character reveals why museum experiences can be so memorable and enhancing, and how they can impact on self-identity.

8

Pupils' learning outcomes: the teachers' views

This chapter examines teachers' perspectives on their pupils' learning outcomes. Their views of the extent to which their pupils will have attained each of the five Generic Learning Outcomes are explored in turn. The quantitative data in the last chapter showed that pupils value the enjoyment, inspiration and creativity that they find in museums and that teachers consider this to be the most important learning outcome of the visit. But at one level this seems very superficial; is it just for fun that teachers bring their pupils to museums? Given the effort that teachers have to make to take a class out of school, especially at secondary level, this seems improbable.[1] What else do teachers think their pupils will have gained from their museum visit? And why is enjoyment so significant?

Anderson suggests that the educational worth of a field trip may be heavily dependent on the agenda of the teacher leading it, primarily in finding the balance between focused learning and enjoyment.[2] But, as he points out, very few studies of teachers' perceptions have been carried out. Much American research has focused on children learning in museums and much of this has tried to show cognitive gain, identifying what facts and information children have learnt. But the RCMG research shows that what teachers want is the enjoyment, inspiration and creative thinking that museums can generate and which are essential in opening up the mind to enable new ideas and perceptions to enter.

The main aims of each of the three linked RCMG studies (RR1: 2003, RR2: 2005 and DCMS/DfES1: 2004) were to measure the outcome and the impact of museum-based learning. 'Outcomes' encompasses learning that can be identified in individuals, while 'impact' considers what this learning might mean in the longer term, at the level of the social. Impact can only be addressed after the outcomes have been mapped and considered in depth. In all three linked RCMG studies, the research focused on learning outcomes, and from the findings, a first view of the impact of learning in museums was derived and reported. Here, in a book-length discussion, the analysis can be taken a little further. This chapter reviews teachers' attitudes to their pupils' learning, and the next chapter uses the pupils' voices to set out what they felt about their own learning. From this evidence it will be possible to analyse more deeply the impact of learning in museums at the beginning of the twenty-first century and to ponder the implications and potential of this impact, bearing in mind legacies of older ways of thinking that still resonate in many museums.

There were a number of questions in the teachers' questionnaires that focused specifically on the extent to which teachers felt their pupils had achieved or would achieve each learning outcome as a result of the museum visit. All five Generic Learning Outcomes were included and each was presented in the form of a small number of sub-categories. These sub-categories were devised from the research team's experience of learning in museums combined with a review of evaluation studies from the UK. Other sub-categories of course exist and if research based on the idea of Generic Learning Outcomes is undertaken in future, it may be that new or modified sub-categories arise from the research itself, as the character of museum-based learning is explored in more depth. At the present time, the sub-categories used in the RCMG research offer ample evidence of teachers' views about each of the GLOs, and evidence for the attainment of each GLO can be easily found in the pupils' work.

There were 3,113 teachers who completed questionnaires (Form A) over the three linked RCMG studies; of these there were 936 in RR1: 2003, 1,632 in RR2: 2005 and 545 in DCMS/DfES1: 2004. In the discussions that follow, the statistical data derived from the teachers' questionnaires in RR2: 2005 is given depth, texture and context by using the comments teachers made during case studies and focus groups. In some instances, evidence from the pupils is also included, but on the whole, the pupils' voices are held over until the next chapter where they will make up the main focus.

Enjoyment, Inspiration, Creativity

When teachers were asked to rate the importance of each GLO, in all studies, it was Enjoyment, Inspiration, Creativity that stood out as the most significant learning outcome for teachers. There were two detailed questions that asked teachers about Enjoyment, Inspiration, Creativity. The first of these addressed the way pupils might feel about the visit, asking teachers: 'To what extent do you think your pupils have enjoyed or been inspired by their museum visit?' This had a number of sub-categories, covering the enjoyment of the experience as a whole, excitement because of new ways of learning, new interests aroused, inspiration to progress to further learning and inspiration to make something creative. Table 8.1 presents teachers' responses in the second *Renaissance* study, RR2: 2005.[3]

There were 82 per cent of teachers who stated that it was 'very likely' that their pupils would have enjoyed the visit, and more than half of the teachers thought it 'very likely' that their pupils would have new interests aroused (56 per cent), be inspired to learn more (54 per cent)and be excited by new ways to learn (53 per cent). Slightly less than half of the teachers (46 per cent) thought it 'very likely' that their pupils would be inspired to make something creative. Teachers were very confident that their pupils had enjoyed the experience as a whole, which they could easily observe, and were a little more cautious about other aspects.

120

Table 8.1 'To what extent do you think your pupils have enjoyed or been inspired by their museum visit?' (RR2: 2005)

	Enjoyed the experience	Excited by new ways of learning	New interests aroused	Inspired to learn more	Inspired to make something creative
TOTAL	1,632	1,632	1,632	1,632	1,632
Very likely	1,337 82%	869 53%	913 56%	880 54%	748 46%
Quite likely	277 17%	645 40%	643 39%	670 41%	631 39%
Neither	1 0%	59 4%	32 2%	31 2%	134 8%
Quite unlikely	2 0%	17 1%	5 0%	10 1%	43 3%
Very unlikely	1 0%	4 0%	4 0%	2 0%	10 1%
Don't know	0 0%	7 0%	6 0%	9 1%	27 2%
Not stated	14 1%	31 2%	29 2%	30 2%	39 2%

However, the difference between 'very likely' and 'quite likely' is a subjective one; in both cases, these are positive responses, and one of the surprising factors about the research as a whole is the very tiny percentages of negative responses. The general optimism of teachers about the outcomes of the visit becomes very evident when reviewing the positive responses as a whole. The percentages of teachers who ticked either 'quite likely' or 'very likely' for each of the sub-questions are given below:

- 99 per cent – enjoyed the museum visit
- 95 per cent – have new interests aroused
- 95 per cent – be inspired to learn more
- 93 per cent – be excited by new ways to learn
- 85 per cent – inspired to make something creative.

Teachers were more unambiguously confident about the pleasure generated by the experience; they were also virtually unanimously confident that their pupils would have had new interests aroused, have been inspired to learn more and have been excited by new ways of learning, but they were a little less sure that this would result in actually producing something creative.

These positive figures are very high; teachers overwhelmingly endorse the potential of museums to inspire enjoyment and further learning. It is very surprising, and gratifying for the museums in the study, to see that 99 per cent of teachers think it quite likely or very likely that their pupils will have enjoyed their visit. One of the other national studies provides a useful comparison. The CEI evaluation of MGEP2 reported that 84 per cent of teachers and accompanying adults said that pupils responded to their museum experience 'very positively', and a further 15 per cent said pupils had responded 'satisfactorily', giving a total of 99 per cent of teachers in this study that were confident about the good experience of their pupils.[4]

The question: 'To what extent do you think your pupils have enjoyed or been inspired by their museum visit?' was a new one in 2005. It had been a surprise in 2003 to find that Enjoyment, Inspiration, Creativity was the most important learning outcome for teachers, and it was felt that the one question that related to this GLO, 'To what extent will you be using the museum experience to promote creativity?' (which also remained in 2005), did not really probe far enough in relation to enjoyment. While evidence from the focus groups about enjoyment and inspiration seemed very strong, the research in 2003 did not have the quantitative evidence to support the powerful qualitative evidence. The new, very specific, question has provided strong positive results, which, when linked with the earlier CEI study, offer consistent quantitative evidence that teachers use museums because of the power of museums to generate pleasure and inspiration through new ways to learn and new things to think about and do.

In discussion with teachers in 2005, it was clear that teachers saw pleasurable experiences as central to effective learning and that they used the museum visit as an opportunity to generate enjoyment:

> I try to make learning fun . . . The museum experience is about learning through having fun.[5]

Teachers explained how the enjoyment experienced by pupils enabled them to relax, immerse themselves in the new experiences and thus learn more:

> Enjoyment opens children up to learning.[6]

The second question on Enjoyment, Inspiration, Creativity appeared in all three linked RCMG studies. Teachers were asked: 'To what extent will you be using the museum experience to promote creativity?' and here the focus was more on how teachers felt they could use the motivation and enthusiasm generated by the museum visit. The answers can be compared across the three linked studies (Table 8.2). It is interesting to see the consistency across the studies in relation to which of the suggested activities teachers might be using, but any interpretation of variation between the studies can only be speculative, and would need to be related both to the ages of pupils in the samples and to the themes being studied by the groups at the museums.

Teachers are most optimistic about exploring new ideas and think they are least likely to be using dance or drama when they return to the classroom. However, even here, nearly half the teachers think this might be one way they might work with their pupils to follow up the visit. It is significant that the balance is the same across the three studies.

122

Table 8.2 'To what extent will you be using the museum experience to promote creativity?' Teachers ticking 'very likely' and 'quite likely'. Comparing the three linked RCMG studies

Enjoyment, Inspiration, Creativity	'Very likely' and 'quite likely' all museums RR2: 2005	Very likely' and 'quite likely' all museums RR1: 2003	Very likely' and 'quite likely' all museums DCMS/ DfES1: 2004
Exploring new ideas	88%	89%	92%
Creative writing	74%	79%	73%
Designing and making	76%	75%	88%
Other forms of creative work	70%	75%	74%
Dance/drama	49%	45%	41%

The slight variations in response are interesting but difficult to explain conclusively. The DCMS/DfES1: 2004 programme involved higher numbers of secondary pupils than in the two *Renaissance* studies, and there were higher numbers of teachers working with art-related and science-related themes. In this study, during the analysis of the questionnaires the responses were cross-tabulated with other questions. In the DCMS/DfES1: 2004 research, teachers using the museum visit for art or cross-curricular themes were more likely to report that they would use the experience to explore new ideas, with 68 per cent (art) and 71 per cent (cross-curricular) ticking 'very likely'. Other themes seemed less focused on new ideas, with 52 per cent of teachers working on historical themes and 43 per cent of teachers working on science and technology ticking 'very likely'. In relation to intentions to promote creativity through designing and making, in the DCMS/DfES1: 2004 study, it is perhaps not a surprise to find 63 per cent of teachers working on art and only 30 per cent of teachers working on history ticking 'very likely'; however, when both positive categories ('very likely' and 'quite likely') are combined, 86 per cent of teachers working on art and 74 per cent of teachers working on science thought they might encourage their pupils to design or make something on return to the classroom.

As can be seen, the statistical findings are sensitive to small differences of degree of enthusiasm or optimism, which teachers express through responding either 'very' or 'quite' likely. Teachers' attitudes to their pupils' museum experiences are likely to vary according to a considerable number of factors, including school culture, attitudes to specific groups of pupils, experience of museum teaching, individual personality and biography, contingent events and so on. What is striking is that the vast bulk of responses are positive, with very few responses that are negative.[7]

Knowledge and Understanding

Most of the teachers who were involved in the three linked RCMG studies used museums because they knew that knowledge could be painlessly absorbed through the enjoyment and immersion of the visit. In the questionnaire, teachers were asked in the three studies: 'To what extent do you think your pupils have gained facts and information during their museum visit?' The sub-categories were facts that were subject-specific; interdisciplinary or thematic; about museums; or about themselves and/or the wider world. A catch-all 'other' sub-category was also added.

Teachers ticked 'quite likely' and 'very likely' that their pupils would have gained facts and information as shown in Table 8.3. The vast majority of teachers in all three studies were very confidant that their pupils would have gained subject-specific and interdisciplinary facts, over three-quarters were optimistic that information about museums would have been absorbed and considerably more than half thought that their pupils would have learnt more about themselves and the wider world.

When all the positive responses are considered together, the general optimism of teachers is evident. However, when the 'very likely' and 'quite likely' categories are disaggregated, the much stronger optimism in relation to the acquisition of subject-specific information is revealed in all three studies. This is presented for the DCMS/DfES1 study only (Table 8.4), but the pattern is very much the same in the other two studies.

The DCMS/DfES1: 2004 research analysed the statistics a little further and showed that in relation to the acquisition of subject-specific information by their pupils, primary teachers (with 68 per cent ticking 'very likely') were slightly more optimistic that secondary teachers (63 per cent), and teachers on history or cross-curricular visits (71 per cent) were more optimistic than science teachers (60 per cent). However, more secondary teachers (45 per cent) than primary teachers (29 per cent) anticipated the acquisition of interdisciplinary or thematic facts; and in fact, apart from the acquisition of subject-specific facts, secondary teachers were generally more optimistic about their pupils' knowledge acquisition than primary teachers. Considering teachers' confidence in their pupils' acquisition of know-

Table 8.3 'To what extent do you think your pupils will have gained facts and information during their museum visit?' All positive responses compared across the three linked RCMG studies

Knowledge and Understanding	'Very likely' and 'quite likely' all museums RR2: 2005	Very likely' and 'quite likely' all museums RR1: 2003	Very likely' and 'quite likely' all museums DCMS/ DfES1: 2004
Subject-specific facts	95%	97%	96%
Interdisciplinary or thematic facts	80%	86%	85%
Facts about museums	76%	78%	81%
Facts about themselves and/ or the wider world	65%	68%	66%
Other kinds of facts	77%	83%	81%

Table 8.4 'To what extent do you think your pupils will have gained facts and information during their museum visit?' Teachers' responses in the DCMS/DfES1: 2004 study

	Subject-specific facts	Inter-disciplinary and thematic facts	Other kinds of facts	Information about museums/galleries	Facts about themselves, their families or the wider world
Very likely	67%	33%	30%	27%	23%
Quite likely	29%	52%	51%	54%	43%
Neither	2%	8%	7%	11%	17%
Quite unlikely	1%	2%	3%	3%	9%
Very unlikely	0%	0%	0%	1%	2%
Not stated	2%	6%	9%	4%	5%

ledge and understanding, in all respects, it was those teachers working on science-related themes (which made up a larger group than in the two *Renaissance* studies) who were the least confident of all teachers (see Table 8.5).

Teachers were very confident across the three studies that their pupils would have absorbed information during their museum visit, with about 95 per cent of teachers saying it was quite likely or very likely that subject-specific facts would have been gained and between 80 per cent and 85 per cent thinking pupils would have gained interdisciplinary or thematic information. In discussions with teachers, the reasons for this confidence began to emerge. Teachers were very ready to point out how engagement with museum collections conveyed information in a very straightforward manner:

> They could see clearly the difference between a butterfly and a bird – it's physical and tangible.

> Seeing a Spitfire – they get a sense of the size, of how flimsy it was . . . they learn facts about it in situ.

> They see the relative size of stuffed animals, who was eating who and understand more about the food chain.[8]

Table 8.5 'To what extent do you think your pupils will have gained facts and information during their museum visit?' Comparing the views of teachers working in different subject areas in the DCMS/DfES1: 2004 study

Teachers ticking 'very likely' DCMS/DfES1: 2004	Subject-specific facts	Inter-disciplinary or thematic facts	Facts about museums and galleries	Facts about themselves and/or the wider world	Other kinds of facts
Art	65%	43%	33%	36%	30%
History	71%	31%	27%	26%	33%
Science/Technology	60%	26%	21%	10%	22%

Teachers understood how their pupils would come to know what something was like through looking at it and comparing it with something else. As an adult, it is easy to forget that children have limited experience, and that museums can, at the simplest level, show children things for real that they have only read about or seen in pictures. Museum collections have a material existence, and the study of this materiality is necessary as part of the development of abstract concepts and comprehension. Having seen something 'for real', children (and adults) are better able to understand it. Many teachers made the point: 'To be able to touch and see and feel, that was a great learning benefit.'[9]

Skills

Teachers seemed rather less enthusiastic about the importance of Skills as an outcome of museum-based learning than they were about Enjoyment, Inspiration, Creativity and Knowledge and Understanding; when asked to rate the importance of Skills in the second *Renaissance* study RR2: 2005, only 46 per cent rated Skills 'very important' compared with the 76 per cent who rated Enjoyment, Inspiration, Creativity 'very important'. The overall positive rating was 89 per cent, however, compared with 94 per cent for Enjoyment, Inspiration, Creativity. From this we can deduce that Skills are important, but not as important as enjoyment, inspiration and creative thoughts and actions.

There was one question on the teachers' questionnaire about Skills: 'To what extent do you think that your pupils will have increased or gained skills during their museum visit?' This was divided into a number of skills, selecting those that from previous research and experience seemed the most appropriate. Table 8.6 presents the data compared across the three RCMG studies.

Table 8.6 'To what extent do you think that your pupils will have increased or gained skills during their museum visit?' Teachers ticking 'very likely' and 'quite likely'. Comparing the three recent RCMG studies

Skills	'Very likely' and 'quite likely' RR2: 2005	Very likely' and 'quite likely' RR1: 2003	Very likely' and 'quite likely' DCMS/DfES1: 2004
Thinking skills	92%	93%	92%
Communication skills	87%	89%	89%
Social skills	86%	87%	85%
Practical skills	72%	67%	76%
Creative skills	69%	70%	71%
Literacy skills	66%	72%	71%
Spatial skills	59%	61%	65%
Other skills	41%	59%	58%
Numeracy skills	23%	29%	24%
ICT skills	10%	n/a	n/a

Teachers were most confident about thinking skills, communication skills and social skills. On the other hand, only a small percentage of teachers were expecting their pupils to have gained ICT skills. This sub-category was added to the Skills question in RR2: 2005 following a request from one museum participant during one of the research planning seminars. It would seem from the responses that many teachers expect their pupils to develop their thinking, communication and social skills during their museum visit as a matter of course, while ICT skills would only be developed or used during workshops that specifically involved these skills.

Teachers working on art-related themes, in the DCMS/DfES1: 2004 research, were the most positive that their pupils would have gained thinking skills, with 66 per cent ticking 'very likely', compared to those who were working on science or technology themes who were least confident, with 47 per cent ticking 'very likely'. The teachers of art appear to be the most confident that their pupils will gain skills across the board, apart from numeracy skills, where only 2 per cent thought it was very likely. This, however, was the only time when teachers of science and technology, 5 per cent of whom ticked 'very likely', appeared more confident than the teachers working on other themes (and even here 5 per cent of teachers working on history also ticked 'very likely'); in the main, these teachers were the least confident about their pupils' learning as a whole. Secondary teachers seemed more confident than the primary teachers, and this was especially marked with creative skills, social skills and spatial skills.

In the teachers' questionnaires in the first *Renaissance* study, RR1: 2003, teachers consistently rated Skills at a lower level of importance than the other learning outcomes. In the focus groups of the second study, therefore, teachers were asked to discuss this further. On asking for a 'skills audit' of the skills that pupils gained as a result of a museum visit, teachers provided a very substantial list of diverse skills:

- Social skills
- Working in teams
- Analytical skills
- Synthesising
- Role-playing
- Empathy
- Self-analysis
- Self-expression
- Verbal skills
  - descriptive language
  - questioning language
  - talking to adults
- Enquiry
- Concentrating
- Making judgements
- Listening
- Looking
- Improvising

- Research skills
- 'Museum skills'.[10]

Some teachers have pointed out that skills can be developed in the classroom, and that there are other things that can only be experienced at the museum, and so skills are less important than the more intangible aspects such as atmosphere, and as we have seen, inspiration and enjoyment. In answering a question about progression in the teachers' questionnaire, however, approximately one-third of teachers in all three studies said it would be very likely that they would be working with their pupils using the new skills gained on the museum visit.

One of the DCMS/DfES1: 2004 case studies focused specifically on skills. It shows not only how skills can be developed in a museum context, but also how skills are integrated with other learning outcomes. *Anim8ed*[11] involved a partnership between the National Museum of Photography, Film and Television, Cartwright Hall in Bradford and the Castle Museum in York which was formed to explore the potential of animation as a learning tool for delivering a variety of subjects across the National Curriculum. The project used collections of paintings, shadow puppets, early optical toys such as clockwork automata and animated magic lantern slides to inspire young people to create their own animations through working with an artist. The focus for the *Anim8ed* project was to explore the use of ICT and animation technology and the aim of the case study in the research was to analyse the impact on skills learning. Two primary schools were involved in the case study: one of these was from inner-city Bradford and the other was from a semi-rural location. A second aim of the project was to introduce the children from these two different social worlds to each other, but this could not be examined as part of the research at this time. In common with all the museum projects in all studies, there was an enormous depth that could not be explored because of time and resource constraints and the limits of the aims of specific studies.

Anim8ed as a project emphasised the development of skills and evidence was found that this was a strong outcome. Skills included ICT, teamwork, communication, using animation across the curriculum, and life skills (meeting a new school, different cultures and names). Learning about a complex process together as a group required the use of planning skills, visualisation, sequencing, process and project management, integration of a range of views, and the initiation and completion of work. One of the teachers said:

> They had to think ahead, and envisage what was going to happen before they began . . . It's quite complicated, understanding that 12 frames go into one second but they all did it, regardless of ability.

But as part of the process of learning specific skills, the children also absorbed facts, and developed their understanding of those bits of information because they were needed to do something. The children could see the facts in action – how a close-up can be used in telling a story through pictures, for example. Because the children were able to be successful in using the new skills and information (and that says something about the way the workshop was planned,

Table 8.7 The Generic Learning Outcomes the children achieved as a result of the project *Anim8ed*

Skills	Keyboard skills – how to use the control and arrow keys Maths skills related to the time factor in animation production How to use the pipette How to manipulate the figures Communicating with new peers (learning new names from new cultures) Working in groups Planning, sequencing, managing processes
Knowledge and Understanding	How TV cartoons are made What side-views and close-ups are It takes 12 pictures a second for an animation New vocabulary (animation stamps, frames, short-cuts) Ganesh and Shiva Even a static picture tells a story How feelings can be shown in a picture
Attitudes and Values	Increased feeling of individual self-confidence Positive attitudes to new friends Positive attitudes to culture Feeling of ownership of animation processes
Enjoyment, Inspiration, Creativity	Inspired by the paintings at Cartwright Hall Enjoyed the visit and the work there Enjoyed the whole project Used their imaginations and creativity throughout the project
Action, Behaviour, Progression	Increased confidence in their practical skills All of the children from the inner city school expressed a wish to go back to Cartwright Hall (the other school was not visited by the researchers as part of the case study)

structured and delivered), their attitudes to learning, themselves and the children they did not know were positive. They enjoyed themselves. They thought they might have another go at another time, or maybe visit the museum again. The five GLOs reinforce each other, and show how a workshop such as this can produce a complex of learning outcomes. Table 8.7 summarises these outcomes.

Attitudes and Values

As the short example above shows, Attitudes and Values are deeply entwined around and within other outcomes of learning. As pupils made their drawings, worked with others and successfully achieved their aims, their attitudes to learning, each other and museums became more positive. One teacher in the *Anim8ed* project described how the activities enabled a specific pupil to find her place in the class:

Plate 8.1 Some of the group who participated in *Anim8ed* show the drawings derived from a painting at Cartwright Hall which will be used in their animations

> Jasmine was new to the school just before Christmas . . . She really designed 'Bluey Mooey' (and it was) quite obvious that it went down well with the rest of the group . . . that really established her in the class.[12]

Children developed their skills, and consequently their attitude to learning became more confident:

> Well, at the beginning I didn't know what were what and all the buttons, and she showed us what, all the buttons and now I can just do anything to animate now.

> We practiced and now . . . we know how to do it.[13]

There was one question on the teachers' questionnaire in all three linked RCMG studies about Attitudes and Values: 'To what extent do you think that the museum visit will have enabled your pupils to feel more positive about any of the following?' The sub-categories were: learning, museums and galleries, other people/communities, and themselves and their abilities. Comparing all positive values in all three studies shows that teachers were most confident about their pupils' more positive attitudes to learning and to museums and galleries, but were also very optimistic that pupils would feel more positive about both themselves and other people (Table 8.8).

Table 8.8 'To what extent do you think the museum visit will have enabled your pupils to feel more positive about any of the following?' Teachers ticking 'very likely' and 'quite likely'. Comparing the three linked RCMG studies

Attitudes and values	'Very likely' and 'quite likely' RR2: 2005	Very likely' and 'quite likely' RR1: 2003	Very likely' and 'quite likely' DCMS/DfES1: 2004
Learning	92%	94%	92%
Museums and galleries	90%	92%	92%
Other people/communities	81%	91%	78%
Themselves and their abilities	83%	83%	87%

Table 8.9 'To what extent do you think the museum visit will have enabled your pupils to feel more positive about the following?' (DCMS/DfES1: 2004)

	Museums/ galleries	Learning	Themselves and their abilities	Other people/ communities	Anything else
Very likely	47%	44%	30%	28%	11%
Quite likely	45%	48%	57%	50%	36%
Neither	4%	4%	8%	14%	22%
Quite unlikely	1%	1%	2%	4%	2%
Very unlikely	0%	–	0%	0%	0%
Not stated	3%	3%	3%	4%	29%

The DCMS/DfES1: 2004 study (see Table 8.9) illustrates the pattern of teachers' confidence; there were higher levels of confidence in relation to feeling more positive about museums and galleries and learning than in relation to attitudes to self and other people. This pattern was also found in both the *Renaissance* studies.

In the DCMS/DfES1: 2004 study where the results were further analysed, secondary teachers seemed more confident than primary teachers that their pupils would feel more positive about themselves and their abilities as a result of the museum visit, with 40 per cent ticking 'very likely' compared to 28 per cent of the primary teachers.

Museum workshops that are shaped around the exploration of specific attitudes and values are perhaps not very common. However, this is an area of growing interest, especially for older pupils. One example is the third case study in RR2: 2005, which was designed to expose pupils to Victorian attitudes to poverty, morality and social responsibility through experiencing different points of view about the Victorian workhouse, focusing specifically on the unmarried mothers who lived there. The project was developed through a close partnership between the teacher and the museum education officer. The museum education officer described their approach:

> We're provoking attitudes and values and we unashamedly look at the unmarried mothers because that . . . is an area where students of this age can identify with and why they were treated so differently and why they were singled out for special attention. So yea, I suppose its building on their emotions and where they are at the minute in order to understand history in terms of people and in terms of the attitude of the time.[14]

The teacher was convinced that the class learnt by 'being with the actors, by going round and visualising themselves, seeing the beds, the dormitory conditions and all those things actually made it come to life'.[15] She went on:

> Following the visit, I think it really has quite an impact . . . I think about themselves and other people and the world, you know, and they do, I think during the visit they are encouraged to think and reflect and put themselves into somebody else's situation. I think they do become more reflective and they've got a lot more empathy, talking to them I think that's quite clear.[16]

The pupils' questionnaires and the interviews with the pupils indicated that the teacher was right to expect the drama to have powerful effects. For example, Dave, aged 15, found the drama almost overwhelming; rather to his surprise he 'almost cried. Seriously.'[17]

Action, Behaviour, Progression

Action refers to the things that people do as a result of learning; and Behaviour is a more sustained set of activities, such that they become part of regular behaviour rather than a single action. Progression refers to moving on as a result of doing things differently, but it can also refer to thinking about things in a different way as it is difficult to separate actions from the thought that informs those actions.

Teachers as a whole found it more difficult to assess this action-related GLO than the other GLOs, and, as discussed previously, in RR2: 2005 15 per cent of teachers left this box blank. The quantitative results consistently indicated that teachers rated Action, Behaviour, Progression slightly less highly as a learning outcome of a museum visit than other learning outcomes, and discussions with teachers began to suggest why this might be:

> We don't always see Action, Behaviour, Progression immediately; these are long term aims so it might be one reason why they are not considered important.[18]

It is hard to tell immediately after a museum visit whether there will be outcomes in the medium to long term. When teachers were completing their questionnaires in the museums immediately following the museum visit and before they left to go back to school, the short-term impact of the visit was already apparent and teachers were, as has been discussed previously, very positive about enjoyment, knowledge gain and, to a slightly lesser degree, change in attitudes. It was less easy at this point to see medium- or long-term impact, and teachers were not always prepared to react to questions that asked for future predictions.

In the focus group and case study discussions, teachers talked about specific and recent experiences, but also used their experience of working with museums over the long term. Here, when teachers were asked questions that enabled them to draw on all and any, rather than a specific, use of a museum, a clearer picture emerged. In these discussions it was found that teachers both expected significant progression from their pupils as a result of a museum visit and had experienced this progression. This was particularly so for pupils who, for whatever reason, were not good at academic or written work, as their teachers believed that the museum gave them an opportunity to display their capacities in other ways. Teachers felt that the impact of the museum for these kinds of pupils was particularly significant:

> Museum visits give opportunities for those kids who are not academically strong on paper to shine.

> Everyone gets to shine at the museum in a different way.[19]

Two questions in the teachers' questionnaires in all three RCMG studies dealt with teachers' views of the extent to which museum visits could enable new experiences that could lead to progression for their pupils. One of these questions focused on the teachers' views of the development of the pupils: 'To what extent do you anticipate that the museum visit will support pupil development?' The sub-categories were 'subject-related understanding', 'increased motivation to learn', 'cultural understanding', 'increased confidence', 'learning across the curriculum' and 'in their assessed work'. Taking all positive responses, teachers in all studies seem very positive about all these aspects of development and progression, apart from 'in their assessed work' (Table 8.10).

Table 8.10 'To what extent do you anticipate that the museum visit will support pupil development?' Teachers ticking 'very likely' and 'quite likely'. Comparing the three recent RCMG studies

Action, Behaviour, Progression	'Very likely' and 'quite likely' RR2: 2005	Very likely' and 'quite likely' RR1: 2003	Very likely' and 'quite likely' DCMS/DfES1: 2004
In their subject-related understanding	94%	94%	96%
In increased motivation to learn	88%	90%	88%
In their cultural understanding	78%	84%	78%
In increased confidence	83%	84%	83%
In learning across the curriculum	83%	85%	85%
In their assessed work	61%	67%	63%

Table 8.11 'To what extent do you anticipate that the museum visit will support pupil development?' Teachers ticking 'very likely'. Comparing the three linked RCMG studies

Action, Behaviour, Progression	'Very likely' RR2: 2005	Very likely' RR1: 2003	Very likely' DCMS/DfES1: 2004
In their subject-related understanding	69%	71%	60%
In increased motivation to learn	41%	49%	40%
In their cultural understanding	35%	38%	34%
In increased confidence	35%	38%	34%
In learning across the curriculum	35%	35%	30%
In their assessed work	19%	24%	16%

A review of the 'very likely' categories shows how much more confident teachers were that their pupils would have progressed in their subject-related under-standing than they were about the other suggested aspects of progression. Only a very small percentage of teachers anticipated that the visit would be 'very likely' to support pupils' assessed work (Table 8.11).

The lack of expectation in relation to how museum visits might help pupils in their assessed work is surprising. It may suggest that teachers do not always use museums in relation to work that will be assessed, but as we have seen, 90 per cent or so of teachers use museums for curriculum-related purposes. The apparent lack of confidence in relation to support for assessed work may, however, indicate that teachers first value the inspirational aspects of a museum visit more highly and more directly, and only second wish to link museum visits to work which is specifically assessed.[20] There are questions here for further research, and there are also issues for museum and school practice.

Although the overarching picture produced by the questionnaires indicates strongly that museums are not being used very much for work which is assessed, the qualitative findings of the RCMG research found a range of examples of museum visits being closely tied to assessment. For example, a teacher in one of the focus groups for the first *Renaissance* study, RR1: 2003, described how pupils' GCSE grades improved as a result of using a visit to Aston Hall. He said:

> Without the museum visit we would not be able to deliver the [history] syllabus and exam marks would fall . . . Students tend to get better marks in coursework related to the museum visit than in exams.[21]

The third case study, which used the Victorian workhouse, focused on a museum project for secondary pupils that lasted over a whole day and was built around an assignment. The museum education officer pointed out that the fact of doing an assignment meant that the visit would be more worthwhile for the secondary school teachers whose use of the museum represented a substantial investment in time, money and energy. She described how secondary schools would frequently wish to involve a whole year group in a museum visit, consisting of a large number of students (200 to 300 pupils) which could be spread over two or three days. The normal pattern of the school day, with its regular change of subject matter and involvement of a number of different subject teachers, would need to be renegotiated. The amount of work required to bring older pupils meant that the inclusion of an assignment made it all the more productive. Discussing the value of the project to the pupils and the school, the museum education officer said:

> I think first of all, they answer a written assignment at the end which can be used as an assessed assignment and I think that's very important because that hits the schools' buttons and it embeds the learning in what they're doing at school. So that's how you make it sustainable, they'll come back every year.[22]

The pupils who took part in this project were aware both of the value of the museum experience in giving them information that they could use in their work and of the value of learning through drama and experience using the workhouse:

> You take it in more, find it a bit more interesting, like write down your experience sort of thing. Like if you went you'd have more to put in your essay than if you didn't.[23]

> It's very important really because like you've got to sort of relive it sort of because you've got to know what it feels like to get the whole story. . . . You've got to know both sides so that when you come to your essay you can write good things and bad things about it.[24]

Pupils described how they felt that they could do better than usual in their work because of the immersive, unusual, first-hand experience:

> Well it means I can know about the workhouse in more detail so I can get a higher mark.

A number of pupils were recorded as doing better than normal on their museum-based assignment.[25]

The second question on Action, Behaviour, Progression was more action-related: 'To what extent do you think that the experience of the museum will result in you working with your students in a different way?' This was broken down into sub-categories as follows: undertaking new activities, using their new skills, enabling them to work with their peers in new ways and other new ways of working in the classroom (Table 8.12).

While the overall positive ratings are encouraging, the proportions of teachers thinking it was 'very likely' that new ways of working would occur following the visit were in fact relatively small at around one-third of teachers, as Table 8.13 shows.

The DCMS/DfES1: 2004 research again showed that the secondary teachers were more positive about expecting learning outcomes than the primary teachers, with, for example, 28 per cent of primary teachers and 37 per cent of secondary teachers thinking it was likely that they would work with pupils using their new skills. Again, teachers working on science-related themes were consistently less positive than the teachers working in other areas.

Table 8.12 'To what extent do you think that the experience of the museum will result in you working with your students in a different way?' Teachers ticking 'very likely' and 'quite likely'. Comparing the three linked RCMG studies

Action, Behaviour, Progression	'Very likely' and 'quite likely' RR2: 2005	Very likely' and 'quite likely' RR1: 2003	Very likely' and 'quite likely' DCMS/DfES1: 2004
Undertaking new activities	78%	79%	83%
Using their new skills	78%	76%	79%
Enabling them to work with their peers in new ways	68%	65%	65%
Other new ways of working in the classroom	61%	62%	63%

Table 8.13 'To what extent do you think that the experience of the museum will result in you working with your students in a different way?' Teachers ticking 'very likely'. Comparing the three linked RCMG studies

Action, Behaviour, Progression	'Very likely' RR2: 2005	Very likely' RR1: 2003	Very likely' DCMS/DfES1: 2004
Undertaking new activities	31%	36%	30%
Using their new skills	33%	35%	30%
Enabling them to work with their peers in new ways	23%	22%	20%
Other new ways of working in the classroom	23%	22%	18%

The teacher in the third RR2: 2005 case study had noticed progression in the group of secondary pupils over the day-long project:

> As the day progressed, it was very obvious within the group that they'd gained confidence and were prepared to question. Early on in the day, hardly anybody spoke and then as they found their feet and, you know, got settled if you like and relaxed and probably as they met more situations where they were getting maybe some opposition of views, they felt stronger and more able to reflect or put in, word, their reflection.[26]

Conclusions

The general level of enthusiasm for museums is very high. Those teachers who participated in this research are extremely enthusiastic about them, especially in relation to the enjoyment experienced by their pupils and the increased motivation to learn that follows. The teachers have high expectations that the pleasure felt by their pupils during their museum visits will 'open them up to learning'; this is regarded as of major importance and achievable for all pupils. Approximately one-third of the teachers in each of the three linked RCMG studies represented schools in deprived wards in England where the pupils were classified as eligible for free school meals; in many of these schools individual pupils were likely to have limited exposure to outings that would expand their view of the world. In the special schools in the studies, many children would have learning difficulties.

Teachers enjoyed using museums, since in the museum all their pupils can achieve in some way because: 'everyone gets to shine in a different way'. Teachers were of the view that museums act as powerful teaching tools because of the materiality of collections and the physical qualities of objects and specimens, combined with the tangibility of the museum experience and the opportunity to access information and feelings through the senses.

However, while teachers are enthusiastic, the research shows that not all teachers feel the same confidence in using museums. A lack of confidence is suggested by the responses of teachers working in science and technology; in the DCMS/DfES1: 2004 study this was very marked.[27] These teachers were consistently considerably less expectant concerning their pupils' learning outcomes than teachers working on other themes. Further analysis[28] showed that 94 per cent of these teachers were working at primary level. In contrast, the teachers working on art themes were much more evenly spread across the primary (53 per cent) and secondary (46 per cent) sectors. Teachers working on art seemed a great deal more confident and had higher expectations of their pupils than the other teachers. It is possible that the science teachers were primary school generalists, working outside their main areas of expertise, and that the art teachers, especially those at secondary level, were much more firmly placed within their specialist field and therefore, feeling more confident about their teaching, had higher expectations of their pupils.

Almost all teachers seemed to have limited expectations when it came to using the museum for assessed work. This is difficult to explain and it would be useful to explore this further. Pupils are able to absorb additional information because they find learning through first-hand experience aids comprehension and the retention of facts; this provides good material for their assessed work. But teachers are perhaps not using this as much as they might; comparisons between the teachers' and the pupils' expectations of positive learning outcomes showed that the pupils were regularly more optimistic about this than the teachers.[29]

The research begins to throw light on the GLOs and their interrelationships. Where discussions were held with teachers and pupils in the case studies, and where a deeper level of analysis of the outcomes of learning was carried out with specific groups of pupils, it became clear that while each of the GLOs can be identified as having their own characteristics, any one event, as, for example, the *Anim8ed* project, will result in a group of interlinked learning outcomes. Although one of the main objectives of this workshop was to develop the specific skills needed for animation, and the pupils' work demonstrated that they had acquired these skills, pupils also achieved outcomes in relation to the other GLOs. The GLOs work together to stimulate and reinforce each other.

A further issue arises in considering this specific case study, and it concerns the focus of the learning. The *Anim8ed* project, like many other museum workshops, was not centrally focused on teaching information about the collections at Cartwright Hall as an end in itself. The pupils were introduced to the paintings and sculptures because they needed source material for their animated films. Spending a whole day in the art gallery, the pupils studied *Nursery Rhymes for Dmitri* by Balraj Khanna because it had been produced using multiple cut-out shapes, and from this, the children could begin to understand how animation might work. The artwork was used as a source of inspiration and knowledge for a specific purpose, and children's interest in the painting was aroused because they were going to use it in their own creative work.[30] They were not expected to manifest an interest in the painting's history, place in twentieth-century art, or in the life or style of the artist in an abstract cognitive way; they used the painting as a solution to a problem, and thus it had relevance for them. Because of this relevance, they became involved with the painting, looked at it carefully, learnt about how colour and shape was used, and how the image was put together. The end result was learning about the collections, but because it was needed to solve a child-focused problem.

Some matters of research method are worth pointing out. Using teachers' questionnaires at the end of a museum visit to ask about the outcomes of that visit illustrates some interesting issues concerning questionnaires. The immediate pleasure and enthusiasm of pupils could be observed as an outcome of their experience, and to some extent so could the acquisition of knowledge, skills and a change in points of view. But longer-term outcomes could not be seen at that point. Discussions with teachers that enabled them to use their past experience as well as their more recent experience gave a more accurate representation of their views. Face-to-face interviews were also useful to clarify why teachers seemed less enthusiastic about skills as an outcome, and to some extent this was to do with the language used in the questionnaire, which did not map completely onto the language used in schools. In a face-to-face situation, a number of terms can be used until the one best recognised is identified; when the term 'skills audit' was used, teachers understood better what the researchers were asking about and a richer response resulted. While questionnaires are useful in producing the large-scale numerical data required by policy makers, and are able to present a 'big picture', it is important to use other methods to check details, confirm interpretation and modify tools where misunderstanding might arise.

9

Pupils' learning outcomes: pupils' voices

Teachers are very optimistic about the learning that their pupils achieve as a result of their museum visits, but what do the pupils themselves think? Pupils may feel enjoyment and inspiration following their museum experience, but what does that achieve? Is there any relationship between this and other learning outcomes? What did the research tell us about the outcomes of learning experiences in museums? Are there strong interrelationships between the GLOs? And can any specific characteristics of museum-based learning be identified?

The statistical data from the pupils' questionnaires gives evidence of how pupils responded to specific GLO-related statements. From this data, it was obvious that pupils enjoyed their museum visits immensely and that the vast majority thought that they had learnt about new things, picked up new skills, increased their motivation to learn and found new ways to think about their school work. This statistical data does not, however, give any indication of what was so exciting, why pupils thought they had learnt things, or how (or whether) the inspiration and the learning came together. The qualitative data from the open statements does throw light on these essential matters.

The pupils' questionnaires allowed any who wished to do so to write free text or to draw in response to a stimulus statement, and most of the 56,810 pupils who completed questionnaires also filled in the space at the bottom. These free textual and visual expressions provide powerful graphic evidence of what individual children and young people felt about their museum visit and this evidence illuminates the statistical data from the pupils' and the teachers' questionnaires.

These thousands of texts and pictures can, at present, only be placed in limited contexts. The pupils' work can be linked back to the class, the school and the museum through a numbering system; this presents the opportunity to research the characteristics of the school and to discover more detail of the workshop session that stimulated the writing and drawing. Where the pupils' visual and written comments have been published in the flipbooks,[1] this was done to some degree. The case studies for the second *Renaissance* study, RR2: 2005, and the DCMS/DfES1: 2004 research explored the contexts of pupils' learning outcomes in considerable depth and in some cases, therefore, the drawing and writing on the bottom of the pupils' questionnaires can be located in a very detailed context. In the case studies, interviews with teachers and pupils, observations at museums and in the classroom, and the review of documents provided ample contextual material. However, most of the contexts for open statements from the pupils remain somewhat fragmentary, but the statements themselves provide a large and comprehensive databank of spontaneous responses from pupils of all ages at the end of their museum visit.

This chapter reviews the evidence from the pupils in relation to the five GLOs, using both the quantitative data from the questionnaires that was presented in summary form in Table 7.7 and Table 7.8 and the qualitative evidence from the pupils' words and pictures at the bottom of the questionnaires.

'The whole trip was inspirational'[2] (Enjoyment, Inspiration, Creativity)

Very high percentages of pupils (91 to 94 per cent of younger pupils and 86 per cent of older pupils) completing the questionnaires agreed that they enjoyed their visits and their textual and visual statements give examples of some of the things they found enjoyable. These included museum buildings and collections, and the activities that pupils participated in at the museum.

Many pupils enjoyed different aspects of the museum buildings and the sites, especially the size and the scale. As one child in one of the RR2: 2005 case studies put it: 'I'm not used to seeing mansions.'[3] The scale of the house made it memorable. Another child remembered the garden for the same reasons: 'It was big and massive.'[4] These large, elaborate and rich environments are outside the experience of many of these children. They are special because a visit is unusual and possibly not likely to be repeated. As one secondary-age pupil put it, the experience was exciting: 'Because you don't go out every day to a museum do you.'[5]

Roma, aged 10, has drawn her impression of Aston Hall, a Jacobean stately home in Birmingham,[6] complete with rather forbidding fence in front. She quite enjoyed being rather scared by the attic rooms (Figure 9.1).

Hassan, aged 9, also visited Aston Hall in Birmingham, but found the exhausting stairs the most amazing aspect. He has drawn the long winding stairs and gives an impression of the height from which he is looking down on them, having climbed all the way up (Figure 9.2).[7]

Some pupils used the opportunity of the space at the bottom of their questionnaires to produce a catalogue of what they had seen:

> I'm amazed by everything, the rooms, ceiling, the panneling on the walls, paintings, beautiful staircase and even the attic was amazing.

This child has developed intentions to show others and share the experience:

> I would definetly bring my family here and have a proper look at everything.[8]

Other aspects of museum sites were found to be exciting and enjoyable. Sean, aged 7, for example, enjoyed riding in the working tram at Beamish Museum.

Figure 9.1 Roma, aged 10, enjoyed her trip to Aston Hall

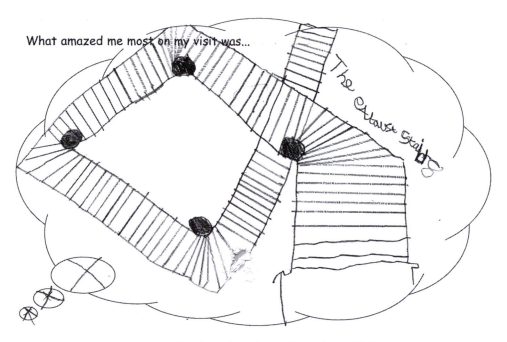

Figure 9.2 Hassan was amazed by the exhausting stairs at Aston Hall

Everyone is crammed in, with the lucky ones on the top; Sean particularly liked the fact that the tram was high (hay). He carefully draws the rod connecting the tram to the electrical wires, the outside stairs to the upper deck and the driver with his peaked cap (Figure 9.3).[9]

Collections were also enjoyable and sometimes inspirational. Pupils frequently recorded how they had been fascinated by the things that they saw. They felt special because they were allowed to touch things that were very, very old:

> What amazed me most at the museum today . . . was that we got to hold things that were older than 3,000 years old. This is the best ever trip.[10]

Huma, aged 7, wrote:

> I was amazed that we were allowed to touch things that were 2 thousand years old. Everything amazed me. This was my first visit to a museum and I loved it.[11]

Many pupils were very surprised by what they saw, and found some collections awesome. Alex, for example, was 'wierded out' by Roman skulls at the Museum of London[12] (Figure 9.4).

Some pupils enjoyed the stories they heard. Kirrika, for example, loved the story about Boudicca that she heard at Colchester Castle Museum, where she saw a replica of the chariot of the Queen of the Iceni tribe. She has produced a confident and energetic drawing of Boudicca and her two daughters speeding along in their wooden-wheeled chariot, with their hair and robes flowing in the wind[13] (Figure 9.5).

Figure 9.3 Sean, aged 7, rides the electric tram at Beamish Museum

Figure 9.4 Alex, aged 9, is 'wierded out' by Roman skulls at the Museum of London

Figure 9.5 Kirrika enjoyed the story she heard at Colchester Castle Museum

143

Many pupils who encountered works of art found them inspiring for their own creative projects. Georgia, aged 17, for example, who was working towards AS art and design, visited Birmingham Museum and Art Gallery and afterwards described what she found inspiring for her own work[14] (Figure 9.6).

Some pupils were very explicit about how they enjoyed doing different activities. Aimee, aged 11, went on a class visit to Manchester Art Gallery[15] during the period of the RR2: 2005 research, and afterwards she wrote:

> What amazed me most on my visit was . . .
> I enjoyed doing the old dancing, it was really fun and enjoyed doing the drama where we had to walk through piccadilly garden that was really fun as well and I really enjoyed pretending there was an airaid and singing run rabbit that was really funny thanks to chloey. Thank you for letting us come to the Art gallery. The Art gallery was a great birthday present.

She popped in a little drawing of a rabbit and another of an air-raid warden with a hat on. Aimee begins to illustrate what it is that pupils enjoy. She has been involved physically; her experience included a varied range of physical activities, including drama with dancing and singing, and visiting two different locations, the Art Gallery and nearby Piccadilly Gardens. She had to use her imagination to pretend that she was living during an air-raid in World War Two. She enjoyed doing things with her friend Chloe, and clearly was not alarmed by the pretended air-raid, probably because she was with her teacher, her class group and her

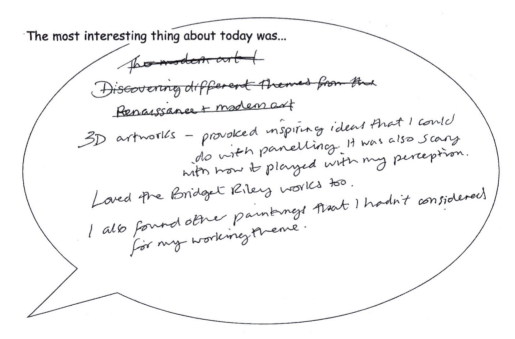

Figure 9.6 Georgia is inspired at Birmingham Museum and Art Gallery

friends, and so although she could enter into the role-play, she also knew she was safe. Her enjoyment has been produced by a well-constructed workshop that has enabled her immersion in new, exciting and purposeful experiences. She shows the degree to which she has made these experiences her own by claiming them as her birthday present.

In discussions with primary-aged pupils, many talked about 'having fun' at the museum and frequently this was because the activities they took part in gave them ideas about things they could do in the future. Two 7-year-olds from the second RR2: 2005 case study, for example, talked about how their museum experience influenced their thinking:

Pupil:	They're fun.
Researcher:	They're fun, why do you think they're fun?
Pupil:	Cos I like activities. Cos when I grow up I want to be an artist.

[The other child being interviewed said:]

Pupil:	And me.
Researcher:	You want to be an artist as well, why?
Pupil:	Cos I like doing art.[16]

The expression 'fun' was used a great deal as a shorthand and where the younger pupils had no other terms to use to describe their feelings. Some secondary-level pupils were able to be more analytical about what they had experienced. Pupils in the third case study for RR2: 2005, for example, described how the immersive experience of the dramatic session in the workhouse enabled them to learn because of the sense of presence that they felt. Being there, seeing it and touching it made it all much easier to understand:

> I think, like, the whole experience was interesting cos this was something different, you sort of take it in a bit more than if you're sitting in the classroom. Sort of there and they're telling you about it and you can see it and touch it sort of thing.[17]

Another pupil who had also visited the museum a week before explained how the involvement worked through enabling her to imagine the experience and feel as she might have felt had she actually been one of the inmates of the workhouse:

> It was really good and it like helped, taught me a lot about what it was actually like and it was really good. And it sometimes actually felt like I was actually one of the people that used to work there cos it was so good and everything.[18]

A third student who had taken part in this case study used the free space on their questionnaire to describe the experience of the role-play. The actors in costume had presented different points of view and because s/he could link these to specific characters, it made the opinions more comprehensible and memorable. Issues concerning the quality of life for young people in the nineteenth-century workhouse suddenly came alive and became meaningful. The text read:

145

> The most interesting thing about today was . . . seeing the actors in costum, this gives an more instresing way for the different opinons, at school you learn things in books but this made it funner & stuck in my head more.[19]

Here again, the word 'fun' is used by the pupils to convey the way in which learning works which engages mind, body and emotions. This is more 'fun' than using books. The museum education staff talked about experiences which should be 'engaging and challenging' and 'hopefully exciting but not necessarily fun'.[20] 'Fun' is a term used by the pupils to describe experiences that demand active physical participation, that are unusual and thus provoke attention and curiosity, and that are found to be of personal relevance and therefore interesting and worth thinking about. This is 'serious fun'.

From the evidence presented here, enjoyment and inspiration stem from new experiences in exciting spaces where pupils take part in unusual events, using a range of diverse learning styles, that they can make sense of because of the work they are doing at school. The strangeness of some of these events is not frightening, as it could be, as they are experienced with a familiar group (the class), and under the control of a known authority (the teacher). The imaginations of the pupils are fired by these new experiences, which involve extraordinary things they feel privileged to see and touch. In the first *Renaissance* study in 2003, it was found that although it was essential for most teachers that the museum visit could be linked to the curriculum, this on its own was not enough. The museum visit was also expected to be highly enjoyable, memorable and catalytic. Teachers in the focus groups in RR1: 2003 described how their pupils were taken beyond their everyday experience during their museum visits, which had the power to jolt latent learning capacity into action.[21] Pleasure acted as a catalyst to a range of other learning outcomes. It made learning seem more relevant, more achievable. These findings were echoed in the second *Renaissance* study, RR2: 2005, and in the DCMS/DfES1: 2004 research. The MGEP2 research also found that enjoyment and subject learning were closely associated.[22]

'When I came away my brain was full of things'[23] (Knowledge and Understanding)

Many of the pupils in the case studies talked about the 'reality' of the museum, referring both to the materiality of the objects and specimens they observed and to the physical character of the spaces and places they experienced. Being able to witness, observe and touch made it easier to absorb facts and information. There were many examples in the free writing and drawing of the materiality of things impressing pupils, as they learnt facts about things, their characteristics and relationships.

Harry, aged 7, for example, was amazed at having handled a piece of armour because:

> The ring mail had 50,000 rings on it. And how heavy it was.

Figure 9.7 Michael learns facts about the python (and how to spell it!)

Michael, aged 8, found the python amazing when he was visiting the Hancock Museum in Newcastle-upon-Tyne, and could easily understand why it was dangerous[24] (Figure 9.7).

Tundun aged 10, who participated in the RR2: 2005 research, was amazed by:

> All the animals and the skeletons and knowing that the skeletons inside of the animal creates the shape of the body. And knowing lots of facts.

He drew a snake and next to it, what he thought its skeleton probably looked like.

Some children demonstrated an astounding capacity to absorb facts of all sorts during their visit. Daisy, aged 6, for example, experienced the Victorian school room at Beamish Museum and was full of information afterwards. She thought the teacher was rather naughty and remembered that the toilet was outside. She recalled that rich people went to school and that the poor had jobs that were often unpleasant. She noted that boys had more opportunities than girls. And to cap it all, she was amazed at the false teeth![25] She could barely get it all down, and has surely increased her writing skills through her powerful need to use them (Figure 9.8).

Some pupils increased their understanding of technical matters, through close observation and probably a demonstration of how particular things worked. Mohammed, aged 9, for example, struggled with his spelling, but was determined to do a technical drawing of the amazing Tudor mouse-trap. He has documented

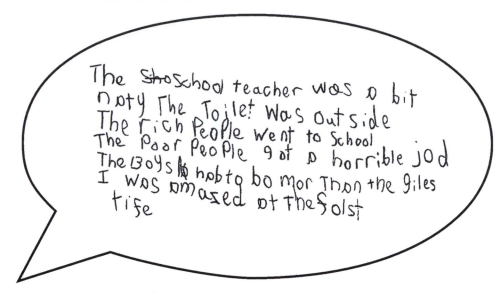

The Shoschool teacher was a bit
noty The Toilet Was outside
The rich People went to School
The Poor People got a horrible job
The Boys hobto bo mor Than the giles
I was amased ot thefolst
tife

Figure 9.8 Daisy was amazed after her experience in the Victorian schoolroom at Beamish Museum

the materials (because he couldn't spell 'cord' he has substituted 'string') and shown how the cheese is placed in the trap under a heavy weight. He has drawn the mouse in the trap too and has made a good attempt to show how all the components operate[26] (Figure 9.9).

Another child, visiting the same museum two years later, worked out how a sun dial showed the time:

> '[In] Tudor times the Tudors never, they didn't have clocks and . . . so they never knew what the time was. And in the gardens there's this massive rock and there's this blade and if when the sun would rise up and it would be touching the blade, they knew when it was noon. And then if it went down they knew what the time was when it was night. And in the morning they would know because it's on one side where there's light, where there's the sunshine because the sun actually moves. And then when it goes down the moon comes up, so that's how they knew the time.'[27]

The curiosity of pupils was aroused according to their individual interests, such as how people lived and how things worked. The cultural backgrounds of pupils also influenced what they found surprising and memorable. The deputy headteacher in the first case study of RR2: 2005 pointed out that although in general, in her view, the museum service did not do enough on black or Asian culture or heritage, when her ethnically mixed group had visited the Tudor manor house:

> the Asian girls in particular liked the garden part of it because in their culture it would be herbs and spices that are used by them . . . it's something they can relate to, something they find surprising.[28]

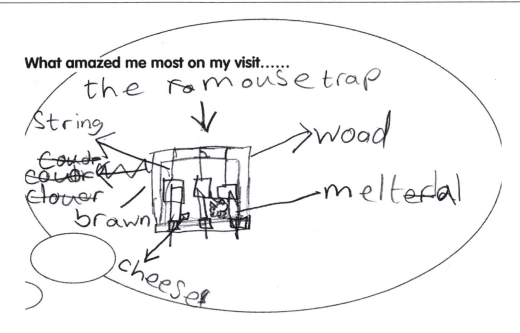

Figure 9.9 Mohammed is amazed at the Tudor mouse-trap

One of the girls in the class described what this had meant to her:

> Well actually that amazed me most . . . I didn't know what herbs meant. But when we went in, when me and the teacher went in and . . . went outside to look at herbs. And in the olden times they used to use like most herbs, some of the herbs in for food like mint, rosemary and lavender.

She described how she used sage and mint in cooking at home.[29] And after the visit to the Tudor house museum, she had used the free space to record the herbs she remembered, including rosemary, lavender and mint.[30]

Some children began to absorb information that enabled them to take a position and make judgements about specific bodies of knowledge. For example, one primary-aged child, having spent some time with the Pre-Raphaelite paintings in the Birmingham Museum and Art Gallery, was very articulate about the superiority of the work of Ford Madox Brown compared to his contemporaries:

> What amazed me most on my visit . . .

> I was amazed how lots of things were still in good condition. The paintings were very colourful even though most of them were black and white. What amazed me most was Ford Madox Brown and how he used people to model and they had to wait until he had finished. The other artists such as Arthus Hughes, Sir Edward Coley Burne Jones, William Holman Hunt Frederick Sandys and Emma Sandys never inspired me with their paintings unlike Ford Madox Brown.

Information was readily absorbed as pupils participated in workshops, visited galleries and historic homes, and encountered collections of items that they found interesting and often inspiring.

Many museum staff structured the information that the pupils encountered in relation to the lives of children in the past and, judging from the pupils' visual and written statements, this proved a very effective teaching strategy, enabling the pupils to imagine themselves in similar situations. There were many examples of pupils who had related what they had learnt to their own lives, learning through linking the new information to what they knew already. Elliot, aged 10, for example, visited Preston Manor in Brighton to study the Victorians. He was surprised to see that children of his age would have been allowed to drink beer. He imagines ordering a pint of the frothy stuff, and this order being accepted. We do not know whether he realised that children could drink beer because the water was not clean enough to drink[31] (Figure 9.10).

Through empathy, the projection of the self back into time and the imagining of the self in the historical situation, children developed their knowledge and understanding of the past. This technique was sometimes used to address world events in terms that pupils could understand. Neelam, aged 10, visited the Herbert Museum and Art Gallery in Coventry to study World War Two. Coventry was badly hit during World War Two, and the city centre was demolished. Neelam had been struck by many of the items she saw: a gas siren, an air-raid siren and a gas mask for a baby. She understood how chemicals were filtered through the gas mask, and she noted that during air raids, children might hide under the stairs.

Figure 9.10 Elliot, aged 10, imagines ordering beer for himself

Figure 9.11 Connections are made between the experience of a child, a city and the wider world

She is connecting to these past events in the city through her imagination, but she is also able to go further through information about Hiroshima and the mushroom cloud explosion[32] (Figure 9.11).

There were many examples of pupils making links between what they could imagine easily in the past, such as eating and drinking, and bigger, more cataclysmic matters. The text in Figure 9.12 gives an example of a primary-aged pupil linking everyday life aboard ship to the purposes of the voyage, to trade slaves.[33] Many pupils appreciated this broader view of history that they were sometimes exposed to during their museum visit. Myyles, a 13-year-old pupil, wrote after a visit to the Museum of London:

> The most interesting thing about today was . . .
>
> The play – how the characters they played were very strong especially the freed slaves and the black history exhibit. I learnt about a lot of new Black heroes.[34]

Pupils made links with prior knowledge in their own ways and at their own levels. Megan, aged 15, wrote after a visit to Manchester Art Gallery:

> The most interesting thing about today was . . .
>
> Dressing up and looking in funny mirrors. Also some pieces were very inspiring on important subjects like homosexuality and HIV. Also racism.[35]

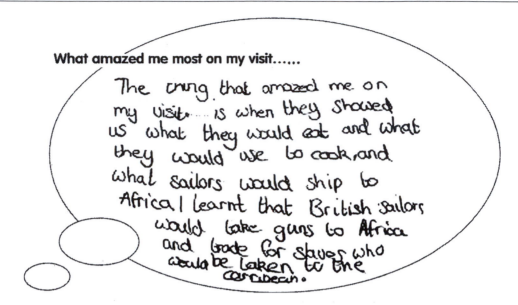

What amazed me most on my visit......

The thing that amazed me on my visit.... is when they showed us what they would eat and what they would use to cook, and what sailors would ship to Africa I learnt that British sailors would take guns to Africa and trade for slaves who would be taken to the caribbean.

Figure 9.12 A pupil links everyday life aboard ship to the shocking purposes of sailing

Pupils appreciated the imaginative teaching which helped them increase their understanding of complex matters. Harriet, aged 13, shows graphically how debates which opened up different perspectives on rural settlements and gave a human face to geography have aided her subject-related understanding[36] (Figure 9.13).

Some pupils were able to reflect on how their Knowledge and Understanding had progressed during a museum visit. Two 9-year-old pupils in the first case study described how the flow of the activity enabled them to tolerate not knowing what specific words meant until the context revealed their meaning. This tolerance of imperfect understanding which entails keeping the mind open to new ideas and a faith that understanding will eventually arrive is an essential learning skill:

> Well I actually thought like a bit hard because when she said all these kinds of words that I've never heard before, at the beginning I never knew what she meant . . . when she said more, I got the understanding and then I knew what she meant.

> It was a bit alright cos I didn't know at first what she was on about cos I didn't know things about the stuff . . . And then as she was going on I learnt about what there was and that.[37]

Words such as 'tapestry' were new to the children, but in a context where they could see 'the blankets on the walls with pictures on them'[38] they could see what the words meant. In examples such as this, it is the flow and pace of the event combined with the situated character of the learning that enables the growth of information and understanding.

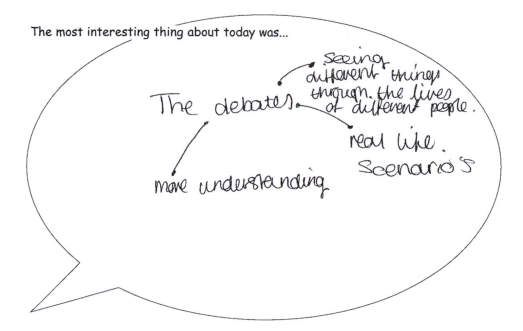

Figure 9.13 Teaching which challenges teenagers to assess different points of view increases their understanding

Pupils also learnt about museums and what they did. Iqra, aged 8, for example, drew two Roman coins very carefully, putting in considerable detail of the heads, and wrote:

> What amazed me was that most of these atrefacts are old and you have managed to keep them save for us to come and see. I have drawn some roman coins wich I found quite amazing.[39] (Figure 9.14)

During their museum visits, pupils increased their knowledge and understanding through linking new facts and information to their own lives and to what they could easily imagine because they had seen the 'real' thing or been in a 'real' place. They absorbed facts of all sorts, including facts relating to the subjects they were studying and facts about world events. They broadened their knowledge of art, history and culture, sometimes seeing these through different perspectives. Because the information they were exposed to was contextualised by objects, spaces, people and events, it made sense and could be remembered.

'It helped my social skills'[40] (Skills)

The older pupils were confident that a museum was a good place to pick up new skills, with large percentages agreeing with this idea (RR1: 2003, 62 per cent; RR2: 2005, 68 per cent; DCMS/DfES1: 2004, 70 per cent). It was felt that younger pupils would not be sufficiently objective about their learning to be able

Figure 9.14 Iqra, aged 8, is impressed by the achievements of the Museum of London

to respond in a meaningful way to this question and consequently it was omitted from their questionnaire.

There were fewer free text and visual statements in the research data as a whole that concerned skills in a direct manner. Some pupils described the skills they had used during their museum workshops in their questionnaires during the second *Renaissance* study (RR2: 2005). After a visit to Birmingham Museums and Art Gallery, for example, a 12-year-old pupil wrote that the most interesting thing was: 'Being an art critic and looking at the symbolism used in the paintings, and paintings in different styles and points of view.'[41] These are complex analytical skills that, for this pupil, have been stimulated because the role of an art critic demanded their use. A 17-year-old wrote about the practical skills developed during a visit to a stately home. The most interesting thing was: 'Visiting Temple Newsam and learning and improving on my skills for hand embroidery.'[42] And Nichole, aged 16, who had been surveying visitors at a Roman fort near Newcastle, wrote that the most interesting thing was: 'Asking the questionnaires to people as it helped my social skills.'[43]

In relation to art, there were some workshops that focused specifically on skills development. Toby, aged 11, described his learning outcomes following a session at Bolton Museum:

> The most interesting thing about today was . . .
>
> that I learnt about using white to blend light colours together. The best area of the museum was the aquarium because you had to draw quicker to catch an image.[44]

154

Although the younger pupils were not asked a direct question about skills, there was a small amount of evidence in the free statements of their awareness of having improved their skills. One example was Alex, aged 11, who had also visited Temple Newsam where she had met an artist.[45] Alex shows graphically in the drawing how she has understood how to use light and shade to improve her work. While she has not shown that she has learnt the specialist terms to discuss this approach, she is confident enough to think that she might be an artist herself one day. The experience of successful skills learning has opened up a whole range of new possibilities, and the specialist terms can come later (Figure 9.15).

Some of the children's work shows how museums enable specific expertise to be used. Sam, aged 10, visited Ironbridge Gorge Museum, where he was struck by the candle-maker:

> who said she could make 300 candles a day but in Victorian times they made 3,000 to 5,000 a day because those days they didn't have electricity so they needed candles and they only had one or two candle shops a town so a lot was needed.[46]

Sam has used high-level numeracy and deduction skills to competently describe the relationships between supply and demand in specific circumstances.

Skills development can occur in a very natural way in a museum setting, as observations carried out for the DCMS/DfES1: 2004 research discovered. Children participating in the *Partners in Time* project who visited the Imperial War

Figure 9.15 From scruffy to shadow pictures: Alex learns about chiaroscuro

Museum Duxford used the aeroplanes, the hangers and their own bodies to consider the characteristics of structures, which need to be strong, stable and stiff; in small groups, they built a structure that could demonstrate these characteristics. The pupils were taught the concepts in the morning through looking at the museum and its collections and in the afternoon they demonstrated their understanding of symmetry and balance, and design and construction skills by building structures. Their class teacher commented: 'They would not have made all these structures with triangles before – they've absorbed that from this morning.' The building skills were complemented by the skills of team-working. The activity was managed through group-work, with negotiation, compromise and shared workloads being critical to its completion.[47]

Some museum workshops in the RCMG studies introduced children and young people to the skills connected to the collections with which they were working. As an outcome following a visit to Arbeia Roman Fort, Tyne and Wear, Haneen could depict in detail the skills and processes used by archaeologists as they map out the terrain, dig down in layers, sift through the soil and set up trays of finds. She imagines herself and her classmates in professional roles[48] (Figure 9.16).

The quantitative data suggests that teachers are less interested in using museums in relation to developing existing skills or introducing new ones. However, in discussing this with teachers, and in reviewing the statements of the pupils, it

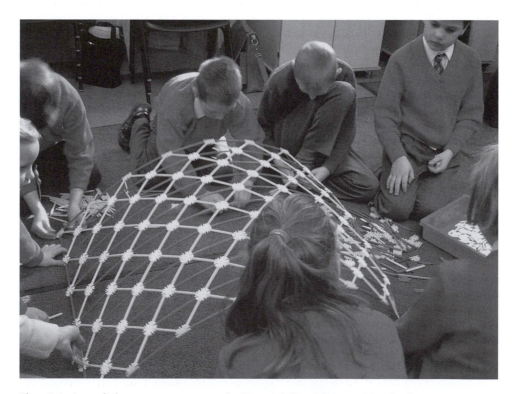

Plate 9.1 A workshop on structures at the Imperial War Museum, Duxford

Figure 9.16 Learning professional skills in the museum

seems that pupils are able to learn new skills and also to use their existing skills and learning preferences to make sense of their experiences.

'I never thought art was interesting or cool, but now I will have to consider that idea'[49] (Attitudes and Values)

Attitudes to knowledge are shaped as information is acquired. This occurs through unconscious responses to the way the subjects matter is presented, to the language that is used in discussion and to the ways in which peers and the interpretive communities close to the learner react to what they hear. Prior knowledge works to shape attitudes to new ideas. While feelings may be weak or strong, diffuse or well defined, as information is absorbed attitudes towards that knowledge come into being or are modified. It was clear from the pupils' voices in the three linked RCMG studies that the development or modification of feelings was one of the outcomes of successful gathering of information. The strongest evidence concerned attitudes to culture and learning from cultural heritage, attitudes to other people, and attitudes to the self.

Teachers were confident that their pupils' attitudes to museums and galleries would have become more positive as a result of their recent experience and there were two statements in the younger pupils' questionnaires that concerned their attitude to museums: 'This is an exciting place'; and 'A visit is useful for school work'. In all three studies between 83 per cent and 87 per cent of pupils agreed with these statements. Older pupils were asked to respond to the statement: 'A museum is a good way to learn in a different way to school' and between 82 per cent and 86 per cent agreed that it was.

There were some examples in the free writing and drawing that showed how the museum visit had changed the attitudes of pupils. Emma, aged 8, initially thought that a visit to Birmingham Museums and Art Gallery would be 'boring because it is for school homework' but changed her mind after the actual visit.[50] Ruth, aged 8, was studying a science topic on Moving and Growing at Bolton Museum.[51] She has drawn two pictures that show how she was confused when she arrived, but was full of ideas after her visit. She draws herself under a question mark and an exclamation mark as a way of depicting her feelings (Figure 9.17). Renuka, aged 10, describes how her visit to Leeds City Art Gallery has changed her mind about art, which she now thinks could be interesting[52] (Figure 9.18).

Many of the pupils' voices showed how a museum visit had changed their initial ideas about art and culture so that they considered these more relevant and interesting to them. There were very few negative responses; however, Vincent, aged 18, had clearly not enjoyed his visit. He wrote (changing the stimulus statement to suit what he wanted to say):

The most uninteresting thing about today was . . .

Not that the gallery was bad because I am sure boaring people love to pine over things like that all day, I have better things to do than ask questions about a picture. Its very boaring – also I think a lot of the so-called art in this museum is over pretencious and hence depresses me, this art gallery has given me an insight into other peoples boaring and drab lives, and it will make my life feel a lot more fulfilling.[53]

Figure 9.17 Ruth felt completely different after her visit to Bolton Museum

What amazed me most on my visit was...

All the artists there are in the world and all the fantastic art they did! I never thought art was intersting or cool, but now I will have to condicer that idea! Thanks alot.
I had a great time!!

Figure 9.18 Renuka has to modify her ideas after a visit to Leeds City Art Gallery

It is perhaps some consolation that, after the visit, he feels that his own life is much more interesting in comparison with those people who use boring museums.

The pupils' statements included examples of how the museum workshops had affected pupils' attitudes to other people. October is Black History Month in England and many museums took part in this by offering workshops about black histories and cultures. Sobis, aged 12, took part in one of these workshops at the Museum of London, and wrote briefly afterwards:

> The most interesting thing about today was . . .
>
> Learning about how people felt when people were getting abused.[54]

The secondary school case study in the second *Renaissance* project RR2: 2005 included many examples of pupils reflecting upon their attitudes to others. This museum project, which used a Victorian workhouse, was structured specifically to focus on attitudes and values, partly as a method of engaging teenagers in learning, as was described in Chapter 8, and clearly this worked well. The focus on the unmarried mothers (the 'jacket women') was successful in allowing the pupils to engage with the issues and consider their views.

> Well you learnt like that not all people were treated the same, because like the jacket women, they were treated harshly because they weren't married and so they got treated much differently and they got kept away from the other people . . . I thought it was a bit wrong because it's not their fault they haven't got married yet.[55]

159

The third RR2: 2005 case study included an interview with a small group of pupils two years after their visit to the workhouse. These pupils described their feelings about what they had learnt two years earlier:

> Well, when you, like, heard that children and how they work and don't really get paid, little food, sort of feel angry about that.

> There was a woman, I can't remember what she was exactly, she was just a woman who got separated from her children and her husband, I felt sorry for her doing that.[56]

Clearly the experience was memorable, and from the discussions with the pupils, the focus on values and attitudes had enabled them to retain information in the mid-term. One of the group described how becoming engaged through using the emotions had made it easier to understand the issues:

> Being in the conditions that there were at that time, you actually felt emotions that they would be feeling at the time and it's easier to understand how things were if you're actually doing it and seeing.[57]

Another pupil said:

> Cos we went there and actually experienced it, it just made it better to learn, because I think if you're enjoying it.[58]

The discussion with this group revealed how understanding, enjoyment and feelings, stimulated by an absorbing and immersive experience, came together to produce powerful memorable learning experiences.

In addition to evidence of developing views about other people, the three linked RCMG studies found strong evidence of impact on attitudes to the self. Ivie, aged 12, for example, took part in a handling session with musical instruments at the Horniman Museum in South London. She wrote afterwards:

> The most interesting thing about today was . . .

> Was sketching all the different instruments. Also I think the handling session was interesting and I was very proud because some of the instruments were from my country (Nigeria).[59]

One of the case studies carried out for the DCMS/DfES1: 2004 research provides a more sustained example of the power of museums to touch and shape views about the self. Individuals are in part products of their history and culture, although this is not always evident when that culture has been rendered invisible through the historical processes of domination. The power of knowledge about culture and history to shape attitudes to life potential and future is revealed in the following example.

The project *Understanding Slavery* involved the National Maritime Museum, National Museums Liverpool, Bristol City Museums and Art Gallery and the British Empire and Commonwealth Museum in Bristol. It was developed to address the legacy of slavery through piloting methods and resources for teaching slavery to teenagers as part of their history curriculum.[60] One of the museums, the British Empire and Commonwealth Museum in Bristol, brought together a collection of replica slave items, videos, artists and actors. The teenagers who visited the museum to take part in this project were involved in four one-day workshops where they handled and discussed the slavery-related objects, took part in role-play activities, visited the galleries where slavery was addressed and wrote a script for a story to be produced in the recording studio of the museum. Later this was to be performed at school.

Research into the impact of the project involved interviewing three students from a school in inner-city Bristol that was facing threat of closure. One teenage pupil was particularly articulate in her discussion of her experience.

> We'd look at objects, [like] slave whips . . . I was quite shocked. I knew it was cruel but I didn't know how cruel, I never could imagine . . . I thought about it in a different way. We actually got to see it and experience what it would have been like. I did know quite a lot but *I* wasn't able to picture it.

Handling objects enabled her to imagine the experience of slavery in a new way – history became picturable. For this pupil, a Black British girl of Afro-Caribbean origin, imagining slavery increased her determination to prove herself:

> If I wasn't gonna try before, I would try now, because the sort of people who didn't believe in black people, I would try just to show them,

Plate 9.2 Pupils examine replica slave artefacts at the Empire and Commonwealth Museum in Bristol

wherever they are . . . I'd try at schoolwork; just try a little bit harder . . . It makes you think more openly, it gives you more determination . . . because they didn't believe that black people could do things as well as white people, or that they weren't worth having, so they used them as slaves. So, [I'd try] to do things for myself, to push myself harder and prove that I can do something. [The experience] inspired me in a different way that I haven't been inspired before. It makes you feel that learning, pushing yourself is actually worth something. Sometimes you think, what's the point, but if you went to the museum, you think well it is actually worth something, that pride and dignity that they took away from the slaves, it's worth giving it back to them.

Through identifying with the experience of enslaved people, this young woman developed an increased sense of individual purpose. The museum project adopted a specific approach to the legacies of the slave trade, emphasising resistance and resilience where possible, and this enabled this pupil to feel that she too could act in the world.

The museum education officer explained her perspective:

A subject like slavery can be very sensitive to certain race groups. It can also be a learning experience. One group of Afro-Caribbean kids were totally in awe. They didn't know that slavery existed. Their families don't talk about it at home . . . it gave them an insight, yes, this is our culture; this is who we actually are. For that race group it's very beneficial.[61]

From the evidence above, it is clear that the museum workshops were enjoyable and inspiring, that pupils were able to immerse themselves in them and as a result their feelings opened up to new ideas and experiences. Pleasure taps directly into feelings and emotions, and as these were harnessed, information became more meaningful. Pupils felt more positive about what they could do and about the material they were studying. Some of the feelings which were evoked linked specifically to identity, both cultural identity and identity as a learner.

Museums are places where cultural stories are produced which can affect how individuals feel about themselves and their place in the world. Matters of identity, how individuals understand themselves and their capabilities, are of extreme significance and because of this, ethical issues arise. The decisions that are made by curators about how to present the past, which objects to include and which to omit, which perspectives to emphasise, and which visual narratives to construct, can shape self-perceptions that will open up or close down life-chances.

'After it got explained to me, I understood it[62] (Action, Behaviour, Progression)

One of the outcomes of learning is action, learning how to do something, doing something new or in a different way, or sustaining a change in behaviour in the mid- or longer term. Progression in learning generally requires that things are carried out in a different way.

The RCMG research found examples of pupils who were pleased with their own progression during the visit. Daniel, aged 11, was a bit worried about making peg dollies at Bilston Craft Gallery, Wolverhampton, where his class were exploring Victorian crafts. However, after he was shown what to do, he understood and enjoyed it. His view of himself has been enhanced as a result of a successful and enjoyable learning outcome[63] (Figure 9.19).

Some of the pupils in the third RR2: 2005 case study described how the experience of the drama changed their attitudes to living in the workhouse over the course of the session:[64]

> When (my teacher) was explaining it, it sounded really bad, but when you actually got there it was a bit scary cos like it is so big and, but, then from like the beginning of the day to the end of the day I had completely different like opinions about it.

Sometimes intentions to do something are developed as an outcome of learning. Most pupils were enthusiastic about what the museum visit might encourage them to do in future. About three-quarters of the younger pupils agreed that: 'Visiting has given me lots of ideas for things I could do' and 'The visit has made me want to find out more'.

Some of the pupils' writing and drawing show the kinds of intentions they might develop. Kirstie, aged 8, for example, had been grinding corn at the Royal Albert Museum in Exeter. She intended to try it out later at home[65] (Figure 9.20).

For some pupils, the museum visit had a potential impact that went beyond their school work. Shanez, aged 13, after a visit to the Museum of London, was inspired by the achievements of Black people in history; she says that she hopes 'we continue what they did'.[66]

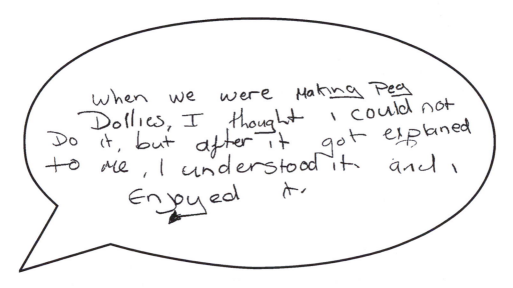

Figure 9.19 Daniel increases his self-confidence through successful learning

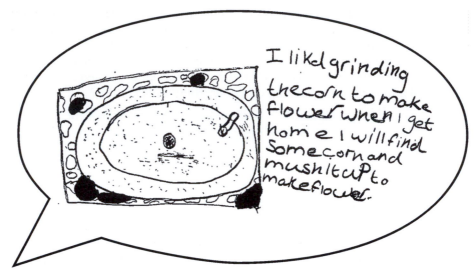

Figure 9.20 Kirstie plans some future actions

Beatrice, aged 17, found inspiration from the way in which a visit to the Horniman allowed her to put a human face to history and from this she was considering how she could make her performance more international:

> The way that costumes and masks have a history and a story behind each one – in a way its another human being! The workshop has helped me as I am now thinking how we can include certain areas from around the world in our themed performance![67]

Between 58 per cent and 59 per cent of the older pupils agreed that they had left the museum more interested in the subject than when they came. And in the third case study for RR: 2005, many pupils were certain that they would do better in their assignments because they knew more. William, aged 13, wrote at the bottom of his questionnaire:

> The most interesting thing about today was . . .

> learning about the school and on the farm. I also enjoyed the role plays about their point of view, it was very realistic. I think it will help my essay because I have actually been and experienced a workhouse. I heard the good and bad point of views about it.[68]

Over half of the older pupils in all three linked studies agreed that they would come again.

Conclusions

This chapter has presented evidence of the outcomes of learning in museums drawn from the views of teachers and pupils in the RCMG studies. The voices of the pupils revealed their pleasure and excitement as they wrote, drew or talked about their experiences in museums. They had taken part in stimulating activities which were fresh, new and beyond their everyday experience. Being involved with different adults, in rich environments, using fascinating artefacts, hearing strange stories, doing new things and being successful, were especially powerful for those pupils whose lives were likely to be narrowly circumscribed. Many pupils felt privileged because they were allowed to use their imaginations and their senses, work together with their friends and make a noise. Pupils rarely wrote about feeling bored or unhappy. In the case studies some evidence was found of poor provision but even in these instances, many pupils presented evidence of good learning outcomes.[69]

Pupils learnt about the past through imagining events and feelings which became more real because of objects and images that they had seen, and because the information about historical events was presented in ways that they could relate to their own lives. They learnt about art by looking at paintings and sculpture and using them as inspiration for their own work, by learning specific new art and craft skills, and by developing methods of art appreciation. Science and technology became meaningful because they saw how things worked, observed, questioned and tried out techniques for themselves.

The evidence shows that museum experiences can spark powerful reactions, including curiosity, surprise and increased self-esteem, and for many pupils the response is so strong it can be recalled and reused for a long time afterwards. This is a consistent finding. Asked to describe her visit to the Booth Museum of Natural History a year earlier, one primary school child involved in the MGEP1 research said:

> We saw stuffed animals, birds, fishes, insects, unicorns, mermaids, a
> peacock, a whale . . . On the floor there was a glass with a badger, snake,
> insects, butterflies under. There was a snake – big and curled up – it could
> eat us.[70]

Four very strong conclusions emerge from the detailed analysis of learning outcomes in this chapter and the previous one. The first is that although it is possible to separate learning outcomes at a conceptual level, and in relation to museum policy and practice it has been necessary to do so in order to count and measure museum-based learning, at the level of the individual learner, the five Generic Learning Outcomes cannot be disaggregated. They all work together in combination, and the closer the links, the deeper the learning seems to be.

The second conclusion which is quite inescapable is that in learning in the museum, mind and body work together. It is crystal clear from what the pupils tell us that they learn best when their bodies are immersed in physical experiences which engage their feelings and emotions and allow their minds to open up to new ideas.

And this brings us on to the third strong finding. Museum learning is not the tightly focused spotlight learning that Claxton describes, but at best involves the open, diffusely focused attention that enables new ideas to flow, new emotions to be felt and lateral thinking to occur.

Fourth, in many examples, it was clear how what the pupils learnt worked to shape their views about themselves. We are what we learn.

An example can enable us to reflect upon these important ideas a little further, prior to opening up the discussion of the character and significance of museum learning in Chapter 10.

The example arises from a primary school visit to Exeter Museum. It demonstrates the immersive, performative and embodied character of museum learning. An interview with a group of children from one of the schools visited as part of the research for RR1: 2003[71] demonstrates how museum visits enable facts and information to be retained. The facts are subject-related (history), but clearly derive from experience with collections (Egyptian artefacts). The transcript illustrates how the excitement of seeing the old objects, together with creative teaching (the experience of the role-play which is the basis for the comments made by the group of children) has enabled the children to use their minds, bodies and imaginations to learn very specific facts about Egyptian customs. The children's memories of the event reveal the integrated, holistic and performative character of learning in the museum. The excitement, enjoyment and inspiration felt by the children as a result of their active learning has provoked and is intertwined with the factual knowledge; it is clear that it is *because* of the remarkable museum experience that the children recall and understand the information. A further point to note is that the pupils themselves are confident that they have learnt something and also that they had seen and done amazing things, well beyond their normal everyday experience. The wonder in Josh's voice, as he repeats the age of the things he saw (3000 years) and holds on to his memories of the hieroglyphics throughout the long discussion, can almost be heard in the transcript. The drawing that follows illustrates the power and impact of museum pedagogy[72] (Figure 9.21).

Figure 9.21 The powerful events that pupils experience in museums are highly memorable

JD:	*Ben, what do you think would have been different by doing it in the museum?*
Ben:	*I think it was actually quite different if we hadn't gone because we wouldn't know as much.*
JD:	*What wouldn't you have known?*
Ben:	*That (pauses) . . .*
JD:	*What would have been different do you think?*
Ben:	*It would have been different because we wouldn't know half the things that we would know now.*
	. . .
JD:	*Was there anything about what you saw in the museum – tell me about the things that you saw.*
Ben:	*I saw (inaudible) . . .*
JD:	*Tell me about the coffin.*
Ben:	*The coffin, it was highly decorated with (pauses)*
JD:	*What was the decoration like? How was it different?*
Ben:	*It was decorated with bits – hieroglyphics and . . .*
JD:	*Tell me, what are hieroglyphics Josh?*
Josh:	*Egyptian writing.*
JD:	*What was special about seeing them and Josh – when you actually went to the museum what was special?*
Josh:	*Touching them – you could touch them, they felt really weird, all liney and bumpy.*
JD:	*All liney and bumpy . . .*
Child:	*And it's hard to sketch them.*
JD:	*And you had to sketch them as well – can you tell me a little bit more about how old were the things that you saw when you went to the museum?*
Josh:	*They were 3,000 years old.*
Ben:	*Some of them were but then some of them were copies of the real thing.*
JD:	*Say you hadn't gone to the museum what do you think you wouldn't have known about the Egyptians?*
Child:	*That they were covered in 20 layers of bandage.*
Child:	*Their (inaudible) were blue.*
JD:	*Jody, anything you think that you wouldn't have known? Bethany?*
Bethany:	*Bodies take 40 days to dry.*
	. . .
JD:	*. . . And you all took part, you all had roles when you went through the mummification didn't you so tell me the sorts of roles that you had?*
Children:	*(all speaking at once) – I was the . . .*
JD:	*Let's do Josh first.*
Josh:	*I was the worker, I had to help the painter.*
JD:	*So what did you have to do?*
Josh:	*I had to paint the coffin. Help paint the coffin.*

JD:	*Great okay – Ben next and then Jody.*
Ben:	*I had to cut – not really – but cut Bethany.*
JD:	*Pretend to cut Bethany and then what were you pretending when you were cutting her, where did you cut her?*
Ben:	*On the side, the side of her body.*
JD:	*What was the idea of cutting that, what was it you wanted to get out of her body?*
Ben:	*The stomach, the intestines, the liver and the lungs.*
JD:	*Okay so it's to take all these things and what were they going to put all these things into?*
Jody:	*Canopic jars.*
JD:	*Into the canopic jars and you've been making . . .*
Ben:	*First they would – first they would actually be put in the same salt as the body would be put in and they'd be wrapped up and then put in . . .*
JD:	*But eventually – and you've made some, you've got some beautiful canopic jars here which you've made out of pottery is that right?*
Children:	*Yes.*
JD:	*So do you think that any of these were inspired by what you saw in the museum?*
	(Problem with closing one of the jars)
JD:	*Did anybody take any of these symbols? Did you see those when you went to the museum?*
Children:	*Yes.*
Jody:	*I did some work and I had to pour all these smells on, all the er nice smelling things on Bethany.*
JD:	*That was a nice thing to be able to do then wasn't it? Ben, what were you?*
Ben:	*I was a priest.*
JD:	*You were a priest so what did the priest have to do?*
Haydn:	*I'd like (pauses) . . .*
Ben:	*Mumble things.*
Haydn (over):	*Hum.*
JD:	*Hum and mumble things and Jody, what did you have to do?*
Jody:	*I um . . .*
JD:	*Oh you put the oils on and Tamara, what did you do?*
Tamara:	*I was Anubis.*
JD:	*Yes, and so what did that mean?*
Tamara:	*I had to check to see if everyone's doing it right.*
JD:	*Yes, so you had to check that these things were right.*
Child:	*And we have to pray to it.*
	. . .
Josh:	*We had to draw an artefact.*
JD:	*What's an artefact? Anybody know what an artefact is – it's a very grown-up word?*
Child:	*Somebody's made something.*

	. . .
JD:	*Josh?*
Josh:	*I like the fact from the video – the River Nile flooded for six whole weeks and it left behind black soggy mud.*
	. . .
JD:	*What did you say to your mum and dad about the visit?*
Bethany:	*I got wrapped up.*
JD:	*You told them all about it?*
Josh (over):	*3,000 year old . . .*
JD:	*You said that you pretended to be dead and been wrapped up in the museum – what did they say?*
Josh (over):	*3000 year old Egyptian writing . . .*
JD:	*So you told them all about the 3000 year old Egyptian writing?*[73]

10

The characteristics and significance of learning in museums

The last four chapters have presented the findings of the three linked RCMG studies. Very strong evidence of pupils learning in museums has been reported. It is clear that museum workshops can provide excellent conditions for successful learning. But what are the characteristics and significance of learning in museums? And how can learning in museums contribute to government schooling policies?

At the end of the last chapter, four tentative conclusions about learning in museums were identified on the basis of the evidence of the RCMG research. These were that the conceptually distinct learning outcomes are integrated rather than distinct in practice; that learning occurs through mind and body working together; that museum experiences both demand and generate learning; and that museums can impact powerfully on identity. This chapter explores these issues more deeply. It goes on to suggest how the particular power of learning in museums can be used to promote creativity, build personalised learning and help with enabling all children to be successful.

The power of museum learning

For the school pupils, learning using museum collections was exciting. The materiality of collections combined with imaginative and often very unusual activities produce an immediacy of engagement that pupils and their teachers found compelling and intriguing. As one teacher in the RCMG research said:

> Children are engaging in a direct relationship with the subject.[1]

The headteacher from the second case study in RR2: 2005 described the impact of a visit to a Tudor house on her pupils and herself:

> I think it brings history alive, they can actually feel what it would be like because they've seen the clothes. It's not just a dry subject . . . it's picturing it, isn't it . . . If they can visualise it, it makes it more real, it does for me.[2]

Much of the evidence has concerned active learning where pupils were engaged in workshops. Learning theorists are convinced that settings which enable active physical engagement, where the tasks and activities are carefully selected, designed and paced to match the capacities and interests of the participants provide excellent, if not optimum, conditions for learning.[3] Immersion in experience is an unconscious and natural way to learn.[4] Claxton describes how this is the first way in which babies come to find out about the world;[5] during the early years, learning through immersion lays the foundation for the development of other ways of learning.[6] But these multiple modes of learning, underpinned by learning through experience, are used throughout life. Experience-based learning is vital in kick-starting learning skills, and this can happen at any stage.

One example shows the richness of a museum workshop, the multiple levels on which one child has responded, and the way in which she combined her experiences to make sense on her own terms. Achese, aged 9, gave a very complete written account of her response to a visit to Leeds City Art Gallery as part of the RR2: 2005 research. She described how she was amazed by the Henry Moore statue, which she thought must have been very hard to make. She wanted more information about how long it took the artist to make it. She was impressed by the realism of one of the paintings she saw, which enabled her to use her imagination and inspired her to want to make her own paintings. She described how she enjoyed doing a large-scale drawing, which she describes as 'fun'. At the end of her museum visit there are multiple interlinked outcomes. Achese has enjoyed herself and produced a large drawing; she has observed some artwork which has led to a need for more facts and the inspiration to make something creative herself; she has used her imagination and developed an intention to do something later on, and she has written a coherent account of it all.[7] The rich workshop, with varied and carefully paced activities, has clearly been a highly productive learning experience for this bright and articulate 9-year-old (see Figure 10.1).

The museum-based learning which was discussed in Chapters 7 to 9 was almost entirely concerned with physical immersion in carefully designed experiences where exploration of objects and sites stimulated bodily engagement. Pupils touched things, explored houses and gardens, climbed the stairs, rode the tram, drew and built things. During this immersion, they used their senses and their bodies as resources for learning, naturally and unconsciously relating what they experienced to their own physical being. One child thought: 'The python was dangerous as it could wrap round my body.' Another felt the tram was 'high' compared with his size. A third was encouraged and modified his view of himself as a learner once he grasped how to use his hands to make the corn dollies. Physical, bodily engagement was the key in many different ways to enjoyment and the subsequent retention of facts, development of skills and enhancement of self-esteem.

The embodied character of learning in museums is one key to its power. As we discussed in Chapter 6, the conscious processes of verbal experience, which involve speaking, reading, listening, are not enough to engender true learning; the feeling processes, which are largely unconscious, must also be engaged and the way to do this is through bodily action.[8] The research data shows the power of active bodily engagement to generate enjoyment, knowledge, understanding and enhanced self-confidence. One of the teachers in one of the research focus groups pointed out how pupils were able to ask better questions, 'more genuine and more real', when they were able to draw on the museum experience for

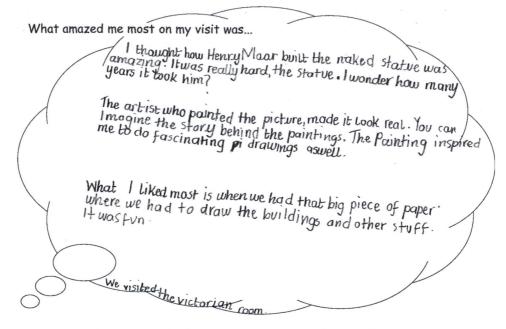

What amazed me most on my visit was...

I thought how Henry Maar built the naked statue was amazing. It was really hard, the statue. I wonder how many years it took him?

The artist who painted the picture, made it look real. You can Imagine the story behind the paintings. The Painting inspired me to do fascinating pi drawings aswell.

What I liked most is when we had that big piece of paper where we had to draw the buildings and other stuff. It was fun.

We visited the victorian room.

Figure 10.1 Achese has a multi-dimensional experience in the art gallery

information.[9] The embodied character of learning in museums which results from immersion in physical experiences is essential to the development of knowledge and understanding. This is as true of the sciences as of the arts and humanities.

While embodied immersion is the earliest mode of learning to develop, Claxton points out how the ability to learn through experience remains essential throughout life and in some instances intuition and experiment may provide more effective learning strategies than rational thought.[10] However, there is a well-established and still widely held view, which can be found in the work of Piaget, that active learning, learning through experience or through play, is only appropriate for very young children and that as young people mature they should move from learning in a concrete way to learning which involves abstract analytical and symbolic thinking rather than physical doing. Contemporary learning theorists point out that this view is mistaken, and that rather than leaving behind experience-based intuitive exploration and response, this remains one among many strategies for learning.[11] The importance and value of embodied and immersive experiences for young learners is well demonstrated by the research data, but this mode of learning is equally as important for learners of all ages.

The use of differentiated modes of attention in learning was introduced in Chapter 6. Using the metaphor of the spotlight and floodlight, Claxton described how the floodlight mode of attention is not tightly focused, but remains open and receptive, able to detect patterns and connections. As the default mode of the brain, this form of attention is essential for coping with unfamiliar environments and also for creativity and the generation of new ideas.[12] The research data shows how immersion in unusual bodily activities in unfamiliar spaces required students to adopt a receptive and open attention in order to navigate and make sense of the events as they occurred. As minds were opened, new ideas could be admitted and absorbed.

The RCMG studies found a great deal of evidence of this open-minded receptiveness, and evidence of how unselectivity enabled pupils to become aware of new ideas that might broaden their perceptions and/or change their opinions. Pupils wrote: 'I never knew', 'I will have to reconsider'. This seemed particularly evident in art galleries, where pupils' preconceptions about art were pleasurably challenged ('art involves more things than I knew about before and is more fun than I thought'). As the body was immersed and activities were undertaken, so the mind and the emotions were engaged. Feelings were stimulated, the mind opened up to new ideas, the imagination freed up, and the self became entirely engrossed in the experience. Barriers to learning came down and new ideas were generated.

Beyond the boredom of not enough to do and the anxiety of too much that is too hard, pupils often seemed, from what they wrote or drew afterwards, to enter what Csikszentmihalyi calls 'a state of flow' during their museum visits. 'Flow' describes a specific quality of experience that involves total immersion in an activity, such that action is spontaneous, the self can be freely and fully expressed, and a process of learning about the self, its capacities, and its relationship to the external world ensues. During the museum workshops we saw that, carried along by the flow of events and the flow of their own spontaneous responses, pupils increased their efforts, tried harder, were tolerant where they did not understand at once, and reached levels of achievement that surprised and pleased themselves and their teachers. Often, in a state of flow, learning can come as a surprise – the discovery of who one is and what one can actually do.[13] Creative inspiration strikes when the mind is playfully relaxed.[14]

Csikszentmihalyi has written at length about the relationship between 'flow' and intrinsic motivation.[15] He states that when complex information is presented in a way that is enjoyable it becomes intrinsically rewarding and this then motivates further learning. Learning is intrinsically motivated when it is spontaneous and when attention is paid simply because things are found to be interesting and important. Learners who are intrinsically motivated have higher achievement scores and higher levels of creativity.[16] Perhaps the strongest evidence in all studies was that of the spontaneous enjoyment that pupils experienced in museums. Pupils continually wrote that 'it was fun', 'I enjoyed it'. Edwards and Knight, discussing the teaching of young children, point out that learning should be enjoyable and that children should get a sense of achievement when they master something.[17] This seems to me to be of wider relevance, an important insight into the relationship between learning and fun. And as Edwards and Knight also point out, it takes skilled educators to engender those feelings of fun and being in control. In the carefully planned museum workshops, pupils felt excited but not threatened; they were relaxed and confident.

In the museum workshops, pupils found ways to learn that were not always open to them at school, and this was especially noticeable with those who found

173

learning hard. Teachers continually described how museums, in contrast to the classroom, enabled all their pupils to 'shine'. Shy children lacking in confidence became more open and self-confident:

> The children changed from not being able to look you in the eye to being able to do radio interviews.[18]

Although there was not much opportunity in the RCMG studies to explore post-museum assessment, where this was examined, improved assessment scores were found.[19] However, the second *Renaissance* study, RR2: 2005, also found that when pupils' and teachers' opinions about the extent and range of the pupils' learning outcomes were cross-tabulated, the pupils were consistently more optimistic about their learning than the teachers.[20] It could be that teachers are not maximising the learning potential of their museum visits.

The children and young people responded to their museum experiences with what one educational theorist has called 'the wild energy' of their thinking[21] partly because the experience was a new one. For a good number of the pupils in all the research studies, the visit to a museum with their schools was the first time they had been inside any museum and even the building must have been in stark contrast to their normal surroundings. For example, in the MGEP1 research one teacher who took her class to Cartwright Hall in Bradford said:

> (It) was a good experience I should like to repeat every year. Too many of our children have never been to a gallery before. The building and the artworks excited them.[22]

It is also possible that the self-confidence and motivation that pupils' found in museums was because they were being successful in a new environment, with unfamiliar adults:

> If anyone visited the site, any pupil could explain what they were doing. They were confident in their own ability in a new way because they were being seen off site and because of the praise.[23]

For many years, educational theorists have given warning about the ways in which teachers' perceptions of their pupils' abilities can shape those abilities.[24] Labelling a pupil a 'slow learner', for example, and making this label known to the pupil has a strong propensity to produce a learner who lacks confidence in their own abilities. It is possible that one of the reasons that some children 'shine' more brightly in museums than teachers normally expect is because museum educators do not know the children as the teachers do and so do not have the same preconceptions. However, this was not probed by the RCMG research and it remains a question for further work. It is certainly also highly probable that pupils who 'shine' unexpectedly in museums are reaping the benefit of being able to use a range of learning styles and resources that are not always available in the classroom. There was much evidence of teachers' thinking along those lines:

> Especially for the poor readers, objects broaden the range of resources available to them. Objects seem to be more memorable. They reinforce memory.[25]

The museum workshops opened up new worlds to the pupils, worlds where they could be inspired and taken beyond their everyday experience. They became aware, often for the first time, of the tremendous scope of culture, the fascination of cultural artefacts and the power and diversity of art:

> Art is 3D stuff; art is fun things too. I used to see art as just painting pictures. I didn't think it was big sculpture, fun things.[26]

They also began to be aware of some of the ways in which they might make their own relationships with the things that they saw.

The integrated domains of learning

The analysis of teachers' and pupils' views of the outcomes of learning in museums shows how the five Generic Learning Outcomes operate together, in an integrated manner. The pleasure felt in hearing the story of Boudicca enabled recall of the details of her family and her chariot. The teenagers who became angry in the workhouse remembered the details of the lives of the inmates because their emotions had been aroused. Information about the role of the Museum of London in saving Roman coins amazed one young pupil. The enjoyment felt in making flower (flour) led another to develop plans for later on. The improvement of drawing skills led to enjoyment for another. The GLOs are conceptually distinct, but combine together in practice; learning in museums is multi-dimensional.

Many contemporary educational theorists describe how emotions are inevitably bound up in learning. Csikszentmihalyi proposes that the learning experiences involve the whole person, including the intellectual, sensory and emotional faculties.[27] Claxton states that learning is intrinsically emotional, with feelings being integral to learning.[28] Sotto points out that tacit learning is so powerful because the feelings are engaged.[29] And Drummond and Pollock, discussing the assessment of children's learning, firmly assert the importance of including the emotional domain.[30]

The RCMG research found many references to the feelings and emotions, especially during the second *Renaissance* study, RR2: 2005. Teachers talked about an emotional and a personal connection as being central to learning:

> It's about emotions, if emotions are triggered it helps you to learn whether it's negative or positive.
>
> Emotional response is the catalyst because it is real.[31]

Some teachers were of the view that being able to use the emotions makes learning more enjoyable, even where the subject matter was difficult:

> But very often it's not a positive experience; what makes it enjoyable is the making contact and having feelings about things . . . doing about WWII is like that . . . learning about the horror is not fun.[32]

Emotions are personal; they are our way of claiming something as our own. An involvement without emotion is distant, unengaged, essentially *uninvolved*. The stimulation of feelings indicates acceptance and engagement in a situation; it means that participation has occurred, and it is because we feel that we think we know, whether what we think we know is right or wrong. Being able to use the emotions activates other strategies for learning.

Museum-based learning pulls together the past, present and future. In order to interpret new experiences in the present, learners must use their existing learning skills and their existing knowledge. These are the tools that enable them to appropriate and make their own their museum experience. As they do so, they lay down experiences and tacit knowledge that may be called upon in the future.

Some teachers talked about how museum experiences provide latent learning, learning that could be activated in the future. Because much museum-based learning happens at the tacit and unconscious level, it remains latent. Felt-knowledge, tacit knowledge, which is laid down during active experiences, produces knowledge which is encoded in a non-verbal way, laid down in a compacted manner; it requires effort to bring tacit knowledge out of this non-verbal state so that it can be used. This raises issues for museums when trying to provide evidence of museum-based learning. As the museum education officer in the third RR2: 2005 case study pointed out, if the participating pupils were to be able to challenge their own and others' preconceived attitudes in relation to contemporary issues as they had in relation to nineteenth-century issues: 'We would need to rely on the school to pick up and reinforce some of the things . . . outside the day.'[33] Museums are dependent on teachers to maximise their pupils' learning, and if pupils' are not encouraged and helped to verbalise or otherwise represent their experiences (through drawings or role-play, for example) much potential learning may be lost.

Contemporary learning theory shows how facts and information only make sense to learners when they can be seen as part of a pattern that already has some familiarity and resonance.[34] Learning is not a simple process of calmly adding one logical fact to another in an unemotional manner; while some learning may be like this and some learners may feel comfortable learning in this manner, much of the time learning is a much more hit or miss affair, one that requires emotional commitment, resilience and desire. In some ways, it is a process of *bricolage* – a picking up of bits and pieces to produce something that seems to suit for the moment. If a hole appears in the edifice, it can be patched, or another bit built on. If it keeps on working, it will not be changed.

Learning is basically a process grounded in desire. If there is no desire to learn, learning will not happen. The stimulation of interest and the desire to learn is one of the most important things that museum workshops can offer the learning process. Brains work best when the intellect combines with intuition and imagination and when it can make patterns based on experience.[35] And in teaching, fantasy and the imagination, which play such a large part in children's lives, are important factors to be considered in addition to intellectual abilities.[36]

The museum workshops provided genuine and convincing contexts for learning. When skills are needed for immediate use to make something, when knowledge is necessary to make sense of what is in front of your eyes, and when emotions result in empathy with others, the context demands that learning takes place. This means that cognition and rationality must be understood as contextual rather than as single independent elements. The acquisition of facts and information and the increase in knowledge and understanding that the research data illustrates occurred as part of multi-faceted, multi-dimensional learning events. For the pupil visiting Birmingham Museum and Art Gallery, information about the Pre-Raphaelite painters was bound up with attitudes to them and personal judgements about which were the best. Taking part in debates where different points of view were articulated and discussed led to increased understanding in geography. Empathising with the plight of unmarried mothers in nineteenth-century Norfolk enabled teenage girls to grasp historical issues. In these examples, the body and the mind work together, and feelings and emotions assist the intellect in developing understanding.

Where information is simply presented as true without any debate and without alternative perspectives, the motivation to delve deeper and learn more is stunted; there does not seem to be any point, and there is nothing to discuss or evaluate.[37] Opportunities to take decisions, make judgements and practise skills and ideas in a supportive environment are vital for progression and development.[38] And as Fay points out: 'Knowing consists not in experience itself, but in grasping the sense of that experience.'[39]

One of the main reasons that the young people were able to articulate and develop their views was because they were able to relate their workshop experiences to

Plate 10.1 Older students found it motivating to have the opportunity to debate whether the workhouse was really so bad at Gressenhall, Norfolk

their own lives. The best learning occurs when learners can relate new experiences and information to what they already know. Museum workshops typically involve a range of diverse events and activities which can be interpreted in many different ways. It is the kaleidoscopic character of the experience, the overlapping and unpredictable combinations of facts, emotions and images that means that different pupils can use them in different ways that are relevant to themselves. There are many different ways of making sense of multiple sensory inputs; the elements of the experience can fall together, combine and overlap to produce an infinite number and range of interpretations.

Learning within the museum workshops was therefore highly personalised; the multi-dimensional events which operated across different domains of learning were open to individual interpretation. Unpredictable links and connections were made. For example, an education officer from a county archive office who participated in the MGEP1 research reported that:

> The power of the objects was really significant: for example, from on ID (card) one child found that an Asian family had lived in his house during the war. The sense of cultural connection was significant for this Asian child.[40]

The three linked RCMG studies revealed many examples of the personalised character of learning. Pupils wrote and drew about how they were inspired to be creative, to make something, or to become something (an archaeologist or an artist, for example). Being immersed in new experiences, secure with their familiar teachers and peers, relaxed and enjoying themselves, the children and young people were able to project themselves into the events in which they participated and interpret them in ways that were meaningful to themselves. Facts and information fell into patterns of significance and became significant because of the feelings they inspired or the activities they stimulated. The identity-related qualities of the writing and drawing of the pupils remind us that children and young people in formal education are at a stage of becoming and that museums are therefore feeding into what they might make of themselves. The processes of self-actualisation are one form of what Giddens calls 'life-politics'.[41] He also points out that personal meaninglessness, the feeling that life has nothing to offer, is a fundamental problem in contemporary times. Museum workshops, on the evidence of the research discussed in this book, appear to be able to engage children and young people and thereby enable them to find personal meaning in some aspects of the past or present. This raises important moral issues about the social responsibilities of museums.

Learning and identity

One of the most significant characteristics of learning in museums is its power to shape identities. Edwards and Knight view self-concept and self-esteem as elements of identity, and describe identity as 'an organising principle for action'.[42] The discussion above has proposed that learning in museums is embodied and immersive, demanding the use of an open-minded, receptive attention and involving experience, emotions and intuition as well as and perhaps more than analytical thought and the intellect. Through experience, feelings become engaged and response is direct, apprehending the experience and the related knowledge in an immediate and sensory way. This can be deeply formative. Tacit learning shapes subjectivities:

> Experiential learning is the process of creating and transforming experience into knowledge, skills, attitudes, values, emotions, beliefs and senses. It is the process through which individuals become themselves.[43]

There has been a great deal written about identity and culture in recent times and it has become one of the most popular fields for cultural research,[44] but there has been much less written about learning, identity and culture and this is one area that needs development as soon as possible. Some post-modern educational theorists have suggested that museums provide experiences and spaces for the shaping of new identities[45] and the RCMG research provides considerable support for this assertion.

Identity gives a stable core to the individuality of a person. At one level, it is about belonging, about being able to feel at home and to recognise that home as your place. Being able to make connections to local knowledge may be very important for the reinforcement of individual identity. Following a school visit to the Museum of London, a 15-year-old pupil wrote:

> Getting to know about the regeneration and of the history of the dockland where I live. I also liked the fact that you get a break and while your out you discover something I didn't no. And know how the people that lived in docklands feel makes me realise what life used to be like. I also liked the information given.[46]

From this statement, it seems that this young person has found that his/her everyday knowledge of their local area has been validated through being given a historical and peopled context. The deepening of a sense of place and belonging provides a powerful personal reinforcement. The writer has appreciated both the information that has been gained, which has produced a sense of being situated in a community, and has also been pleased with the opportunity to learn in a different and more relaxing way from school, through 'a break'.

Many of the statements made by the pupils in the three linked RCMG studies showed how they appropriated meaning from their museum experiences. Cultural theorists have been concerned with theorising the links between meaning and identity. Hall tells us that being able to construct meaning is central to identity, as it gives us our sense of who we are and where we belong,[47] and Weedon states that identity is central to the desire to be a knowing subject, in control of meaning.[48] Identity, meaning and self-determination are key issues in the production of a powerful sense of an active self. A person is active when what she says and does stems from her own beliefs and convictions; she is reactive when she acts or chooses what to do on the basis of what others want her to say and do. In being active, actions are generated from within; in being reactive, actions are a response to something outside you. Only by being active is one self-determining rather than passive, an independent agent.[49]

179

There was some evidence in the three linked RCMG studies of museum experiences provoking pupils to become more of themselves, more active and self-determining. Handling slave goods and participating in workshops about slavery made one young woman determined to work harder because she linked the subject matter of the workshop directly to her own sense of self. She became prepared to invest more of herself in her school work, 'try a little bit harder' and 'think more openly'. She became more resilient, more determined and more resourceful in her approach to learning. There were a considerable number of comments from the pupils in the three RCMG studies about how being introduced to Black history and culture was significant and important. Where a sense of belonging and empowerment has been aroused because workshop content links directly to specific lives and cultures, questions are raised about what happens when these links are not made. These are questions of ethics, which link to issues of social inclusion.

Claxton discusses the need for resilience and resourcefulness in learning and these tie into the relationship between learning and identity. Successful learning increases resilience which leads to an enhanced capacity to take things forward when the going gets tough. Resilient learners are able to resist difficulties and maintain momentum. Resourceful learners are confident, able to shift from one method of making sense to another.[50] Resilient and resourceful learners have strong and active self-images. Participating in experiences that involved challenging and potentially frightening information may have helped pupils become more resilient. Learning about children during World War Two, experiencing a bomb shelter, or imagining children at the time of the explosion of the atom bomb at Hiroshima could have made pupils anxious or afraid, but this did not seem to have happened. Learning about potentially frightening events was possible within a context where pupils were among known friends and peers and accompanied by familiar teachers, who could be relied upon to keep the group safe. This combination of danger and safety, which involved new and challenging things within contexts where pupils felt secure, was powerful and likely to have increased resilience.

Experiences that engaged the emotions and the imagination, made children and young people feel special and demanded total immersion and trust, were instantly memorable and made an impact on pupils' ideas of who they were, what they could do and who they might become. As one child said after a project at the V&A during MGEP1: 'I felt proud. I didn't think I could produce that kind of work. I think I could do more – better than I thought before.'[51]

The RCMG finding that museum education can impact on identity is supported by an evaluation carried out by NFER of the Image and Identity scheme at the V&A that was part of the DCMS/DfES *Strategic Commissioning Museum Education Programme*. One conclusion from this study is that:

> It would appear that the opportunity offered by galleries as the location of cultural resources and expertise, led not only to an enhanced understanding of both cultural difference and individual identity, but also to an understanding of the relationship between the two . . . the rich

Plate 10.2 Exposure to potentially alarming objects, information and experience felt safe within a known group of peers

cultural resource embodied in the participants themselves and the extent to which this was acknowledged and explored in the projects, combined with the rich cultural resources contributed by the galleries, generated a potent learning experience, often within very limited time frames.[52]

Becoming visible (to government) through performance

The outcomes of learning in museums that have been identified as a result of the RCMG studies have resulted from a particular approach to museum pedagogy involving interactive workshops, many of which were designed to be innovative, and all of which were devised in a climate of special funding and a prioritisation of education as a response to a particular political situation in England at the beginning of the twenty-first century. These workshops were designed by skilled and experienced experts so that all children could succeed. This success was necessary for the sake of the pupils themselves, many of whom were not ordinarily successful learners, as, because of government policies of social inclusion, much of the educational work targeted those in deprived locations, or who had Special Educational Needs. However, perhaps a greater priority that drove the museum workshops was the demonstration that learning in museums could itself be successful. The period during which the research discussed in this book was undertaken (2000 to 2006) was seen by many in museums in England, and especially those involved in the educational role of museums, as one of extraordinary opportunity, where failure was not an option. In addition, those museums in the phase 1 hubs were charged (at the time of RR1: 2003) with demonstrating how regional museums could develop, given the resources, and thus they saw themselves as flag-bearers for regional museums as a whole. Future funding for all hub museums depended on their success, thus the stakes were high. And in the national and independent museums, the additional funding from DCMS/DfES enabled the education departments to raise their internal profiles in a number of important ways.

For all these reasons, the circumstances within which the outcomes of museum-based learning were measured were highly charged and somewhat unusual. The evaluations focused very largely on school pupils (with only a small amount of community involvement); involved schools and teachers from across England, where approximately one-third of schools were located in deprived wards and/or were special schools; and the teaching approach concentrated mainly on high-quality, resource-intensive workshops. The bulk of these teachers (85 per cent RR1: 2003; 86 per cent RR2: 2005) used museums and other cultural organisations on a regular basis. The research therefore presents a picture of school pupils in active learning situations, where most teachers were familiar with the use of museums to complement their classroom-based work and where the museums were working at high velocity to increase the use and quality of their provision for schools. Careful research into the needs of teachers preceded the design of programmes.

The research discussed in this book used the concept of Generic Learning Outcomes as a framework for the generation, analysis and interpretation of evidence of learning, and this approach was fully set out in Chapters 2–4. This concept has worked as an effective research tool, producing reliable evidence of learning in museums. Through asking questions about each of the learning outcomes, the GLOs framed the production of statistical data on pupils' and teachers' perceptions of the value of museums in teaching and learning, and through being used as analytical categories for analysing teachers' and pupils' conversations, they were also successfully used to generate portrayals of experiences. The GLOs can be seen as one example of the positive power of performativity. While many dislike the continuous demand of accountability, being able to offer up museum-based learning to systematic measurement and study has enabled museums to become visible and systematically knowable.[53] We now have a method of representing the educational value of museums using a range of different forms of evidence, and can talk knowledgeably and in detail about learning in museums. This method was developed in conjunction with museum, library and archive practitioners and has been offered, through the MLA Inspiring Learning for All website,[54] as an appropriate and useful approach. Given the general lack of experience in carrying out research in museums and other cultural sites, this has been rapidly adopted as one way to structure evaluation of learning from culture.[55]

The evidence of performance that has been gathered using the GLOs enables museums to place themselves in a position for scrutiny. This is particularly important at a time when government policies continue to demand that museums develop their educational capacity, particularly for schools. During the period of the research, education policies and strategies have been developing rapidly. While rapid introduction may be combined with rapid disappearance, it is worth taking a little time to consider the ways in which museums can contribute to government strategies. At the present time in England, government is open to arguments about how museums promote creativity, how museums can help build personalised learning and how museums can help with enabling all children to be successful.[56]

Creativity is high on the agenda of educational policy makers and schools, but considerable development is still needed for creativity to be embedded into classroom teaching and learning. Museums, however, are already seen by teachers and by pupils as places where creativity can flourish, where new ideas are generated and where experiences can be inspirational. Some schools are incorporating teaching for creativity into classroom work, and a small minority have policy statements on the encouragement of creativity and have developed a collective understanding of this complex concept. However, there are also a considerable number of schools where teachers do not know how to develop creativity in their pupils, are uncertain about the meaning of the term, and do not know how to adapt their teaching.[57] Many teachers assume that creativity is inherently connected with art and design, and do not understand that creativity is a generic quality.

Museums are already valued by some schools for their expertise in promoting creativity.[58] Much museum-based teaching is itself highly creative, using a range of skills and strategies that harnesses the enquiry and enthusiasm of pupils. In addition, however, the planning and development of museum-based workshops are designed to promote creative responses in participants. The research studies discussed in this book show how highly both teachers and pupils value and are using museums for their capacity to stimulate creativity. The work that children do in museums is imaginative and purposeful, setting the scene for innovation and valuable outcomes. While some schools are already using museums as external partners to promote creativity, this research suggests several ways in which this could be extended.

In many schools, cross-curricular opportunities are used to stimulate creativity[59] and some of the most creative work observed by HMI was interdisciplinary.[60] As the second *Renaissance* study, RR2: 2005, showed, the use of museums for cross-curricular work has increased rapidly but was mainly being promoted by primary teachers working on historical themes. Museums have a much wider cross-curricular potential than this and there is some evidence that teachers understand this.[61] Museum displays are thematic and cross-curricular and objects are inherently interdisciplinary; using museum displays and collections, children can make connections and see relationships, reflect critically, and understand how their ideas and feelings have changed during the museum visit. Museums and galleries are already synonymous in the minds of many teachers with creativity; teachers use museums because of their potential to stimulate the imagination, to raise questions in children's minds, and to engage pupils of all ages in critical reflection and emotional responses. This view of museums could be used to develop in teachers' minds a more complex understanding of what creativity can mean and how it can be promoted.

Museums could also enable teachers to broaden their range of teaching styles and develop further their disposition and pedagogy for creativity. Museum educators routinely use a range of teaching styles during one school visit, and experienced museum educators use objects, buildings, sites, materials and specialised individuals such as actors, artists or curators as part of their teaching repertoire. In addition, museum educators are highly skilled at teaching for multiple personalised outcomes through adopting an open-ended, enquiry-based and activity-led approach. Demonstrations and team-teaching could be used to enable teachers to explore some of these creative teaching methods.

The second characteristic of museum learning that can be closely related to government agendas at the present time is its openness to personalisation. One of the major aims of education in England today is to enable each individual child to develop their full potential. The focus on the individual is marked:

> Learning is at the heart of this Government's agenda because it is the key to a rich life for individuals and prosperity for the nation.[62]

The individual focus underpins a great deal of government policy for schooling and for the care of children and young people outside school. One of the key policy documents is the Green Paper *Every Child Matters* which states:

> Our aim is to ensure that every child has the chance to fulfil their potential by reducing levels of educational failure, ill health, substance misuse, teenage pregnancy, abuse and neglect, crime and anti-social behaviour among children and young people.[63]

Personalised learning focuses on the drive to tailor learning to the needs, interests and aptitudes of individual learners. It is a key issue in current debates about educational strategies[64] and the research discussed in this book suggests that museums should be part of this conversation. While museums have already developed strong and effective partnerships with schools, the character of museum-based learning could be further considered within the contexts of personalised learning.

All the research studies contain strong evidence that museums capture the enthusiasm of pupils of all ages and abilities, regardless of their social or cultural backgrounds. In part, this enthusiasm stems from being able to make an individual emotional investment in a museum experience which results in a personalised response to a collective event. Personalised responses lead to the development of individualised relevance – ideas, objects, relationships, events become meaningful. Through this, pupils can flourish as resilient individuals.

One of the key findings of this research study is the very high level of enjoyment and inspiration that pupils of all ages experience in museums and the most

Plate 10.3 The girls have chosen a portrait to work with at Beningborough Hall, North Yorkshire, where they can recognise someone like themselves

important outcome for teachers, and the one they most expect to find in their pupils is enjoyment. Teachers appreciate the generative qualities of museums – how museum experiences generate learning through enjoyment and curiosity. In many museums, the atmosphere induces behaviour for learning and progression. Diverse learning styles can be used in museums, and this is a major strength of a museum visit. The varied learning styles to be found in museum and gallery settings for learning frequently arise through physical activity, and can include object handling, analysis of visual displays, drawing, drama, group discussion, questioning, listening, team-work and problem-solving. Through choosing from the diverse range of learning styles which are on offer during most museum workshops or visits, pupils can respond in ways that confirm their individual learning strategies, some of which are not always validated in classroom situations. This is particularly effective in the case of those who are not strong in conventional academic skills.

The research has found evidence of personal responses which take the form of active making of meaning and taking ownership of learning; the use of prior knowledge to make events meaningful and significant in an individual way; making links with family circumstances; use of preferred learning styles; individual aesthetic response to specific objects or buildings; building of confidence in individual capacity to understand and perform better; stronger relationships between individual pupils and their peers as the result of shared experience. Pupils are aware of the potential of museums for learning, and are frequently confident that they have indeed learnt something. They have also been observed expecting their learning to be manifested in assessed work for which they expect to, and sometimes do, achieve higher grades. Teachers are consistently less confident about their pupils' learning, and this research shows that even where teachers are not confident that their pupils have learnt, those pupils remain confident. The learning potential of museums could be further exploited, especially in relation to the development of strategies to personalise learning.

The third significant contribution of museums to government policies is the role museums can play in relation to government philosophy of enabling all children to fulfil their educational potential through being healthy, staying safe, enjoying and achieving, making a positive contribution and economic well-being.[65] The research discussed in this book shows that museums can enable the vast majority of children to succeed at learning. The tangibility of the experience and the opportunity to access information and feelings through the senses, combined with the possibility of individual emotional engagement makes the museum a powerful teaching tool, especially for those who find more academic approaches difficult. Pupils are able to deploy a broad range of learning styles, and respond to open-ended events in diverse ways. While this makes learning exciting and enjoyable for all pupils, it is an essential pathway to progression for those who find learning a challenge.

Government proposes that organisations must find ways to broaden opportunities for all children to reach their individual potential and museums can be very effective at this, particularly with older pupils. While pupils at KS2 and below are frequently spontaneously enthusiastic, older pupils find this more difficult. However, the research found many instances of older pupils talking about how they found museums cool and interesting, rather to their surprise, and how they would need to change their views about museums. Sometimes older pupils reported their emotional responses to their experiences in museums, again, to their own amazement. The *Key Stage 3 National Strategy*[66] suggests a climate for learning that contains two elements which are important for effective learning. These are the use of diverse learning styles and the acknowledgement of pupils' prior knowledge as a basis from which to build. While museum educators cannot be aware of the prior knowledge that each pupil brings to the museum experience, learning in museums is sufficiently open-ended and interdisciplinary for all young people to use what they already know to make sense of their experience at the museum.

The research demonstrates clearly that museums are significant players in working towards social inclusion, at least for their younger users. The museums in these studies are working with high numbers of schools located in deprived areas, and high numbers of special schools. According to the analysis of schools in relation to the deprivation indices, the 69 museums in the RR2: 2005 study were working with schools located across the social spectrum, but disproportionately more of the schools using museums than would be expected are located in the most deprived areas. Of school visits to museums, 32 per cent are located in the 20 per cent most deprived areas (SOAs) in England. Considering the actual schools visiting museums in relation to the percentages of pupils eligible for free school meals, museums are working with schools with pupils from all social backgrounds, but 38 per cent of these visits are made by schools where more than 25 per cent of the pupils are eligible for free school meals and therefore are perceived by government as at risk.

The use of objects and of learning in a rich and tangible environment, while providing enjoyable, effective and stimulating pathways to learning for all children, has long been acknowledged as especially valuable for pupils with special needs and for those who find learning difficult. The RR2: 2005 research has found that special schools are very much over-represented as museum users in relation to their distribution in England. Where special schools make up 5 per cent of all schools in England, they made up 12 per cent of the schools using the 69 museums in September and October 2005. There is a long-standing and successful relationship between special schools and museums, which this research confirms. Many special schools use museums frequently, and it may in some ways be easier for them to do so because they work with smaller groups of pupils, have easier access to transport than other schools, and have more flexible timetables.

Conclusions

This chapter has reviewed the evidence from the RCMG research and from this discussion some ideas are starting to emerge that begin to explain the power of learning in museums. The five Generic Learning Outcomes were conceptualised as distinct categories for the purposes of analysing the outcomes of learning, using the broad approach to understanding learning that was discussed in Chapter 6. But the five outcome categories, it is now clear, also reveal the dimensions along which learning processes, as well as learning outcomes, may be mapped. They thus provide evidence for the characteristics of museum-based learning. As rich and deep evidence of museum learning outcomes has accumulated through several evaluation research studies, the characteristics of learning in museums have become clearly visible.[67] At one level, the characteristics that have emerged from the data do not come as a surprise, as they have been described and explored in practice for many years. The value of the GLO-based research is that it provides consistent and unequivocal evidence for the existence of these characteristics.

From the evidence we can describe learning in museums, at its best, as immersive, embodied, holistic and pleasurable which together lead to learners adopting an open-minded and receptive outlook. Museums can induce a condition of 'readiness to learn'.

Learning is a serious activity that needs to be fun.[68] In museums, learning seemed to nearly always be fun. 'Serious play'[69] is an idea that is emerging in post-modern pedagogies and it perhaps has value as a way of explaining learning for both adults and children in museums. In performative, participatory learning, students are described as enjoying the activity through taking part, rather than consuming content through learning facts.[70] Learning happens through the activity and the involvement it demands; through experience which becomes personally meaningful when structured to be relevant and enjoyable for the learner.

As the research has shown, learning in museums can affect the ways in which learners see themselves. Different contexts, environments, situations and relationships bring out different elements of the self because they encourage and enable the articulation of different facets of identity.[71] The research suggests that museums are places where self-concepts can be changed, where self-esteem can be increased, and where, potentially, a stronger sense of self can be engendered.

We may now be able to talk about learning in museums as something that occurs through the experience of 'serious play' which both provokes a further readiness to learn and, where that learning is successful, can lead to a more positive self-image for learners. If this is the case, museums can be seen as powerful and significant sites for learning in post-modernity.

The final chapter considers the research findings within the context of museum culture as a whole.

11

Learning in the post-museum: issues and challenges

The post-museum was introduced at the start of this book as a museum form with a number of important characteristics. The post-museum will be shaped through a more sophisticated understanding of the complex relationships between culture, communication, learning and identity that will support a new approach to museum audiences; it will work towards the promotion of a more egalitarian and just society; and its practice and operations will be informed by an acceptance that culture works to represent, reproduce and constitute self-identities and that this entails a sense of social and ethical responsibility. And Marstine suggests that in the emerging post-museum, education will become much more fully integrated into museum practice.[1]

The research findings show in some detail the power and significance of learning in museums for pupils. But the research also found barriers to the realisation of this power in those aspects of museum culture that marginalised educational work[2] and it is to these aspects that we will turn in this chapter.

Considering the school pupils as museum visitors revealed a far more diverse and democratic picture of use than has been reported by recent visitor studies.[3] Where adult visitors to English museums appear to continue to be representative of higher social classes and the most highly educated sections of society, approximately one-third of the schools visiting museums came from locations that were classified as deprived, where a high percentage of the children were, on the government measure of entitlement to free school meals, at risk. Children of all abilities found museum learning appealing, and it was especially pleasing to see that this extended to those pupils who found classroom-based learning difficult. From a school use perspective, museums are acting as inclusive democratic institutions.

The character of learning that the school pupils experienced was enactive and embodied and this was clearly very successful in engaging attention, stimulating curiosity, opening minds to new ideas and, through serious fun, enabling a broad range of integrated learning outcomes. But the experience of most visitors to most museums is limited to a much more restricted approach to learning, one which is based on learning by looking. 'Learning at a glance' has a long pedigree in museums, but the research raises questions about its effectiveness. Consideration needs to be given to whether, if learning modes are broadened, the use of museums might not broaden to match to some degree the inclusive picture presented by the pattern of school use.

One of the most striking findings of the research was the link between learning and identity. If self-identities are shaped by museums, then ethical questions arise about how the 'curriculum' of the museum articulates with different subjectivities. There is a long history of museums privileging a Europeanist world view, but today this has to be called into question. Human rights and the politics of recognition need to be acknowledged as museums construct their displays and consider what narratives to produce for their publics. There are questions to be asked about how these cultural narratives articulate with those who use museums; if stories were told from new perspectives, might a different pattern of use result?

With the current emphasis on education, comments are frequently heard about how museums have always been educational. But what were the educational purposes of museums when the public museum first emerged during the mid to late nineteenth century, and can these purposes really still be relevant today, when so much has changed?

It is clear from the RCMG research that museums have tremendous potential power in relation to pupils' learning, but reviewing that research from the perspective of museum culture as a whole suggests a number of potential barriers to the opening up of similarly pleasing learning experiences for a broader range of visitors. This chapter opens up these issues for discussion.

Learning at a glance

From the end of the eighteenth century, learning in museums was expected to take place through looking. McClellan describes how during the eighteenth century in Europe there was a growing conviction that works of art could be classified in a rational taxonomic manner, inspired by the binomial method of classifying plants and animals by genus and class that had been introduced by Linnaeus and Buffon.[4] In art museums, the organising principles of natural history were paralleled by grouping the artworks by school and chronology and this became the dominant structure of displays of art. Visual taxonomies were produced for didactic purposes, laid out to be observed and studied through the gaze. Through observation, the underlying organisational principles of the display, and thus of the subject matter that shaped it, would be absorbed.

An ideal natural history cabinet had been described in France by Daubenton in 1749:

> (The) arrangement will indicate the principles according to which one should study natural history; only through such an arrangement will those principles be realised. Everything will in fact be instructive; at each glance not only will one gain knowledge of the objects themselves, one will also discover relationships between given objects and those that surround them.[5]

Half a century later across the channel, the same visual didactics were being proposed. Forbes describes in 1853 how provincial museums in English county towns:

> arranged with skill and judgement . . . at a glance tell us of the neighbourhood and activity of a few guiding and enlightened men of science . . . at a glance explanatory of the geology, zoology, botany and ancient history of the locality and neighbouring province.[6]

The collections on display were arranged in a manner that visually demonstrated the structural principles of each field of disciplinary knowledge. It was the task of museum displays to transmit the 'true' structure of science, history or art history[7] and to do this to enable 'learning at a glance'. The eye was expected to quickly take in visual information so that the disciplinary structures and applications of the arts, sciences and history were immediately understood. The eye provided a direct conduit to the mind; it was thought that learning would happen simply by placing specimens, artefacts or paintings in the 'correct' positions on display.

In learning at a glance, the mind was expected to abstract itself away from the body. George Godwin, the Honorary Secretary to the London Art Union, described in 1840 how the fine arts could work as learning experiences:

> The influence of the fine arts in humanising and refining – in purifying the thoughts and raising the sources of gratification in man – is so universally felt and admitted, that it is hardly necessary now to urge it. By abstracting him from the gratification of the senses, teaching him to appreciate physical beauty, and to find delight in the contemplation of the admirable accordances of nature, the mind is carried forward to higher aims, and becomes insensibly opened to a conviction of the force of moral worth and the harmony of virtue.[8]

The body was seen as a potential problem, to be set aside during learning, with the use of the senses perceived as a less reliable way of learning.[9] This approach is based in the long-standing Western philosophical position that mind and body are separate entities, with the mind dominating the body as the foundation of self-identity; the mind was thought to be concerned with universal and higher matters, while the body, with its earthing tendencies, was based in the here-and-now. The rational work of the mind, rather than the bodily sense-organs, was the source of knowledge. Where the senses were acknowledged, they were problematic; it was sight and hearing that could perceive beauty, and touch, smell and taste were insignificant.[10]

Social divisions and hierarchies were based on the mind–body dualism, with those whose lives were thought to be defined by bodily processes and activities, which included women, labourers and the disabled, being seen as of lesser value than those whose lives were defined by intellectual achievements.[11] A strong association between reason, the mind and masculinity existed,[12] with Joshua Reynolds, for example, taking the view that 'liberal society' necessarily excluded women who were incapable of abstract thought because of their gender, and 'mechanics' who were unable to develop intellectual abilities because of the nature of their daily work.[13] Foucault discusses how the 'hysterisation' of women's bodies, which positioned women as pathologically weak, unstable and prone to melancholy, was one of the most powerful strategies of control in the modern period.[14]

Learning through looking was expected to take place in a solitary, silent manner. Trodd describes how abstraction from the physical body into the language of the image was necessary, in Hazlitt's view, in order to understand art.[15] Visiting Angerstein's gallery in Pall Mall in 1822, immediately before it became the National Gallery, Hazlitt envisages the space of the Gallery as a space of pure meaning:

> a sanctuary, a holy of holies, collected by taste . . . (where) we breathe empyrean air; enter into the minds of Raphael, of Titian . . . and look at nature with their eyes; we live in times past, and seem identified with the permanent forms of things. The business of the world at large, and of its pleasures, appears like a vanity and an impertinence. What signify the hubbub, the shifting scenery, the folly, the idle fashions without, when compared to the solitude, the silence of speaking looks, the unfading forms within.[16]

This way of thinking about learning in museums, with its emphasis on contemplative looking, is very different from the performative, embodied approach that the research shows proved so successful for the school pupils. Although new ways of developing exhibitions in museums and art galleries are emerging that acknowledge the full three-dimensional immersive potential of this form of media,[17] contemplative looking is still the experience of most museum visitors. What can be learnt from the effective pedagogic strategies used for pupils and young people in the development of exhibitions in the future?

Museum curricula, identity and the politics of recognition

The RCMG research findings open up issues about how what we have called the 'curriculum' of museums relates to the subjectivities of their visitors. As qualitative research becomes more familiar within the cultural field, evidence is beginning to accumulate that illustrates how museums can be used by people as an integrated and significant part of their lives. Where extended involvement occurs on the basis of mutual respect, museums can have a powerful impact on individuals.[18] One example is the *Represent* project in Birmingham which had some very profound effects on some of the participants, who described how the project had reinforced their self-perceptions while changing their views about museums.[19] One young woman said:

> I would not be caught dead in a museum . . . the project made us feel good, we had gained knowledge, we felt more confident and had our eyes opened to new things. When I was young my mother made me wear traditional African costume. I hated it and felt ashamed. Now I think museums should have things like that in them. I want my culture to be

part of the mainstream culture. I want to see something positive about it, not all the negative things in the slavery gallery Liverpool.[20]

Most visitors to museums experience a fleeting engagement – at least in terms of time. But there is evidence of the way visitors interpret museums from their own perspectives and in relation to their own identities. Worts describes an interesting approach used at the Art Gallery of Ontario, where visitors were asked to fill in 'Share Your Reaction' cards.[21] Many people drew images inspired by their thoughts while observing paintings. Many of the cards reveal how identity is key to meaning-making, and how the individual paintings inspired reflection and personal responses to the displayed artwork. One visitor, for example, wrote about a painting that showed the birthplace of her grandmother:

> My paternal grandmother was born in Glace Bay. For my entire life I have wondered what her childhood was like. Until very recently I have been able only to communicate with her in shouts and sign language. She is 92. She will die soon, but now I have seen her home. Now the words are not as necessary. Thank you.

This is a response that is not informed by knowledge of art or art history, but which is based in the writer's life-experience and personal emotional life. Another visitor recorded her disappointed response to the museum as a whole:

> I would like to know why in this entire Art Gallery, people of colour are not represented. I would like to see more art about the Indian culture and also art on the black race. I am really disappointed that in a city where we are so multicultural, only European cultures are seen in the art gallery. I would not bring my child here, because we are not represented. We are not recognised for any of our talents – I am a black woman, who is Canadian (born).

Here again the paintings in the gallery were viewed through the identity of the writer, with her feelings of rejection and alienation being the main element in her response to the gallery. Museums act as cultural mediators and the relationship of the museum 'curriculum' to the identity of the visitor-as-learner is significant. Individual constructions of identity are affirmed and reinforced when public narratives, such as those found in museums, involve strong and positive representation that can be recognised as relating to or belonging 'to me'. And as Weedon points out, non-recognition and non-identification leaves the individual in a state of non-subjectivity and lack of agency.[22] Where this happens, museums are in danger of facilitating learning which is hurtful and destructive.

As the symbolic power of culture is increasingly acknowledged in museums, the ethical responsibilities for the use of those symbols are beginning to be taken seriously in some museums.[23] But there is a long history of museums constructing narratives on the basis of gendered and racialised social hierarchies. Tony Bennett, for example, describes in some detail the ideas that lay behind the evolutionary museum at the end of the nineteenth century.[24] Belief in continual progress was a key structure of modernity, and evolution was one of the most powerful discourses of progress, one which both produced museum narratives and was produced by them. By the 1840s, the new sciences of geology, palaeontology, natural history, prehistoric archaeology and anthropology had begun to be developed. These new forms of knowledge would lead to new ways of learning about the past, through study of the things themselves, 'reading' the fossils, rocks, pottery and tools. Direct interpretation of the object would enable the investigation of what Bennett calls 'pasts beyond memory', those pasts that could no longer be called up by living people, but which lay hidden in the ground and in the land-scape. New ways of thinking about the earth as historically stratified proposed the ground as a source of historical information in both geology and archaeology. This stratigraphical method was extended to other sciences and histories as the present began to be seen as the result of the slow accumulation of the many pasts stored up within contemporary life.[25] These ideas constituted and were produced by the 'evolutionary museum' where objects were arranged to show the rela-tionships between things which could not actually be seen but which could be inferred.

Bennett suggests that by the end of the nineteenth century the Enlightenment museum, where display had been based on Linnaean principles of the classi-fication through observable similarities and differences of families and classes of specimens, had been superseded by the evolutionary museum, where develop-mental sequences of objects were exhibited to present the long, slow accumulation of those pasts as they shaped the present. The similarities and differences of the surfaces of things were no longer as meaningful as the relationships between things, as sequences and series, often based on small details, were worked out across disciplines which included archaeology, geology, biology, anthropology, art history, medicine and psychoanalysis.[26] Newly discovered pasts emerged, as the techniques of 'retrospective deduction' were applied to read the past *through* the present, identifying past causes from their contemporary effects, and at the same time deducing the character of the whole from the detail of the part.[27]

Ideas about evolution brought new ideas about what should be collected. Where formerly specimens, fossils and lumps of rock had been what most natural history collectors wanted, now artefacts as well as specimens became significant. A 'natural history' of people was proposed by Louis Agassiz writing to Mr Thomas G. Cary in 1863:

> Every day the history of mankind is brought into more and more intimate connection with the natural history of the animal creation, and it is now indispensable that we should organise an extensive collection to illustrate the natural history of the uncivilised races . . . two classes of specimens should be brought together, one concerning the habits and pursuits of the races, the other concerning the physical constitution of the races themselves. With reference to the first it would be desirable to collect articles of clothing and ornaments of all the races of men, their implements, tools, weapons . . . small canoes and oars.

These objects, along with others, were recommended so that they could show how people lived and how far they had progressed. Agassiz considered it was going to be more difficult to collect items that would illustrate 'the physical constitution' of what he called 'the savage races', but he suggested that where possible the 'skulls of the natives of different parts of the world' and 'perfect heads, preserved in alcohol' should be acquired. If these were not forthcoming, 'portraits or photographs may be substituted'.[28]

These kinds of ideas, abhorrent to us today, informed the collecting practices of some nineteenth-century museums. Leone and Little describe how the positioning of indigenous peoples as 'natural' rather than 'social' was an integral element of Peale's museum in Philadelphia in the 1820s.[29] And indeed in many colonial museums the artefacts of colonised peoples were displayed in natural history museums; the Australian Museum in Sydney is one example among many where geology, zoology and anthropology were combined for the purposes of 'science'.[30]

Bennett describes how, in the second half of the nineteenth century, 'the arch-aeological conception of the person' proposed that indigenous peoples were on the lowest rungs of the evolutionary ladder and were therefore incapable of becoming fully civilised.[31] Each step in the evolutionary journey was one of technical and cultural progression, from an absence of cultivation, metals, pottery, cloth and weapons, moving up through successive layers of sophistication to the higher reaches of civilisation represented by the best in art, law, politics and technological innovation. The museum offered a way of establishing equivalence between objects through typological display, so that the stone tools found in the territories of colonised indigenous peoples could be accorded the same meaning as the stone tools of the European stone age, and thus, as Bennett puts it: 'Colonised peoples could be represented as primitive but not ancient, as living relics of the European past but without any history of their own.'[32] Distance in geographical space was transformed into distance in historical time, and the integration of geographically distant peoples into the history of Europe enabled the picturing of those peoples as the still surviving (though only just) bottom-most layer of the archaeological make-up of modern people. Indigenous peoples, through this formulation, took their place among the flora and fauna of the natural history museum.

Intellectual frameworks such as these still permeate much of the thinking that can be found in the museum field today as discussions over the continued validity of the idea of the 'universal museum' indicate.[33] There are increasingly bitter international debates about how far museums should recognise and respond to the often bloody histories that lie behind their collecting activities, and the extent to which the legacies of the social circumstances within which past collecting took place should be addressed. The cultural narratives of museums are constructed today at a time when museums are expected to act as critical thinkers in the context of human rights,[34] and at a time when the politics of recognition demands that attention is paid both to cultural representation and to patterns of the distribution of culture.

The purposes of museums and education

As education is prioritised in museums, statements can be heard about the long-established educational purposes of museums. 'Museums in the United Kingdom have always been seen as educational institutions', asserts Anderson at the start of his influential report, *A common wealth: museums and learning in the United Kingdom.*[35] Similarly, Hein proposes at the start of his important book *Learning in the Museum*: 'Education as a crucial museum function has been recognised as long as there have been public museums.'[36] But to what extent can nineteenth-century claims made about the educational purposes of museums be valid today? What did they really mean, and how far were museums 'educational'?

Looking back to the nineteenth century, it seems plain that the idea of the moral capacities of museums and the arts resonated throughout the period in England. For many, museums were seen as part of what Bauman has called an 'early modern illusion'; a desire for a good and just society, where everyone knew their place, and was content with it, and where everything could be known, ordered and controlled.[37] The themes of morality, social improvement, education, taste and the arts were strongly linked throughout the nineteenth century.[38]

Ideas about the educational power of museums can be found in many of the statements about why museums should be established. For example, educational purposes were clearly set out in the philosophy behind the South Kensington Museum (the embryo Victoria and Albert Museum) in the 1850s. In the first report to the Department of Science and Art, Henry Cole declared:

> Indeed, a museum presents probably the only effectual means of educating the adult . . . By proper arrangements a museum may be made in the highest degree instructional . . . an impressive schoolroom for everyone.[39]

A strong conviction that the arts, through museums and education, could bring the different parts of society together and could alleviate social problems formed the basis of these arguments.[40] One example of this can be found early in the century. Peel suggested to parliament in 1832 in a discussion about the funding of a building for the National Gallery that while the rich had their own pictures to look at, the poor might be 'softened' through exposure to paintings in a public gallery:

> In the present times of political excitement, the exacerbation of angry and unsocial feelings might be much softened by the effects which the fine arts had ever produced on the minds of men. . . . The rich might have their own pictures, but those who had to obtain their bread by their labour, could not hope for such an enjoyment . . . He therefore, trusted that the erection of the edifice would not only contribute to the cultivation of the arts, but also to the cementing of the bonds of union between the richer and the poorer orders of the State.[41]

Twenty years later, speaking at a lecture held at the Museum of Practical Geology in 1853 about the desirability of a national system of local museums, Edward Forbes proclaimed:

> Every shilling granted judiciously by the State for the purposes of education and instruction, for the promotion of schools, libraries and museums, is a seed that will in the end generate a rich crop of good

citizens. Out of sound knowledge spring charity, loyalty, and patriotism –
the love of our neighbours, the love of just authority, and the love of our
country's good. In proportion as these virtues flourish, the weeds of
idleness, viciousness, and crime perish.[42]

Forbes had well-developed ideas about museums and education. Museums, he
thought, are most effective when working together with other organisations, as
'museums, of themselves alone, are powerless to educate. But they can instruct
the educated, and excite a desire for knowledge in the ignorant.' However, Forbes
thought that museums were likely to be of little use unless they were 'connected
to systems of public teaching' and although in well-arranged museums, the
collections will be instructive 'at a glance', lectures would also help the museum
realise its educational promise. Forbes considered that those who thought
museums should stand alone, 'on their own exclusive merits, and be mainly places
of personal study and consultation', were only thinking about museums in
relation to 'men' who are already 'men of science, historians or connoisseurs'.
'Competent teachers' were needed to open up the museum to 'those who (are) as
yet ignorant (but) desire to learn' and 'those in whom it is desirable that a thirst
for learning should be incited'. Forbes longed for a 'well-organised museum' in
every British town of even moderate size, which would be free to all classes, both
adults and the 'youthful and childish population'. Civilisation could not be
claimed, he thought, until each town had a park, an art gallery, a museum, a
library and public statues of the great and the good. These ideas about museums
and their educational purposes are firmly located within more general views of
the social purposes of education. In discussions about the establishment of
elementary schools in England, for example, Selleck tells us that the purposes of
education are to improve the 'lower orders', reducing crime through the spreading
of information. Elementary education, in the view of the middle-class reformers,
would train and inform future voters and thereby preserve and maintain the social
structure.[43]

If many of the statements made about the purposes of education in museums
focused on the 'lower orders', the arts and museums were also seen as one way
in which the aspiring sections of the bourgeoisie could distinguish themselves
from these very 'lower orders' of society.[44] Culture and education could be
positioned as that to which the bourgeois class had a natural right and affinity
because of their educated minds and cultivated natures. Learning at a glance,
disembodied learning, could be practised by those cultured and educated people
who had been trained in how to achieve it, but it was also on the basis of this
method of teaching that museums were expected to act as vehicles of mass
communication to the working classes. This was, of course, inherently contra-
dictory. At the same time as the educational value and purpose of the museum
was being proposed on a broad social front, museum pedagogies operated to
promote specific styles of learning that were thought to be beyond the natural
capacities of many of their visitors.

There was no single view of the educational purpose of museums, and not all
museums were perceived as having the same kind of educational capacity.
Distinctions were made between what local museums and national museums

might be expected to achieve in respect of education. John Ruskin, for example, writing in the 1850s, was clear about the distinction between educational museums for the 'lower orders' and national galleries of art:

> A national museum is one thing, a national place of education another; and the more sternly and unequivocally they are separated the better each will perform its office – the one of treasuring, the other of teaching.[45]

The role of national galleries of art seems to have been particularly ambiguous in relation to its educational role. While Trodd points out that a government report in 1853 suggests that the National Gallery should be a 'complete school of art' rather than the sort of collection 'a private gentleman might want to possess',[46] Taylor suggests that clear distinctions were made between the South Kensington Museum, which was designed to be 'popular and educational', and the National Gallery in Trafalgar Square, which was expected to be 'elevated and selective'.[47]

Hill suggests that the commitment to education was weak in many municipal museums,[48] which acted instead as spaces where the middle classes could display their cultural authority rather than as didactic spaces for improvement. Hill suggests that in some regional museums, especially those such as the Harris Museum, Preston, which relied heavily on the South Kensington loan scheme and where the art collections were more significant than the natural history collections, the pedagogical function was barely visible, with the art collections being used instead to signify the classical knowledge of the middle classes.[49] The 'educational' purposes of museums were ambiguous. If the Harris Museum was 'didactic', presenting the whole development of Western Art, as Waterfield describes,[50] this was perhaps intended less to teach the urban poor and more to enable the middle classes to display their connoisseurship.

During the nineteenth century, when the idea of the public museum was new, the dream of a perfect society provided the rationale for museums as educational institutions. The idea that a good and just society could be achieved was a key theme of the nineteenth century; many believed that a 'state of perfection' could be reached, even though there was no single view as to how this might be attained. What was common across many groups and individuals was a vision of the *possibility* of a just and conflict-free society, described by Bauman as:

> of steady equilibrium between supply and demand and satisfaction of all needs; of perfect order, in which everything is allocated to its right place, nothing out of place persists and no place is in doubt; of human affairs becoming totally transparent thanks to knowing everything needing to be known; of complete mastery over the future – so complete it puts paid to all contingency, contention, ambivalence and unanticipated consequences of human undertakings.[51]

One of the principal icons of 'heavy' modernity, which Bauman describes as characterised by obsession with order, institutionalised norms, habitualised rules, assignment of duties and supervised performance,[52] was the Fordist factory, but museums, with their classification systems, focus on order, desire for durability and insistence on perceived neutrality, can also be described as emblematic of this 'heavy' stage of modernity. They formed part of the modernist proposition for a healthy society, introduced along with systems of sanitation, transportation and communication.[53]

Bauman suggests that in post-modern times, or what he calls 'liquid' or 'fluid' modernity', the belief in the possibility of 'the good society' (this 'early modern illusion') has virtually collapsed. The idea of a social arrangement based on perfect order with everything in its place, where everything could be known, and where the world and its future could be mastered, is no longer seen as possible today.[54] The concept of a totally ordered life with fixed reference points is no longer tenable.[55] Today, lives are much more fluid and changeable and situations are experienced as contingent rather than permanent. Life is much less predictable, and people are no longer 'born into' their identities.[56] And the idea of a fixed society made up of diverse groups with different levels of social privilege but which remain harmonious, all holding the same values and objectives, seems hopelessly naive at a time when many societies face civil war, territorial fragmentation, and when ethnic and religious conflicts seem impossible to resolve.

During the nineteenth century, the task of education was perceived as enabling the control of the social and natural world. The values of critical reason, individual autonomy and benevolent progress underpinned education which was seen as a form of enlightenment, an induction into the canon, 'a gift bestowed by educators'.[57] Educational discourses thus shaped and maintained the project of ('heavy') modernity through the development of educational systems where subject disciplines were clearly defined, and where space and time was monitored and controlled with the aim of producing bounded, centred and autonomous selves who were fit for specific pre-allocated roles. Differentiation of teaching was shaped by the purposes for which the curriculum was designed, rather than by the abilities or specific needs of the child. It was assumed that citizenship had to be taught or achieved through appropriate forms of education, access to high culture, and thus discernment and the capacity to distinguish worth. Museums, among other organisations such as universities, assumed the task of educating for citizenship, of producing the rational 'man' who was able to reason in an abstract way and to imagine abstract concepts.[58]

The universal meanings and approved curricula that formed the basis for modernist education are no longer viable. Increasingly, nineteenth-century disciplines are breaking down as new disciplines emerge and subject boundaries blur. And there is increasing acknowledgement of the value of experience and of the senses in education.[59] Knowledge in post-modernity has different purposes, which include utility, pleasure and the fulfilment of desire, and learning as lifestyle consumption which involves the forming of new identities.

Today, learning is expected to be enjoyable, foregrounding play and desire, rather than a search for a proscribed pre-determined end; a desire rather than a discipline.[60] The self is understood as embodied, with experience and emotion available as a resource in the teaching and learning process. Learning is about individuation and choice, and about a lifelong aptitude; in post-modern times (or

199

light modern times), individuals are presented with a large range of life-choices and are expected to pursue their own pathways through life, making their own best choices and remaking them as necessary. Fitting individuals to a pre-allocated lifelong position is no longer the purpose of education. Education is now more strongly focused on producing individuals with strong personal identities, strong self-esteem, confidence, and the ability to evaluate and make judgements about their own best interests. Adult learners focus their learning agendas according to their individual desires.

Issues for the future

Today, museums are searching for ways to respond to the considerable changes that have occurred since their social and educational role was last declared important. The discussion above suggests that the platform on which the educational purposes of the public museum was initially constructed no longer holds firm and that new ideas about the educational use and potential of museums are needed.

The research questions with which the research discussed in this book began were: Does learning happen in museums, and if so, in what way and to what purpose? What is the character of learning in museums and what are the outcomes and impact of this learning? This overarching question underpinned the three national research programmes; the research methods and the analysis and interpretation of the findings were structured using the GLOs, the conceptual and interpretive framework that was devised through the Learning Impact Research Project (LIRP).

The power of museum pedagogy can now be clearly seen; this is one of the positive aspects of the post-modern emphasis on accountability and performativity. While increased government intervention is often felt to be burdensome, it has, for the time being at least, enabled museums to gather and present evidence of their effectiveness, efficiency and efficaciousness in educational work. The research evidence has shown how museums can match and exceed government expectations, can respond to government desires for social inclusion, and can complement the state's provision of educational systems.

The outcomes of this learning have been identified on several levels. The most valued outcome of museum-based learning, in the views of both the teachers and the pupils, was Enjoyment, Inspiration, Creativity. Learning in museums resulted in pupils of all ages, and with a range of capacities for learning, feeling motivated to learn and enjoying learning. The second most important outcome for teachers was their pupils learning more about the subject matter. In addition, learning in museums opens up cultural experience for pupils. Museum visits showed pupils a world beyond their everyday experience, and successful learning within this new cultural world enabled pupils to begin to find ways to claim this world as their own. Chapter 10 identified the impact of learning museums as the production of positive and enthusiastic learners; increased success for those who find school-based learning difficult; and the experience of new ways of thinking about history, the arts and the sciences.

When the research evidence is considered in relation to museum culture as a whole, important questions about the purposes of museums today, about modes of teaching and learning and about how museums can reposition themselves for the future are raised. It has been suggested that the pedagogic power revealed by the research locates the museum as a key site for learning in the new century, but relationships between nineteenth- and twenty-first-century ideas about the educational purpose and pedagogy of museums, in the context of the analysis of contemporary educational performance as presented here, suggest that new ways of articulating the educational values of museums are needed that acknowledge the shifts and continuities that characterise post-modernity.

Questions about educational purpose, pedagogy and performance come together in post-modern times, placing the museum in a swirling vortex of ambiguity, confusion and potential opportunity. These questions, if considered honestly and answered with analytical clarity, will enable the emergence of diverse approaches to the post-museum.

Notes

1 Museums: learning and culture

1 The use of the term 'museum' is intended to include museums and galleries.
2 Bauman, 2000: 28.
3 See for example, Resource, 2001; Graubard, 1999; Welsh, 2005.
4 Abercrombie and Longhurst, 1998; Henning, 2006; Storey, 1999.
5 Price, 2002.
6 Bauman, 2000; Ross, 2004.
7 Hooper-Greenhill, 2000a.
8 Marstine, 2006: 19; Sandell, 2007b: 9.
9 Chaney, 1994; Easthope and McGowan, 2004.
10 Ray and Sayer, 1999: 22.
11 Hall, 2005: 28.
12 Chaney, 1993: 15.
13 Hooper-Greenhill, 2000a.
14 Thistlewood, 1993: 8.
15 Hutcheon, 1989: 62.
16 Hooper-Greenhill, 2000a.
17 Wenger, 1998: 215.
18 Giddens, 1991.
19 Department for Culture, Media and Sport and Department for Education and Employment, 2000: 4.
20 Friere, 1972; Illich, 1973.
21 Harrison, 1950, 1970; Marcouse, 1961; Winstanley, 1967.
22 Usher et al., 1997, describe how this has happened in adult education.
23 For a discussion of some of the relevant terms, see Hooper-Greenhill, 1999.
24 See Jarvis et al., 1998; and Joyce et al., 1997.
25 See Falk and Dierking, 2000: 9–10.
26 See for example, Friere, 1972; Gardner, 1985, 1991; Giroux, 1992.
27 Falk and Dierking, 2000: 2.
28 Pringle, 2006: 7.

29 A discussion of different styles of display and the different educational philosophies and approaches to communication that underpin them is useful in exploring this point. See Hein, 1998 and Hooper-Greenhill, 2000a.
30 Pringle, 2006; Hooper-Greenhill and Moussouri, 2002, describe the position of research into learning in museums in Britain in 1999.
31 Miers, 1928 and Markham, 1938, give a good overview of the situation.
32 Hooper-Greenhill, 1991: 51.
33 Carter, 1984.
34 American Association of Museums, 1992.
35 Boodle, 1992.
36 American Association of Museums, 1984.
37 Boodle, 1992: 1.
38 Museums Association, 1993.
39 Hooper-Greenhill, 199b.
40 This was the first ministry for culture in the UK; later it became the Department for Culture, Media and Sport (DCMS).
41 Anderson, 1997: iv.
42 Ibid.
43 Anderson, 1999.
44 Ibid.: 37.
45 Ibid.: 39–40.
46 Department for Culture, Media and Sport and Department for Education and Employment, 2000: 7.
47 There have been a large number of reports and papers on this theme in recent years: Department for Culture, Media and Sport, 1998, 2000, 2001; Department for Culture, Media and Sport and Department for Education and Employment, 2000.
48 MLA, The Museums, Libraries and Archives Council (formerly known as Resource) replaced the Museums and Galleries Commission (MGC) and the Libraries and

Information Commission (LIC) in April 2000 (www.mla.gov.uk, accessed 25.01.06).

49 MLA, 2006b. Anderson reviewed the situation across Britain, but the MLA report focuses on England only, following devolution.

50 Hooper-Greenhill, 2006b, analyses the field of museum visitor studies, including educational evaluation.

51 Selwood, 2006b.

52 I was the founding Director of RCMG from 1999 to 2006 and leader of the research teams that carried out the research discussed in this book. All research reports are available on the RCMG website: www.le.ac.uk/museumstudies/research/rcmgpublicationsandprojects.html (accessed 19.01.06).

53 Babbidge, 2000; Hill, 2005; Selwood, 2006a.

2 Calibrating culture

1 Fyfe, 2006.

2 Babbidge, 2005: 13.

3 Selwood, 2001: 2.

4 Ibid.: 24.

5 Resource, 2001: 27.

6 Wenger, 1998.

7 Resource was established as a registered charity, independent of government. The mission of Resource was set out in their publications; for example: 'Resource provides the strategic leadership, advocacy and advice to enable museums, archives and libraries to touch people's lives and inspire their imagination, learning and creativity', *Resource News*, 4 July 2002. Resource (now MLA) does, however, work with government policies very clearly to the fore.

8 It was tricky at first to know how to talk about the various elements within this newly constructed cultural field. The term 'domain' was adopted to refer to the distinct communities – that is, museums, libraries and archives were referred to as separate 'domains' within one 'sector'.

9 Babbidge, 2000.

10 DCMS, 1998.

11 Selwood, 2001: 1–3.

12 DCMS, 1998.

13 DCMS and DfEE, 2000: 4.

14 David Blunkett, Secretary of State for Education and Employment, June 1999: quoted in Education and Libraries Task Group, 2000: 1.

15 DCMS, 2001: 6.

16 Ryan, 2001: 8.

17 Edgar and Sedgwick, 1999: 425.

18 McGuigan, 2004.

19 Selwood, 2006a.

20 Selwood, 2006b.

21 Ross, 1995.

22 Scott, 2006.

23 Frey and Meier, 2006.

24 Selwood, 2001; NMDC, 2004a; Travers and Glaister, 2004.

25 Price, 2002.

26 Usher et al., 1997: 65.

27 Atkinson, 2000.

28 Wilkinson, 2003a.

29 Wilkinson, 2003b.

30 Jowell, 2004.

31 That is, DCMS.

32 Jowell, 2004: 9.

33 Ibid.: 17.

34 Williams and Wavell, 2001; Proctor and Bartle, 2002.

35 Matarasso, 1998a, 1998b; Allison and Coalter, 2001; Coalter, 2001.

36 Muddiman et al., 2000: ii.

37 McNicol et al., 2002: 9.

38 Anderson, 1997: 1999.

39 DCMS and DfEE, 2000: 7.

40 Pick, 2001: not paged.

41 DCMS, 1998: not paged.

42 Resource, 2000.

43 DCMS, 1999, 2000, 2001.

44 The Inspiring Learning for All framework was developed by Gaby Porter, Anne Murch and Martin Bazley for Resource/MLA (www.inspiringlearningforall.gov.uk, accessed 22.01.07).

45 Members are listed at: www.inspiringlearningforall.gov.uk/introduction/how_have_we/how_have_we/_192/default.aspx (accessed 22.01.07).

46 Education and Libraries Task Group, 2000; Anderson, 1997, 1999; DCMS and DfEE, 2000; Muddiman et al. 2000; McNicol et al. 2002; Pick, 2001.

47 Selwood, 2002a, 2002b.

48 Hooper-Greenhill, 2006b.

49 Selwood, 2006b.

50 Ansbacher, 2002; Motylewski, 2001; Weil, not dated.

51 The cross-domain team that carried out the research included Eilean Hooper-Greenhill, Jocelyn Dodd, Theano Moussouri, Marlene Morrison, Chris Pickford, John Vincent, Catherine Herman, Richard Toon and Ceri Jones. Francois Matarasso was part of the team for the first phase of the research.

52 Brophy, 2002; Hannon et al., 2001; Bryson et al., 2002.
53 Robson, 2002.
54 The concepts and the approach taken to learning outcome measurement by LIRP were discussed at a seminar organised by Resource/MLA for academics and cultural researchers in London in July 2002. Early drafts were presented at the British Sociological Group meeting at Tate Liverpool in October 2002, and as part of the Perspectives lecture series in the Department of Museum Studies, University of Leicester in February 2003.
55 Much of what follows is based on the interim report to Resource/MLA. Hooper-Greenhill, 2002.
56 Robinson, 1996.
57 Moussouri, 2002.
58 Jarvis et al., 1998: 26.
59 www.aallnet.org/prodev/outcomes.asp (accessed 22.01.07) and see Moussouri, 2002: Appendix A.
60 Motylewski, 2001; IMLS, not dated.
61 Lord et al., not dated.
62 The Learning and Skills Council is responsible for the planning, funding, monitoring and quality improvement of all post-16 education and training excluding higher education (www.lsc.gov.uk/Regions/London/ accessed 22.01.06).
63 The term 'non-accredited learning' describes formal and non-formal provision which does not lead directly to any form of external accreditation, award or qualification.
64 LSC, 2003.
65 Miles and Tout, 1994a, 1994b.
66 Economic and Social Research Council, 2002: 1.
67 QCA and DfEE, 1998: 43. The QCA is responsible to government for the development of the curriculum in England (www.qca.org.uk/7907.html. accessed 22.01.07).
68 Quality Assurance Agency for Higher Education, 2000b: 3.
69 Learning and Teaching Scotland, 2002.

3 Conceptualising learning in cultural organisations

1 Jarvis et al., 1998: 1–2.
2 Claxton, 1999: 26.
3 The Campaign for Learning is a national charity: www.campaign-for-learning.org.uk/ (accessed 22.01.07).
4 Holmes, 2000a.
5 See Moussouri, 2002 for details.
6 See Hooper-Greenhill and Moussouri, 2002 for a review of research into learning in museums.
7 Hooper-Greenhill, 2000a. This conceptual framework has informed the work of RCMG since its inception.
8 Hein, 1998: 135.
9 The most useful current books on museums and education are not concerned with this concept. See Falk and Dierking, 2000; Hein, 1998; Leinhardt et al., 2002; Paris, 2002; Roberts, 1997.
10 Hooper-Greenhill, 2004c.
11 Gardner, 1985, 1991. Claxton has critiqued Gardner because of the ways in which he hierarchises learning modes with learning through experience at the bottom and scholastic learning at the top. Those who are non-intellectual learners are characterised by Gardner as 'dysfunctional'. See Claxton, 1999: 61–62.
12 Gunther, 1999.
13 Claxton, 1999: 7–8.
14 Sotto, 1994: 75.
15 Winitzky and Kauchak, 1997: 62.
16 Gallagher, 1992: 120.
17 Sotto, 1994: 75.
18 Jarvis et al., 1998: vii.
19 Claxton, 1999: 6.
20 Wenger, 1998.
21 Claxton, 1999: 11.
22 This is what Howard Gardner refers to as 'the unschooled mind'. See Gardner, 1991.
23 Polanyi quoted in Sotto, 1994: 55.
24 Sotto, 1994: 99–100.
25 Ibid.: 98.
26 Ibid.: 96.
27 Jarvis, et al., 1998: 46.
28 Ball, 2003.
29 Kershaw, 1994, cited in Abercrombie and Longhurst, 1998.
30 Hassan, 1986: 507.
31 Bagnall, 2003.
32 Abercrombie and Longhurst, 1998.
33 Claxton, 1999: 74–75.
34 National Advisory Committee on Creative and Cultural Education (NACCCE), 1999; Council for Science and Technology, 2001.
35 Falk and Dierking, 2000: 11.
36 Ibid.: 12.
37 Ibid.: 29–31.
38 Ibid.; see also Falk and Dierking, 1992.
39 Falk and Dierking, 2000: 164.
40 See for example, ibid.: 8.

41 Ibid.: 9.
42 Ibid.: 39.
43 Ibid.: 41.
44 Ogbu, 1995: 70.
45 Ibid.: 84.
46 Jarvis et al., 1998: 9.
47 Borger and Seaborne, 1966: 16, cited in Jarvis et al., 1998: 21.
48 Jarvis et al., 1998: 22.
49 Falk and Dierking, 2000: 41.
50 Edgar and Sedgwick, 1999: 155–157.
51 Ibid.: 157.
52 Ibid.: 157.
53 See for example, Falk and Dierking, 2000: 113.
54 Ibid.: 49.
55 Ibid.: 43.
56 Hardt, 1992.
57 During, 1993.
58 O'Sullivan et al., 1994: 68.
59 Hooper-Greenhill, 2000a: 10–14.
60 Sotto, 1994: 36.
61 Ibid.: 32.
62 Fish, 1980.
63 Wenger, 1998.
64 Edgar and Sedgwick, 1999: 102.
65 Fay, 1996.

4 The Generic Learning Outcomes: a conceptual and interpretive framework

1 Two papers that give the conceptual and academic framework for the GLO approach were posted on the Resource/MLA website during summer 2002. See Hooper-Greenhill, 2002 and Moussouri, 2002.
2 Moussouri, 2002.
3 Selwood, 2006b.
4 Claxton, 1999: 7–8.
5 Ibid.: 11.
6 This development was led by Gaby Porter and Anne Murch.
7 The ideas were presented to and fully discussed by the staff of the participating museums, libraries and archives at a workshop on 30 May 2002 in Evesham. A consultation workshop with key stakeholders was also held on 3 July 2002 in London. Regular progress meetings were held with staff of MLA (Sue Wilkinson, Gina Lane, Simon Matty and Sue Howley).
8 See Economic and Social Research Council, 2002: 1.
9 Quality Assurance Agency for Higher Education, 2000b.
10 Other examples are also included from earlier research projects, and when this is the case, specific references are given.
11 Desai and Thomas, 1998: 22.
12 Hooper-Greenhill et al., 2001b: 14.
13 Nicol, 2000.
14 The expression 'activity' is used in the GLO diagram on the MLA website (see Figure 4.1). However, the term 'Action' was used in the research and research tools. Both expressions refer to the actions people take and the activities they engage in, and from this point of view the terms are interchangeable.
15 The use of the expression behaviour to describe one dimension of learning and its outcomes does not imply any affiliation to behaviourism. Behaviourism is a philosophy in social science that suggests that behaviour can be interpreted as governed by conditioning rather than internal processes (thoughts, feelings, memories).
16 Kelly, 1999; Hooper-Greenhill, 2000a: 19–20.
17 Tom Mayberry and colleagues at Somerset Record Office. Report of LIRP pilot project.
18 Fiona Williams, Library Services Manager, Poole Libraries. Report of LIRP pilot project.
19 Wenger, 1998; Lave and Wenger, 1991; Sotto, 1994; Claxton, 1999.
20 Holmes, 2000b.
21 See for examples of this Ohta, 1998: 48–58; Hooper-Greenhill and Moussouri, 2001: 24.
22 Fay, 1996; Gallagher, 1992.
23 Usher et al., 1997: 57.
24 Ibid.: 86.
25 Jo Rice, (then) Head of Heritage Education, Warwickshire Museums and Archives. Report of LIRP pilot project.
26 Usher et al., 1997: 61.
27 Bourdieu, 1993: 260.
28 Usher et al., 1997: 66.
29 Giddens, 1991: 20.
30 The Department for Education and Skills is now the Department for Children, Skills and Families (DCSF).

5 The research programmes: background and method

1 Selwood, 2002a, 2002b.
2 Morris, 2005; Davies, 2005.
3 Denscombe, 2002: 118–139.
4 The research reports contain specific details for each of the research studies.
5 I am grateful to Resource/MLA for being

willing to allow the time and resources to do the job properly. This willingness was largely procured by Sue Wilkinson, who was in charge of the educational development work of MLA.

6 Lawley, 2003.

7 Resource, 2001.

8 The members of this task force were Matthew Evans (Chair), Stuart Davies, Deborah Boden, David Fleming, Jane Glaister, Karen Knight, Neil MacGregor, Nicholas Serota and Robert Sheldon.

9 Babbidge, 2005: 12.

10 The Registration Scheme was introduced in 1988 to acknowledge those museums that had achieved minimum standards, mainly focused on the care and management of collections. These museums became eligible for certain kinds of funding and guidance, and were accepted formally into the museum community. Much of the work of Resource/MLA has been based on the development from these rather basic requirements.

11 Resource, 2001: 24.

12 Ibid.: 29–33.

13 Selwood, 2001: 41.

14 Dunlop and Selwood, 2001: 45–53; Davies, 2001: 104–117.

15 Graubard, 1999: vi; Ross, 1996.

16 Resource, 2001: 33.

17 Ibid.: 58.

18 Ibid.: 44.

19 Ibid.: 43.

20 Ibid.: 44.

21 Ibid.: 7.

22 Ibid.: 40.

23 Ibid.: 36.

24 Ibid.: 106.

25 The term 'museum service' is used to refer to the group of museums which share a common local authority governing body. In most large English cities, a number of different museum sites make up the city 'museum service'. The regional hubs therefore consist of a number of city museum services that are located in the same English region.

26 Resource, 2001: 95.

27 Babbidge, 2005: 24.

28 Resource, 2001: 14.

29 Selwood, 2006a.

30 The three pathfinder hubs were in the West Midlands, the North East and the South West of England.

31 Morris, 2003; Lawley, 2003: 85; MLA, 2003a: 4.

32 Babbidge, 2005.

33 Morris, 2003; MLA, 2003a: 1.

34 MLA, 2003a: 4.

35 MLA, 2003b.

36 Babbidge, 2005.

37 MLA, 2006a.

38 Resource, 2001: 36.

39 All research reports are available on the RCMG website: www.le.ac.uk/museumstudies/research/rcmgpu blicationsandprojects.html.

40 Hooper-Greenhill et al., 2004a, 213 pages.

41 Hooper-Greenhill et al., 2004b, 24 pages.

42 Key Stage 2 encompasses children aged 7 to 11.

43 RCMG, 2004.

44 Hooper-Greenhill et al., 2006a, 314 pages.

45 Hooper-Greenhill et al., 2006b, 23 pages.

46 RCMG, 2006a.

47 RCMG, 2006b.

48 Hooper-Greenhill et al., 2004c, 491 pages.

49 Hooper-Greenhill et al., 2004d, 38 pages.

50 Hooper-Greenhill et al., 2004c: 1.

51 Watson, 2004.

52 Clarke et al., 2002: 4.

53 Hooper-Greenhill et al., 2001a, 84 pages.

54 Clarke et al., 2002, 56 pages.

55 Hooper-Greenhill, 2004b.

56 CEI, 2004a.

57 CEI 2004b.

58 Stanley et al., 2004.

59 Galloway and Stanley, 2004.

60 Stanley et al., 2004: 3.

61 Hooper-Greenhill, 2000a, 2006a.

62 Robson, 2002: 4.

63 Mason, 1996: 38.

64 Robson, 2002.

65 Denscombe, 2002: 24.

66 Harvey and MacDonald, 1993: 126.

67 Barnett, 1991: 68.

68 Hooper-Greenhill et al., 2004a, 2004b.

69 Hooper-Greenhill et al., 2006a, 2006b.

70 Hooper-Greenhill et al., 2004c, 2004d.

71 These questionnaires remained more or less the same across the studies. Copies will be found in the appendices of each of the full research reports.

72 Jo Graham, Museum Education Consultant, helped with design of Form B.

73 See following chapters.

74 Familiarisation and observational visits and focus groups were carried out for RR1: 2003 and DCMS/DfES1: 2004 by Eilean Hooper-Greenhill and Jocelyn Dodd, with help from Helen O'Riain; for RR2: 2005, these were

undertaken largely by Jocelyn Dodd and
Lisanne Gibson. Ceri Jones assisted in all
projects; Jenny Woodward assisted during
RR1: 2003 and Emma Sullivan during RR2:
2005, especially on statistical analysis. Dr
Martin Phillips advised on postcode analysis
and statistical analysis.
75 Hooper-Greenhill et al., 2006a: 40–45.
76 National Statistics, http://
neighbourhood.statistics.gov.uk/.
77 National Statistics, http://
neighbourhood.statistics.gov.uk/.
78 A number of the words and images have been
published in the three 'flipbooks'; see RCMG,
2004, 2006a, 2006b.
79 Original spelling!

6 The patterns of school use of museums

1 DCMS, 1999: 4–5.
2 DCMS, 2000: 7.
3 Ipsos MORI, 2006.
4 MLA, 2004: 2.
5 Hooper-Greenhill et al., 2004a: Section 4. The
numbers reported for Ironbridge Gorge
Museum were very large at 20,764 and
represented about one-third of the numbers of
pupil contacts in the three phase 1 hubs
altogether. If this figure is removed, the
increase across the other museums stands at
42.5 per cent.
6 The phase 2 museum services were free to
choose which museums within the service
would take part in this research in 2005; these
were selected because of high levels of
educational use. See Hooper-Greenhill et al.,
2006a: 16.
7 Hooper-Greenhill et al., 2006a: 50.
8 NMDC, no date: 1.
9 DfES, 2006.
10 NMDC, no date: 1–2.
11 Travers and Glaister, 2004: 5, 32; NMDC,
2004a: 4.
12 Travers and Glaister, 2004: 5.
13 Hooper-Greenhill et al., 2004a: 41.
14 Hooper-Greenhill et al., 2006a: 13.
15 Hooper-Greenhill et al., 2004c: 98.
16 Measures were taken to avoid double-counting
any school where more than one class might
have been visiting on any one day and more
than one teacher might have completed a
questionnaire.
17 These are schools where children have special
needs because of learning or other disabilities.
18 Hooper-Greenhill et al., 2001a: 25.

19 CEI, 2004b: 17.
20 DfES, 2005a.
21 For example, in the DfES study, middle
schools have not been included in a separate
category, as in RR2: 2005, but included where
appropriate with primary or secondary
schools.
22 Gardener Smith Associates, 1990a: 15.
23 CEI, 2004a: 34.
24 Robins and Woollard, 2003: 4.
25 Primary school focus group, RR2: 2005, held
at Birmingham Museum and Art Gallery,
12 October 2005.
26 Complete postcode details were not provided
by all schools and where these could not be
ascertained by other means, schools had to be
omitted from this analysis.
27 This was carried out for the second
Renaissance study (RR2: 2005) only.
28 The research team thanks Nicky Morgan and
MLA for negotiating the use of this database
for the research.
29 Hooper-Greenhill et al., 2004a: 44–49.
30 Hooper-Greenhill et al., 2004c: 106–109.
31 See ibid.: 106–109.
32 This is subject to considerable discussion at
present; see Newman et al., 2005; Belfiore,
2002; Sandell, 1998; Levitas, 2004.
33 Not all postcodes that could be ranked using
IMD 2000 could be ranked using IMD 2004.
See Hooper-Greenhill et al., 2006a: 72.
34 See Hooper-Greenhill et al., 2004c:
108–109.
35 In addition, a successful application was made
to ESRC for funding for a PhD studentship (a
CASE award) to study these issues further. The
partners in this project are the Departments of
Geography and Museum Studies, University of
Leicester, and DCMS. The PhD should be
completed by October 2008. The holder of the
award is Anna Woodham.
36 DfES, 2006.
37 The postcode and school meals analyses were
carried out for the research teams in each
study by Dr Martin Phillips, Department of
Geography, University of Leicester, assisted by
Ceri Jones.
38 Gardener Smith Associates, 1990a: 30.
39 Gardener Smith Associates, 1990b: 6.
40 Adams and Cole, 1990: 7.
41 These more detailed questions about use were
new in 2005 and so no comparisons are
possible with the earlier studies.
42 DfES, 2005b.
43 See www.schoolsliaison.org.uk/ (accessed
08.10.06).

44 Hooper-Greenhill et al., 2006a: 101.
45 Gardner Smith Associates, 1990a: 27.
46 Hooper-Greenhill et al., 2001a: 27.
47 This project continues, with a tremendous web-based resource – www.understandingslavery.com (accessed 23.01.07); see also *Museums Journal*, 2006.
48 Winterbotham (2005: 125) found that social and local history was the largest area of study in his doctoral research into museum education services in three English counties.
49 Hooper-Greenhill et al., 2001a: 28–29; Clarke et al., 2002: 12–15.
50 Stanley et al., 2004: 3.
51 DfES, 2003c.
52 Hooper-Greenhill et al., 2006a: 110.
53 Hooper-Greenhill et al., 2006a: 105–109.
54 DfES, 2003c.
55 Anderson et al., 2006: 370.
56 Griffiths, 2006.
57 Gardner Smith Associates, 1990a: 25.
58 Ibid.: 27.
59 Von Wistinghausen et al., 2004: 39.

7 The value of museums to teachers

1 Pupils' voices from the third case study, November, 2005. Researchers Jocelyn Dodd and Lisanne Gibson.
2 Primary school focus group, for RR2, held at Birmingham Museum and Art Gallery, 12 October 2005.
3 The Chi square analysis is presented where relevant in the research report.
4 See Hooper-Greenhill et al., 2006a: 139.
5 Hooper-Greenhill et al., 2004c: 124–132.

8 Pupils' learning outcomes: teachers' views

1 Teachers raised many issues concerning the difficulties in taking their pupils to museums. These are discussed in Hooper-Greenhill et al., 2006a: 156–158. See also Johnsson, 2003: 15; Robins and Woollard, 2003; and Winterbotham, 2005: 38ff.
2 Anderson et al., 2006: 367.
3 The full table is presented here to show how this data is presented in the research report, but the detailed tables for the other questions are represented for the sake of the clarity of the argument. They can be found in the research report. In the tables the results are mostly presented with the highest figures to the left of the table; this does not reflect the

order in which the sub-categories were presented in the teachers' questionnaire.
4 Stanley et al., 2004: 5.
5 Hooper-Greenhill et al., 2006a: 169.
6 Ibid.: 169.
7 These do of course vary a little in each of the GLO-based questions, but on the whole are negligible or very small. The actual percentages are given in the full research reports.
8 Hooper-Greenhill et al., 2004a: 112.
9 First case study, RR2: 2005. Transcript of interview with class teacher, 01.11.05: 3. Researchers Lisanne Gibson and Ceri Jones.
10 Hooper-Greenhill et al., 2006a: 189–192.
11 Hooper-Greenhill et al., 2004c: 342–351. See also the project website at www.anim8ed.org.uk/ (accessed 02.11.06).
12 Ibid.: 346.
13 Ibid.: 346.
14 Interview with museum education officer, 14.11.05. Researchers Jocelyn Dodd and Lisanne Gibson.
15 Transcript of teachers' focus group, 14.11.05. Researchers Jocelyn Dodd and Lisanne Gibson.
16 Transcript of teachers' focus group, 14.11.05. Researchers Jocelyn Dodd and Lisanne Gibson.
17 RCMG, 2006b.
18 Hooper-Greenhill et al., 2006a: 187.
19 Ibid.: 187.
20 Winterbotham (2005: 126) also notes this phenomenon.
21 Hooper-Greenhill et al., 2004a: 131.
22 Third case study, RR2: 2005. Transcript of interview with museum education officer, 14.11.05: 3. Researchers Jocelyn Dodd and Lisanne Gibson.
23 Third case study, RR2: 2005. Transcript of first interview with pupils, 21.11.05:6. Researchers Jocelyn Dodd and Lisanne Gibson.
24 Third case study, RR2: 2005. Transcript of first interview with pupils, 21.11.05: 18. Researchers Jocelyn Dodd and Lisanne Gibson.
25 Hooper-Greenhill et al., 2006b: 17–20.
26 Third case study, RR2: 2005. Transcript of teachers' focus group, 21.11.05: 21. Researchers Jocelyn Dodd and Lisanne Gibson.
27 This was not assessed in the other two RCMG studies.
28 I am very grateful to Jenny Woodward, who

carried out some further statistical analysis for this book after the conclusion of the DCMS/DfES1: 2004 research.

29 See Hooper-Greenhill et al., 2006a: 251–265.

30 Hooper-Greenhill et al., 2004c: 51–52. www.anim8ed.org.uk/.

9 Pupils' learning outcomes: pupils' voices

1 RCMG, 2004; RCMG, 2006a, 2006b.

2 Hooper-Greenhill et al., 2006a: 203, Fig. 7.2e.

3 First case study, RR2: 2005, transcript of pupils' interview on 01.11.05: 4. Researchers Lisanne Gibson and Ceri Jones.

4 First case study, RR2: 2005, transcript of pupils' interview on 01.11.05: 3. Researchers Lisanne Gibson and Ceri Jones.

5 Third case study RR2: 2005. Transcript of interview with second class of pupils on 21.10.05: 18. Researchers Jocelyn Dodd and Lisanne Gibson.

6 www.bmag.org.uk/ (accessed 03.12.06).

7 RCMG, 2006a.

8 Hooper-Greenhill et al., 2004a: 108; original spelling in all cases.

9 RCMG, 2006a.

10 Hooper-Greenhill et al., 2004a: 213.

11 RCMG, 2004.

12 RCMG, 2006a.

13 Ibid.

14 RCMG, 2006b.

15 www.manchestergalleries.org/education/ (accessed 05.12.06).

16 Second case study RR2: 2005. Transcript of interview with pupils 18.10.05: 7. Researchers Jocelyn Dodd and Lisanne Gibson.

17 Third case study RR2: 2005. Transcript of interview with first class of pupils on 21.11.05: 2. Researchers Jocelyn Dodd and Lisanne Gibson.

18 Third case study RR2: 2005. Transcript of interview with third class of pupils on 21.11.05: 9. Researchers Jocelyn Dodd and Lisanne Gibson.

19 Hooper-Greenhill et al., 2006a: 231, Fig. 7.5.1e. Spelling as in original.

20 Third case study RR2: 2005. Transcript of interview with museum education staff, 14.11.05: 4–5. Researchers Jocelyn Dodd and Lisanne Gibson.

21 Hooper-Greenhill et al., 2004b: 17.

22 Stanley et al., 2004: 6.

23 Clarke et al., 2002: 6.

24 RCMG, 2006a.

25 RCMG, 2004.

26 Ibid.

27 First case study, RR2: 2005. Transcript of pupils' interview, 01.11.05: 16. Researchers Lisanne Gibson and Ceri Jones.

28 First case study, RR2: 2005. Transcript of interview with deputy headteacher, 01.11.05: 2. Researchers Lisanne Gibson and Ceri Jones.

29 First case study, RR2: 2005. Transcript of interview with 9-year-olds, 01.11.05: 14. Researchers Lisanne Gibson and Ceri Jones.

30 Hooper-Greenhill et al., 2006a: 217, Fig. 7.4.2g.

31 RCMG, 2006a.

32 Ibid.

33 Hooper-Greenhill et al., 2004d: 17.

34 RCMG, 2006b.

35 Hooper-Greenhill et al., 2006a: 239, Fig. 7.5.2k; RCMG, 2006b.

36 RCMG, 2006b.

37 First case study, RR2: 2005. Transcript of interview with pupils, 01.11.05: 15. Researchers Lisanne Gibson and Ceri Jones.

38 First case study, RR2: 2005. Transcript of interview with pupils, 01.11.05: 15. Researchers Lisanne Gibson and Ceri Jones.

39 RCMG, 2006a.

40 RCMG, 2006b.

41 Hooper-Greenhill et al., 2006a: 247, Fig. 7.5.5c.

42 Ibid.: 247, Fig. 7.5.5d.

43 RCMG, 2006b.

44 Ibid.

45 RCMG, 2006a.

46 RCMG, 2004.

47 Hooper-Greenhill et al., 2004c: 376–384.

48 RCMG, 2004.

49 RCMG, 2006a.

50 Hooper-Greenhill et al., 2006a: 248, Fig. 7.5.6a.

51 RCMG, 2006a.

52 Ibid.

53 RCMG, 2006b.

54 Ibid.

55 Third case study, RR2: 2005. Transcript of interview with second group of pupils, 21.11.05: 19. Researchers Jocelyn Dodd and Lisanne Gibson.

56 Third case study, RR2: 2005. Transcript of interview with fourth group of pupils, 21.11.05: 3. Researcher Jocelyn Dodd.

57 Third case study, RR2: 2005. Transcript of interview with fourth group of pupils, 21.11.05: 2. Researcher Jocelyn Dodd.

58 Third case study, RR2: 2005. Transcript of

interview with fourth group of pupils, 21.11.05: 2. Researcher Jocelyn Dodd.
59 RCMG, 2006b.
60 Hooper-Greenhill et al., 2004c: 47–50.
61 Hooper-Greenhill et al., 2004c: 385–395.
62 RCMG, 2004.
63 Ibid.
64 Third case study, RR2: 2005. Transcript of interview with third group of pupils, 21.11.05: 14. Researchers Jocelyn Dodd and Lisanne Gibson.
65 RCMG, 2004.
66 Hooper-Greenhill et al., 2006a: 245, Fig. 7.5.4c.
67 RCMG, 2006b.
68 Ibid.
69 Hooper-Greenhill et al., 2006a: 265–266.
70 Clarke et al., 2002: 11.
71 Carried out for the research team by Jocelyn Dodd.
72 RCMG, 2004.
73 Hooper-Greenhill, 2004a: 112–115.

10 The characteristics and significance of learning in museums

1 Hooper-Greenhill et al., 2006a: 170.
2 RR2: 2005. Birmingham case study, transcript of interview with deputy head, 1.11.05. Interviewers Lisanne Gibson and Ceri Jones.
3 Edwards and Knight, 1994.
4 Claxton, 1999: 67; Sotto, 1994: 96.
5 Claxton, 1999: 58.
6 Ibid.: 60.
7 RCMG, 2006a.
8 Sotto, 1994, 99–100.
9 RR2: 2005. Birmingham primary teachers focus group, 12.10.05. Researchers Jocelyn Dodd, Lisanne Gibson and Ceri Jones. In this case, the school group had learnt how Egyptian mummies were wrapped up and had drawn upon this experience to form the basis of their questions.
10 Claxton, 1999: 63–66.
11 Ibid.: 61; Edwards and Knight, 1994: 35. Howard Gardner, whose ideas about multiple intelligences have been influential in museums which have tried to broaden their display and pedagogic styles, also appears to place intellectual learning at the top of a hierarchy of value where intuitive learning remains at the bottom (Claxton, 1999: 62).
12 Claxton, 1999: 74–75.
13 Csikszentmihalyi and Hermanson, 1999.
14 Claxton, 1999: 4.
15 Csikszentmihalyi, 1975; Csikszentmihalyi and Robinson, 1990; Csikszentmihalyi and Hermanson, 1999.
16 Csikszentmihalyi and Hermanson, 1999: 147–148.
17 Edwards and Knight, 1994: 3.
18 Cited in Hooper-Greenhill, 2004b.
19 Hooper-Greenhill et al., 2006b: 20.
20 Hooper-Greenhill et al., 2006a: 251–265.
21 Drummond, 1993: 82, citing Egan, 1988.
22 Clarke et al., 2002: 5.
23 Hooper-Greenhill, 2004b.
24 See for example, Edwards and Knight, 1994: 12.
25 Hooper-Greenhill, 2004b.
26 Ibid.
27 Csikszentmihalyi and Hermanson, 1999.
28 Claxton, 1999: 15–16.
29 Sotto, 1994: 98.
30 Drummond, 1993: 42.
31 Hooper-Greenhill et al., 2006a: 170.
32 Ibid.: 170.
33 Third case study, RR2: 2005. Transcript of interview with museum education officer, 14.11.05: 9. Researchers Jocelyn Dodd and Lisanne Gibson.
34 Sotto, 1994: 50; Drummond, 1993: 85.
35 Claxton, 1999: 12.
36 Drummond, 1993.
37 Csikszentmihalyi and Hermanson, 1999: 155.
38 Edwards and Knight, 1994: 33–35.
39 Fay, 1996: 27.
40 Clarke et al., 2002: 9.
41 Giddens, 1991: 9.
42 Edwards and Knight, 1994: 11.
43 Jarvis et al., 1998, 46.
44 Du Gay et al., 2000; Weedon, 2004; Woodward, 2002, 1997.
45 Usher et al., 1997: 16.
46 Hooper-Greenhill et al., 2006a: 148–150 (spelling as in the original).
47 Hall, 1997: 3.
48 Weedon, 2004: 21.
49 Fay, 1996: 19.
50 Claxton, 1999.
51 Hooper-Greenhill, 2004b.
52 Downing et al., 2004: 44.
53 Usher et al., 1997: 74.
54 www.inspiringlearningforall.gov.uk.
55 See for example, Johnsson, 2004a.
56 DfES, 2003a.
57 Office for Standards in Education, 2003: 17–19.
58 Ibid.: 5, 16.
59 Ibid.: 13.
60 Ibid.: 18.

61 Johnsson, 2003.
62 DCMS and DfEE, 2000: 3.
63 DfES 2003a.
64 DfES, 2004.
65 DfES, 2003a.
66 DfES, 2003b: 23.
67 Johnsson (2003, 2004a, 2004b), who has carried out research structured through the use of the GLOs, provides evidence of pupils' and teachers' attitudes that supports much of the RCMG research.
68 Edwards and Knight, 1994: 36.
69 Usher et al., 1997: 22.
70 Morgan and McWilliam, 1995.
71 Edwards and Knight, 1994: 12.

11 Learning in the post-museum: issues and challenges

 1 Marstine, 2006: 30.
 2 Hooper-Greenhill et al., 2004d: 38.
 3 Ipsos MORI, 2006.
 4 McClellan, 1994: 80.
 5 Ibid.: 80.
 6 Forbes, 1853: 14–15.
 7 Hein, 1998: 19–20.
 8 Godwin quoted in 'The Art-Union of London', *Art-Union*, 2 (May 1840): 67, cited in Minihan, 1977: 78–79.
 9 Prior, 2002: 91.
10 Edgar and Sedgwick, 1999: 44.
11 Bennet et al., 2005: 16.
12 Edgar and Sedgwick, 1999: 46.
13 Bennett, 2004: 97.
14 Foucault, 1978: 103–104; Turner, 1984: 98–103.
15 Trodd, 1994.
16 W. Hazlitt, 'The Angerstein Gallery', *The London Magazine*, XXXVI, December 1822: 489–90, quoted in Trodd, 1994: 42.
17 Macdonald and Basu, 2007; Pollock and Zemans, 2007.
18 See for example, Dodd et al., 2002; see also Hooper-Greenhill, 2006a.
19 Pontin, 2001.
20 Hooper-Greenhill and Dodd, 2002: 20.
21 Worts, 1995.
22 Weedon, 2004: 7.
23 Sandell, 2007b.
24 Bennett, 2004.
25 Ibid.: 56.
26 Ibid.: 39.
27 Ibid.: 40.
28 Cited in Carbonell, 2004: 131.
29 Leone and Little, 2004.
30 Strahan, 1979.
31 Bennett, 2004: 63.
32 Ibid.: 63.
33 O'Neill, 2004.
34 Marstine, 2006.
35 Anderson, 1997: iv.
36 Hein, 1998: 3.
37 Bauman, 2000.
38 Minihan, 1977: 43.
39 Ibid.: 112.
40 Ibid.; Hill, 2005.
41 Parliamentary Debates (Commons) July 23 1832, cited in Minihan, 1977: 57.
42 Forbes, 1853. I am grateful to Professor Simon Knell for sharing this paper with me.
43 Selleck, 1968.
44 Knell, 2000.
45 Ruskin, cited in Taylor, 1999: 78.
46 Trodd, 1994: 40.
47 Taylor, 1999: 100.
48 Hill, 2005: 59, 105.
49 Ibid.: 46.
50 Waterfield, 1991: 23.
51 Bauman, 2000: 29.
52 Ibid.: 24.
53 Ibid.: 77; Bennett, 1995.
54 Bauman, 2000: 29.
55 Ibid.: 76.
56 Ibid.: 32.
57 Usher et al., 1997: 23.
58 Chakrabarty, 2002.
59 Ibid.
60 Usher et al., 1997: 17.

Bibliography

Abercrombie, N. and Longhurst, B. (1998) *Audiences: A Sociological Theory of Performance and Imagination*, Sage Publications, London, Thousand Oaks and New Delhi.

Accenture and the National Trust (2006) *Demonstrating the Public Value of Heritage*, Accenture and the National Trust.

Adams, G. and Cole, H. (1990) *Survey of Museum and Gallery Usage by ILEA Schools, 1988–1989*, Inner London Education Authority, London.

Addison, N. and Burgess, L. (2005) The friendly interventionist: reflections on the relationship between critical practice and artist/teachers in secondary schools, in Atkinson, D. and Dash, P. (eds) *Social and Critical Practices in Art Education*, Trentham Books, Stoke on Trent, UK and Sterling, USA, 127–137.

Agassiz, L. (2004) Letter of 1863 to Mr Thomas G. Cary, in Carbonell, B. M. (ed.) *Museum Studies: An Anthology of Contexts*, Blackwell, Oxford, 131–132.

Allison, M. and Coalter, F. (2001) *Realising the Potential of Cultural Services: The Case for Museums*, Research briefing twelve point two, Local Government Association, London.

American Association of Law Libraries (2003) *Writing Learning Outcomes*, Professional Development Committee American Association of Law Libraries, www.aallnet.org/prodev/outcomes.asp (accessed 22.01.07).

American Association of Museums (1992) *Excellence and Equity: Education and the Public Dimension of Museums*, American Association of Museums, Washington, DC.

American Association of Museums (1984) *A Report of the Commission of Museums for a New Century*, American Association of Museums, Washington, DC.

Anderson, D. (1999) *A Common Wealth: Museums in the Learning Age*, Department for Culture, Media and Sport, London.

Anderson, D. (1997) *A Common Wealth: Museums and Learning in the United Kingdom*. A report to the Department of National Heritage, London.

Anderson, D., Kisiel, J. and Storksdieck, M. (2006) Understanding teachers' perspectives on field trips: discovering common ground in three countries, *Curator*, 49 (3), 365–385.

Ansbacher. T. (2002) What are we learning? Outcomes of the museum experience, *Informal Learning: The Informal Learning Review*, 53, March–April, 3–7.

Appleton, J. (2001) Museums for 'The People', in *Museums for 'The People'?: Conversations in Print*, Academy of Ideas, London, 14–26.

Aronowitz, S. and Giroux, H. (1991) *Postmodern Education*, University of Minnesota Press, Minneapolis.

Atkinson, D. (2005) Approaching the future in school art education: learning how to swim, in Atkinson, D. and Dash, P. (eds) *Social and Critical Practices in Art Education*, Trentham Books, Stoke on Trent, UK and Sterling, USA, 21–30.

Atkinson, D. and Dash, P. (eds) (2005) *Social and Critical Practices in Art Education*, Trentham Books, Stoke on Trent, UK and Sterling, USA.

Atkinson, E. (2000) The promise of uncertainty:

education, postmodernism and the politics of possibility, *International Studies in Sociology of Education*, 10 (1), 81–99.

Babbidge, A. (2005) Forty years on, *Cultural Trends*, 14 (1), no. 53, 3–66.

Babbidge, A. (2000) UK museums: safe and sound? *Cultural Trends*, 37, 3–35.

Bagnall, G. (2003) Performance and performativity at heritage sites, *Museum and Society*, 1 (2), 87–103.

Ball, S. J. (2003) The teacher's soul and the terrors of performativity, *Journal of Education Policy*, 18, 215–228.

Barnes, C., Mercer, G. and Shakespeare, T. (1999) *Exploring Disability: A Sociological Introduction*, Polity Press, Cambridge.

Barnett, V. (1991) *Sample Survey: Principles and Methods*, Edward Arnold, London.

Bauman, Z. (2000) *LIQUID modernity*, Polity Press, Cambridge.

Bauman, Z. (1992) *Intimations of Postmodernity*, Routledge, London.

Bazin, G. (1967) *The Museum Age*, Desoer, S.A. Publishers, Brussels.

Belfiore, E. (2002) Art as a means of alleviating social inclusion: does it really work? A critique of instrumental cultural policies and social impact studies in the UK, *International Journal of Cultural Policy*, 8 (1), 91–106.

Belsey, C. (1980) *Critical Practice*, Methuen, London and New York.

Bennett, T. (2004) *Pasts Beyond Memory: Evolution, Museums, Colonialism*, Routledge, London and New York.

Bennett, T. (1998a) *Culture: A Reformer's Science*, Sage, London.

Bennett, T. (1998b) Pedagogic objects, clean eyes, and popular instruction: on sensory regimes and museum didactics, *Configurations*, Johns Hopkins University Press and the Society for Literature and Science, 345–371.

Bennett, T. (1995) *The Birth of the Museum: History, Theory, Politics*, Routledge, London and New York.

Bennett, T., Grossberg, L. and Morris, M. (2005) *New Keywords: A Revised Vocabulary of Culture and Society*, Blackwell Publishing, Oxford.

Best, S. and Kellner, D. (1997) *The Postmodern Turn*, The Guilford Press, New York and London.

Best, S. and Kellner, D. (1991) *Postmodern Theory: Critical Interrogations*, Macmillan, Basingstoke and London.

Bhabha, H. K. (1994) *The Location of Culture*, Routledge, London and New York.

Bicknell, S. and Farmelo, G. (1993) *Museum Visitor Studies in the 90s*, Science Museum, London.

Boodle, C. (1992) *A New Decade: Museums and Education in the 1990s*, National Heritage, London.

Bourdieu, P. (1993) The historical genesis of a pure aesthetic, in Bourdieu, P. *The Field of Cultural Production: Essays on Art and Literature*, edited by Johnson, R., Polity Press, Cambridge, 254–266.

Bourdieu, P. (1984) *Distinction: A Social Critique of the Judgement of Taste*, Routledge, New York and London.

Bourdieu, P. (1971a) Intellectual field and creative project, in Young, M.F.D. (ed.) *Knowledge and Control: New Directions for the Sociology of Education*, Collier-Macmillan Publishers, London, 161–188.

Bourdieu, P. (1971b) Systems of education and systems of thought, in Young, M.F.D. (ed.) *Knowledge and Control: New Directions for the Sociology of Education*, Collier-Macmillan Publishers, London, 189–207.

Bourdieu, P. and Darbel, A. (1991) *The Love of Art: European Art Museums and their Public*, Polity Press, Cambridge. Translation Caroline Beatty and Nick Merriman.

Brophy, P. (2002) *The Evaluation of Public Library Services: Measuring Impact*, www.peoplesnetwork.gov.uk/impact/index.asp (accessed 13.12.03).

Bryant, J. (2003) Talkback: Should museum directors employ fewer staff and pay them more instead of continuing to pay at a lower level – yes, *Museums Journal*, 103 (4), 47.

Bryson, J., Usherwood, B. and Streatfield, D. (2002) *Social Impact Audit*, South West Museums, Libraries and Archive Council, Taunton.

Burgess, R. (1984) *In the Field*, George Allen and Unwin, London.

Carbonell, B. M. (ed.) (2004) *Museum Studies: An Anthology of Contexts*, Blackwell Publishing, Malden, MA, Oxford and Victoria, Australia.

Carter, P. G. (1984) Educational services, in Thomson, J.M.A. (ed.) *Manual of Curatorship*, Butterworths, London, 435–447.

Centre for Education and Industry (2004a) *Learning through Culture is Working! Interim Findings from Evaluation of Museums and Galleries Education Programme Phase 2 (2002–4)*, Department for Education and Skills, ENGAGE (the National Association for Gallery Education), the Group for Education in Museums (GEM), the Museums, Libraries and Archives Council (MLA) and the Centre for Education and Industry, University of Warwick.

Centre for Education and Industry (2004b) *The Impact of Phase 2 of the Museums and Galleries Education Programme*, Volumes 1 and 2, CEI, University of Warwick, www.teachernet.gov.uk/ mgep2 (accessed 22.01.07).

Chakrabarty, D. (2002) Museums in late democracies, *Humanities Research*, IX (1), 5–12.

Chaney, D. (1994) *The Cultural Turn: Scene-setting Essays on Contemporary Cultural History*, Routledge, London and New York.

Chaney, D. (1993) *Fictions of Collective Life: Public Drama in Late Modern Culture*, Routledge, London and New York.

Clarke, A., Dodd, J., Hooper-Greenhill, E., O'Riain, H., Selfridge, L. and Swift, F. (2002) *Learning Through Culture: The DfES Museums and Galleries Education Programme: A Guide to Good Practice*, DfES, London and RCMG, Leicester. Downloadable from www.le.ac.uk/ museumstudies/research/rcmg publicationsandprojects.html www.teachernet.gov.uk/docbank/index.cfm?id=1379 (accessed 01.10.06).

Clarke, K. (2006) *Capturing the Public Value of Heritage*. The proceedings of the London conference 25–26 January. English Heritage on behalf of Heritage Lottery Fund, English Heritage and the National Trust.

Claxton, G. (1999) *Wise Up: The Challenge of Lifelong Learning*, Bloomsbury, London.

Coalter, F. (2001) *Realising the Potential of Cultural Services: The Case for Libraries*. Research briefing twelve point one, Local Government Association, London.

Coombes, A. (2003) *History after Apartheid: Visual Culture and Public Memory in a Democratic South Africa*, Duke University Press, Durham, NC, and London.

Coombes, A. (1991) Ethnography and the formation of national and cultural identities, in Hiller, S. (ed.) *The Myth of Primitivism: Perspectives on Art*, Routledge, London and New York, 189–214.

Corker, M. and Shakespeare, T. (eds) (2002) *Disability/Postmodernity: Embodying Disability Theory*, Continuum, London and New York.

Council for Science and Technology (2001) *Imagination and Understanding: A Report on the Arts and Humanities in Relation to Science and Technology*, Council for Science and Technology, London. Online at www.cst.gov.uk/cst/imagination.htm (accessed 12.02.02).

Csikszentmihalyi, M. (1975) *Beyond Boredom and Anxiety*, Jossey-Bass, San Francisco.

Csikszentmihalyi, M. and Hermanson, K. (1999) Intrinsic motivation in museums: why does one want to learn? in Hooper-Greenhill, E. (ed.) *The Educational Role of the Museum*, second edition, Routledge, London, 146–160.

Csikszentmihalyi, M. and Robinson, R. (1990) *The Art of Seeing*, J.P. Getty Press, Malibu, M.A.

Csikszentmihalyi, M. and Rocheberg-Halton, E. (1981) *The Meaning of Things*, Cambridge University Press, Cambridge.

Dash, P. (2005) Cultural demarcation, the African diaspora and art education, in Atkinson, D. and Dash, P. (eds) *Social and Critical Practices in Art Education*, Trentham Books, Stoke on Trent, UK and Sterling, USA, 117–125.

Davies, S. (2005) Still popular: museums and their visitors 1994–2004, *Cultural Trends*, 14 (1), no. 53, 67–105.

Davies, S. (2001) Local authorities: new opportunities and reduced capacity, in Selwood, S. (ed.) *The UK Cultural Sector: Profile and Policy Issues*, Cultural Trends and Policy Studies Institute, 104–117.

Delanty, G. (1997) *Social Science: Beyond Constructivism and Realism*, Open University Press, Buckingham.

Denscombe, M. (2002) *Ground Rules for Good Research: A 10 Point Guide for Social Researchers*, Open University Press, Buckingham, Philadelphia.

Department for Culture, Media and Sport (2005) *Living Life to the Full*, DCMS, London.

Department for Culture, Media and Sport (2001) *Libraries, Museums, Galleries and Archives for All: Co-operating across the Sectors to Tackle Social Exclusion*, DCMS, London.

Department for Culture, Media and Sport (2000) *Centres for Social Change: Museums, Galleries and Archives for All: Policy Guidance on Social Inclusion for DCMS Funded and Local Authority Museums, Galleries and Archives in England*, DCMS, London.

Department for Culture, Media and Sport (1999) *Libraries for All: Social Inclusion in Public Libraries – Policy Guidance for Local Authorities in England*, DCMS, London.

Department for Culture, Media and Sport (1998) *A New Cultural Framework*, DCMS, London.

Department for Culture, Media and Sport and Department for Education and Employment (2000) *The Learning Power of Museums: A Vision for Museum Education*. DCMS, London.

Department for Education and Science (1973) *Provincial Museums and Galleries* (The Wright Report), HMSO, London.

Department for Education and Science (1971) *Museums in Education: Education Survey*, 12, HMSO, London.

Department for Education and Skills (2006) *Schools and Pupils in England: January 2006 (Final)*, www.dfes.gov.uk/ (accessed 22.01.07).

Department for Education and Skills (2005a) *Schools and Pupils in England: January 2005 (Final)*, www.dfes.gov.uk/ (accessed 22.01.07).

Department for Education and Skills (2005b) *Youth Green Paper, Youth Matters*, DfES, London, www.dfes.gov.uk/publications/youth/ (accessed 22.01.07).

Department for Education and Skills (2005c) *Education Outside the Classroom Manifesto*, www.dfes.gov.uk/consultations/con Details.cfm?consultationId=1370 (accessed 10.11.06).

Department for Education and Skills (2005d) *Harnessing Technology: Transforming Learning and Children's Services*, DfES, London, www.dfes. gov.uk/publications/e-strategy/ (accessed 22.01.07).

Department for Education and Skills (2004) *A National Conversation about Personalised Learning*, DfES, London, DfES/0919/2004.

Department for Education and Skills (2003a) *Every Child Matters: Summary*, DfES, London and the Stationary Office, Norwich. See also www.dfes.gov.uk/ ISA/everychild/greenPaper.cfm accessed 11.08.06).

Department for Education and Skills (2003b) *Key Stage 3 National Strategy: Introducing the Third Year*, DfES, London, 23.

Department for Education and Skills (2003c) *Excellence and Enjoyment: A Strategy for Primary Schools*, DfES, London.

Desai, P. and Thomas, A. (1998) *Cultural Diversity: Attitudes of Ethnic Minority Populations Towards Museums and Galleries*, BMRB International Limited for the Museums and Galleries Commission, London.

Dicks, B. (2003) *Culture on Display: The Production of Contemporary Visitability*, Open University Press, Berkshire.

Dierking, L. (1996) Contemporary theories of learning, in Durbin, G. (ed.) *Developing Museum Exhibitions for Life-long Learning*, The Stationary Office, London, 25–29.

Dodd, J. and Sandell, S. (eds) (2001) *Including Museums: Perspectives on Museums, Galleries and Social Inclusion*, Research Centre for Museums and Galleries, University of Leicester, Leicester.

Dodd, J., O'Riain, H., Hooper-Greenhill, E. and Sandell, R. (2002) *A Catalyst for Change: The Social Impact of the Museum*, Research Centre for Museums and Galleries, University of Leicester, Leicester, www.le.ac.uk/museum studies/research/rcmgpublications andprojects.html (accessed 22.01.07).

Downing, D., Jones, M. and Kinder, K. (2004) 'A Good Image of Myself'. An Evaluation of the Image and Identity Scheme, NFER, Berkshire.

Drummond, M. J. (1993) *Assessing Children's Learning*, David Fulton Publishers, London.

Du Gay, P., Evans, J. and Redman, P. (2000) *Identity: A Reader*, OUP, Oxford.

Dunlop, R. and Selwood, S. (2001) Funding from central government, in Selwood, S. (ed.) *The UK Cultural Sector: Profile and Policy Issues*, Cultural Trends and Policy Studies Institute, 45–53.

During, S. (1993) Introduction, in During, S. (ed.) *The Cultural Studies Reader*, Routledge, London and New York, 1–25.

Easthope, A. and McGowan K. (eds) (2004) *A Critical and Cultural Theory Reader*, second edition, OUP, Maidenhead, Berkshire.

Economic and Social Research Council (2002) *The Teaching and Learning Research Programme – Specification for Phase III*, on-line www.ex.ac.uk/ESRC-TLRP/phase3spec.htm (accessed 17.08.06), www.tlrp.org/manage/pdf/PhaseIIISpecification.pdf.

Edgar, A. and Sedgwick, P (eds) (1999) *Key Concepts in Cultural Theory*, Routledge, London and New York.

Education and Libraries Task Group (2000) *Empowering the Learning Community*. Report of the Education and Libraries Task Group to the Secretaries of State for Culture, Media and Sport and for Education and Employment, Library and Information Commission, London.

Edwards, A. and Knight, P. (1994) *Effective Early Years Education: Teaching Young Children*, Open University Press, Buckingham, Philadelphia.

Falk, J. and Dierking, L. (2000) *Learning from Museums: Visitor Experiences and the Making of Meaning*, Altamira Press, Walnut Creek, California.

Falk, J. and Dierking, L. (1992) *The Museum Experience*, Whalesback Books, Washington, DC.

Fay, B. (1996) *Contemporary Philosophy of Social Science: A Multicultural Approach*, Blackwell, Oxford.

Findlen, P. (1994) *Possessing Nature: Museums, Collecting and Scientific Culture in Early Modern Italy*, University of California Press, Berkeley, Los Angeles, London.

Fish, S. (1980) *Is there a Text in this Class? The Authority of Interpretive Communities*, Harvard University Press, Cambridge, MA, and London.

Flower, W.H. (2004) Local museums, in Carbonell, B. M. (ed.) *Museum Studies: An Anthology of Contexts*, Blackwell Publishing, Oxford, 315–317 (originally written in 1898).

Fontana, A. and Frey, J. (2000) The interview: from structured questions to negotiated text, in Denzin, N. K. and Lincoln, Y. S. (eds) *Handbook of Qualitative Research*, Sage, London.

Forbes, E. (1853) *On the Educational Uses of Museums*, Metropolitan School of Science applied to Mining and the Arts, Museum of Practical Geology, Longman, Brown, Green and Longmans, London.

Foster, H. (ed.) (1983) *Postmodern Culture*, Pluto Press, London and Concord, MA.

Foucault, M. (1978) *The History of Sexuality: An Introduction*, Penguin Books, Middlesex.

Fraser, N. (1999) Social justice in the age of identity politics: redistribution, recognition, and participation, in Ray, L. and Sayer, A. (eds) *Culture and Economy after the Cultural Turn*, Sage, London, Thousand Oaks, New Delhi, 25–52.

Frey, B. S. and Meier, S. (2006) The economics of museums, in. Ginsburgh, V. A. and Throsby, D. (eds) *Handbook of the Economics of Art and Culture*, Vol. 1, North-Holland, Amsterdam.

Friere, P. (1972) *Pedagogy of the Oppressed*, Penguin Books, Middlesex.

Frostick, L. (1985) Museums in education, a neglected role? *Museums Journal*, 85 (20), 67–74.

Fyfe, G. (2006) Sociology and the social aspects of museums, in Macdonald, S. (ed.) *A Companion to Museum Studies*, Blackwell, Oxford, 33–49.

Fyfe, G. (1996) A trojan horse at the Tate: theorising the museum as agency and structure, in Macdonald, S. and Fyfe, G. (eds)

Theorising Museums, Blackwell, Oxford and The Sociological Review, 203–228.

Fyfe, G. (1995) The Chantrey episode: art classification, museums and the state, in Pearce, S. (ed.) *Art in Museums*, Athlone, London, 5–41.

Gadamer, H. G. (1976) The historicity of understanding, in Connerton, P. (ed.) *Critical Sociology*, Penguin Books, Harmondsworth, 117–133.

Gallagher, S. (1992) *Hermeneutics and Education*, State University of New York Press, New York.

Galloway, S. and Stanley, J. (2004) Thinking outside the box: galleries, museums and evaluation, *Museum and Society*, 2 (2), 125–146.

Gardner, H. (1991) *The Unschooled Mind: How Children Think and How Schools should Teach*, Fontana Press, London.

Gardner, H. (1985) *Frames of Mind: The Theory of Multiple Intelligences*, Paladin, London.

Gardner Smith Associates (1990a) *School Visits to the Tower of London and the Royal Armouries and to Other Heritage Sites and Museums. Part 1: Survey among Past and Potential Teacher Visitors to HM Tower of London*, Royal Armouries at the Tower of London.

Gardner Smith Associates (1990b) *School Visits to the Tower of London and the Royal Armouries and to Other Heritage Sites and Museums. Part 2: Survey among Mothers of School Age Children*, Royal Armouries at the Tower of London.

Giddens, A. (1991) *Modernity and Self-identity: Self and Society in the Late Modern Age*, Polity Press, Cambridge.

Giddens, A. (1990) *The Consequences of Modernity*, Polity Press, Cambridge.

Giroux, H. (1992) *Border Crossings: Cultural Workers and the Politics of Education*, Routledge, New York and London.

Giroux, H. (1991) *Postmodernism, Feminism and Cultural Politics: Redrawing Educational Boundaries*, State University of New York Press, Albany.

Graubard, S. R. (1999) America's museums, *Daedalus* (Journal of the American Academy of Arts and Sciences), 128 (3).

Griffiths, G. (2006) Should museums target their schools education programmes solely at the national curriculum? No, *Museums Journal*, 106 (12), 17.

Gunther, C. (1999) Museum-goers: life-styles and learning characteristics, in Hooper-Greenhill, E. (ed.) *The Educational Role of the Museum*, second edition, Routledge, London.

Hall, S. (2005) Whose heritage? Un-settling 'the heritage': re-imagining the post-nation, in Littler, J. and Naidoo, R. (eds) *The Politics of Heritage: The Legacies of Race*, Routledge, London and New York, 23–35.

Hall, S. (ed.) (1997) *Representation: Cultural Representations and Signifying Practices*, Sage, London, Thousand Oaks, New Delhi, in association with The Open University, Milton Keynes.

Hall, S. (1990) Cultural identity and diaspora, in Rutherford, J. (ed.) *Identity: Community, Culture and Difference*, Lawrence and Wishart, London.

Handler, R. and Gable, E. (1997) *The New History in an Old Museum: Creating the Past at Colonial Williamsberg*, Duke University Press, Durham, NC, and London.

Hannon, V., Joubert, M. M. and Kogan, M. (2001) *Research, Cultural and Sports Policies*, a report to the Quality, Efficiency and Standards Team of the Department, Culture, Media and Sport, Centre for Evaluation of Policy and Practice, Brunel University.

Hardt, H. (1992) *Critical Communication Studies: Communication, History and Theory in America*, Routledge, London and New York.

Harland, J., Kinder, K., Haynes, J. and Schagen, I. (1998) *The Effects and Effectiveness of Arts Education in Schools, Interim Report 1*, NFER, Slough, Berkshire.

Harland, J., Kinder, K., Lord, P., Stott, A., Schagen, I., Haynes, J., Cusworth, L., White, R. and Paola, R. (2000) *Arts Education in Secondary Schools: Effects and Effectiveness*, NFER, Slough, Berkshire.

Harré, R. (1983) *Personal Being*, Blackwell, Oxford.

Harrison, M. (1970) *Learning out of School: A Teacher's Guide to the Educational Use of Museums*, Ward Locke Educational, London.

Harrison, M. (1950) *Museum Adventure: The Story of the Geffrye Museum*, University of London, London.

Harvey, L. and MacDonald, M. (1993) *Doing Sociology: A Practical Introduction*, Macmillan, Basingstoke.

Hassan, I. (1986) Pluralism in postmodern perspective, *Critical Inquiry*, 12, 503–520.

Heal, S. (2002) Renaissance arrives – but only for a few, *Museums Journal*, 102 (12), 14–15.

Hein, G. (2006) John Dewey's 'Wholly original philosophy' and its significance for museums, *Curator*, 49 (2), 181–203.

Hein, G. (1998) *Learning in the Museum*, Routledge, London.

Henning, M. (2006) *Museums, Media and Cultural Theory*, Open University Press, Maidenhead, Berkshire.

Hill, K. (2005) *Culture and Class in English Public Museums, 1850–1914*, Ashgate, Hampshire, England and Burlington, USA.

Hirsch, J. and Silverman, Lois, (eds) (2000) *Transforming Practice: Selections from the Journal of Museum Education 1992–1999*, Museum Education Roundtable, Washington, DC.

Holden, J. (2006) *Cultural Value and the Crisis of Legitimacy*, DEMOS, London.

Holmes, L. (2001) Decontaminating the concepts of 'learning' and 'competence': education and modalities of emergent identity. Paper prepared for the Education Stream of Second International Conference on Critical Management Studies, Manchester, www.re-skill.org.uk/papers/contaminated.html (accessed 07.03.05).

Holmes, L. (2000a) Is 'learning' a contaminated concept? Draft working paper prepared for 'Learning and Practice', one-day conference of the Learning and Critique Network, Manchester, 8 November, www.re-skill.org.uk/papers/contaminated.htm (accessed 07.03.05).

Holmes, L. (2000b) Reframing learning: performance, identity and practice, Presented at Critical contributions to managing and learning: second connecting learning and critique conference, Lancaster University, July 2000, www.re-skill.org.uk/papers/lanc00.html (accessed 07.03.05).

Hooper-Greenhill, E. (in press) Education, post-modernity and the museum, in Knell, S., Macleod, S. and Watson, S. (eds) *Museum Revolutions* (draft title), Routledge, London.

Hooper-Greenhill, E. (2006a) The power of museum pedagogy, in Genoways, H. (ed.) *Museum Philosophy for the Twenty-first Century*, University of Nebraska Press, 235–245.

Hooper-Greenhill, E. (2006b) Studying visitors, in MacDonald, S. (ed.) *Companion to Museum Studies*, Blackwell, Oxford, 362–376.

Hooper-Greenhill, E. (2004a) Measuring learning outcomes in museums, archives and libraries: the Learning Impact Research Project (LIRP), *International Journal of Heritage Studies*, 10 (2), 151–174.

Hooper-Greenhill, E. (2004b) Learning from culture: the importance of the Museum and Gallery Education Programme (Phase 1) in England, *Curator*, 47 (4), 428–449.

Hooper-Greenhill, E. (2004c) Musei: didattica, apprendimento ed edutainment, in Valentino, P.A. and Delli Quadri, L. M. R. (eds) *Cultura in gioco: le nuove frontiere di musei, didattica e industria culturale nell'era dell'interattivita*, VI Annual Report, Associazione Civita, Giunti, Fireze, Italy, 51–77.

Hooper-Greenhill, E. (2002) Developing a scheme for finding evidence of the outcomes and impact of learning in museums, archives and libraries: the conceptual framework, RCMG, Leicester. Prepared for the LIRP team and presented to Resource/MLA 26 June. Downloadable at www.le.ac.uk/museumstudies/research/rcmgpublicationsandprojects.html.

Hooper-Greenhill, E. (2000a) *Museums and the Interpretation of Visual Culture*, Routledge, London.

Hooper-Greenhill, E. (2000b) Communication and communities: changing paradigms in museum pedagogy, in Lindquist, S. (ed.) *Museums of Modern Science, Nobel Symposium 112*, Science History Publications/USA and the Nobel Foundation, 179–188.

Hooper-Greenhill, E. (1999) *The Educational Role of the Museum*, second edition, Routledge, London and New York.

Hooper-Greenhill, E. (1992) *Museums and the Shaping of Knowledge*, Routledge, London and New York.

Hooper-Greenhill, E. (1991) *Museum and Gallery Education*, Leicester University Press, Leicester, London and New York.

Hooper-Greenhill, E., Dodd, J., Gibson, L., Phillips, M., Jones, C. and Sullivan, E. (2006a) What did you learn at the museum today? Second study. Evaluation of the outcome and impact of learning through the implementation of the Education Programme Delivery Plan across nine Regional Hubs (2005). Full research report. www.le.ac.uk/museumstudies/research/rcmgpublicationsand-projects.html.

Hooper-Greenhill, E., Dodd, J., Gibson, L., Phillips, M., Jones, C. and Sullivan, E. (2006b) What did you learn at the museum today? Second study. Evaluation of the outcome and impact of learning through the implementation of the Education Programme Delivery Plans across nine Regional Hubs (2005). Research summary. RCMG, Leicester and MLA, London.

Hooper-Greenhill, E., with Dodd, J., Phillips, M., O'Riain, H., Jones, C. and Woodward, J. (2004a) What did you learn at the museum today? The evaluation of the impact of the Renaissance in the Regions Education Programme in the three Phase 1 Hubs (August, September and October 2003). Full research report. RCMG, Leicester. www.le.ac.uk/museumstudies/research/rcmgpublicationsandprojects.html. www.mla.gov.uk/information/publications/00pubs.asp.

Hooper-Greenhill, E., Dodd, J., Phillips, M., O'Riain, H., Jones, C. and Woodward, J. (2004b) What did you learn at the museum today? The evaluation of the impact of the Renaissance in the Regions Education Programme in the three Phase 1 Hubs (August, September and October 2003). Research summary. RCMG, Leicester and MLA, London. www.mla. gov.uk/information/publications/00pubs.asp.

Hooper-Greenhill, E., Dodd, J., Phillips, M., Jones, C., Woodward, J. and O'Riain, H. (2004c) Inspiration, identity, learning: the value of museums. The evaluation of DCMS/DfES Strategic Commissioning 2003–2004: National/Regional Museum Partnerships. Full research report. RCMG, Leicester. www.le.ac.uk/museumstudies/research/rcmg publicationsandprojects.html. www.culture.gov.uk/global/publications/archive_2004/valueofmuseums. www.teachernet.gov.uk/docbank/index.cfm?id=7412.

Hooper-Greenhill, E., Dodd, J., Phillips, M., Jones, C., Woodward, J. and O'Riain, H. (2004d) Inspiration, identity, learning: the value of museums. The evaluation of DCMS/DfES Strategic Commissioning 2003–2004: National/Regional Museum Partnerships. Research summary. RCMG and Department for Culture, Media and Sport, London. www.le.ac.uk/museumstudies/research/rcmgpublicationsandprojects.html. www.teachernet.gov.uk/docbank/index.cfm?id=7413.

Hooper-Greenhill, E., Dodd, J., Moussouri, T., Jones, C., Pickford, C., Vincent, J., Herman, C. and Toon, R. (2003) Measuring the outcomes and impact of learning in museums, archives and libraries: the Learning Impact Research Project end of project paper. www.le.ac.uk/museumstudies/research/rcmgpublicationsandprojects.html.

Hooper-Greenhill, E. and Moussouri, T. (2002) *Researching Learning in Museums and Galleries 1990–1999: A Bibliographic Review*, RCMG, Leicester.

Hooper-Greenhill, E. and Dodd, J. (2002) *Seeing the Museum through the Visitors' Eyes: The Evaluation of the Education Challenge Fund*, RCMG, Leicester.

Hooper-Greenhill, E., Dodd, J., O'Riain, H., Clarke, A. and Selfridge. L. (2001) The impact of the DfES Museum and Gallery Education Programme: a summative evaluation. RCMG, Leicester. www.teachernet.gov.uk (accessed 01.10.06).

Hooper-Greenhill, E., Moussouri, T., Hawthorne, E. and Riley, R. (2001) *Making Meaning in Art Museums 1: Visitors' Interpretive Strategies at Wolverhampton Art Gallery*, RCMG, Leicester.

Hooper-Greenhill, E. and Moussouri, T. (2001a) *Making Meaning in Art Museums 2: Visitors' Interpretive Strategies at Nottingham Castle Museum and Art Gallery*, RCMG, Leicester.

Hooper-Greenhill, E. and Nicol, G. (2001b) *Evaluating Creativity: The Evaluation of the 10 Gallery Education Projects of Encompass 2000*, RCMG, Leicester and ENGAGE, London.

Hooper-Greenhill, E., Sandell, S., O'Riain, H. and Moussouri, T. (2000) *Museums and Social Inclusion: The GLLAM Report*, Research Centre for Museums and Galleries (RCMG), University of Leicester, Leicester, and Group for Large Local Authority Museums, Newcastle-on Tyne.

Huang, K-A. (1999) *New Visions for Museums*, National Museum of History, Taipei.

Hutcheon, L. (1992) Theorising the postmodern: towards a poetics, in Jencks, C. *The Post-modern Reader*, Academy Editions, London/St Martin's Press, New York, 76–93.

Hutcheon, L. (1989) *The Politics of Postmodernism*, Routledge, London and New York.

Hutchinson, J. (1893) On educational museums, *Museums Association Report of Proceedings with Papers Read at the Fourth Annual General Meeting*, London, 3–7 July, 47–63.

Huyssen, A. (1995) *Twilight Memories: Marking Time in a Culture of Amnesia*, Routledge, New York and London.

Huyssen, A. (1992) Mapping the postmodern, in Jencks, C. (ed.) *The Post-modern Reader*, Academy Editions, London/St Martin's Press, New York, 40–72.

Illich, I. (1973) *Deschooling Society*, Penguin Books, Middlesex.

Institute of Ideas (2001) *Museums for 'The People'?: Conversations in Print*, Academy of Ideas, London.

Institute of Museum and Library Services (not dated) *Perspectives on Outcome-based Evaluation for Libraries and Museums*, ILMS, Washington.

Ipsos MORI (2006) *Renaissance in the Regions 2005: Visitor Exit Survey – Final National Report. Research Study Conducted for MLA*, MORI, London.

Jarvis, P., Holford, J. and Griffin, C. (1998) *The Theory and Practice of Learning*, Kogan Page, London.

Jencks, C. (1992) *The Post-modern Reader*, Academy Editions, London/St Martin's Press, New York.

Johnsson, E. (2004a) Stag beetles, greenhouses and plastic bottles: pupils' ideas about local and global environmental issues (summary), London Museums Hub EPDP Research. Front end evaluation. www.mlalondon.org.uk/uploads/documents/HUB_Rpt_env_educ_frontend_research.pdf (accessed 08.11.06).

Johnsson, E. (2004b) Pupils' ideas about museum experiences, EPDP research, London Museums Hub, December 2003 to January 2004, London.

Johnsson, E. (2003) Investigating learning outcomes and impacts of visits to London's Hub museums 2: qualitative baselines: Teachers' ideas about learning in museums, EPDP research, London Museums Hub, October to December 2003, London. www.mlalondon.org.uk/uploads/documents/HUBteacherideas.pdf (accessed 24.01.07).

Jowell, T. (2004) *Government and the Value of Culture*, Department for Culture, Media and Sport, London.

Joyce, B., Calhoun, E. and Hopkins, D. (1997) *Models of Learning – Tools for Teaching*, OUP, Buckingham, Philadelphia.

Jury, L. (2006) Galleries and museums unable to buy new works as funding dries up, *The Independent*, Friday, 12 May, 10–11.

Katriel, T. (1997) *Performing the Past: A Study of Israeli Settlement Museums*, Lawrence Erlbaum Associates, New Jersey.

Kavanagh, G. (1994) *Museums and the First World War: A Social History*, Leicester University Press, Leicester.

Kavanagh, G. (1988) The First World War and its implications for education in British museums, *History of Education*, 17(2), 163–176.

Kelly, L. (1999) Finding evidence of visitor learning. Paper presented at 'Musing on learning' seminar, Australian Museum, Sydney, 20 April. www.amonline.net.au/amarc/research/learning.htm (accessed 22.01.07).

Knell, S. J. (2000) *The Culture of English Geology, 1815–1851: A Science Revealed through its Collecting*, Ashgate, Aldershot.

Knight, B. (2002) Study confirms visitors as main source of museum dust, *Museum Practice*, 20, 11.

Koven, S. (1994) The Whitechapel Picture Exhibitions and the politics of seeing, in Sherman, D. J. and Rogoff, I. (eds) *Museum Culture: Histories, Discourses, Spectacles*, Routledge, London, 22–48.

Landry. C. (2003) Culture's collision course, *Museums Journal*, 103 (1), 16–19.

Lave, J. and Wenger, E. (1991) *Situated Learning: Legitimate Peripheral Participation*, Cambridge University Press, Cambridge.

Lawley, I. (2003) Local authority museums and the modernising government agenda in England, *Museum and Society*, 1 (2), 75–86.

Lawson, J. and Silver, H. (1973) *A Social History of Education in England*, Methuen, London.

Learning and Skills Council (2003) LSC Position paper on recognising and recording progress and achievement in non-accredited learning. Online at www.lsc.gov.uk.

Learning and Teaching Scotland (2002) Education for citizenship in Scotland: national framework paper. LT Online service www.ltscotland.org.uk/citizenship/management-toolkit/planning/paper/index.asp (accessed 17.08.06).

Leinhardt, G., Crowley, K. and Knutson, K. (2002) *Learning Conversations in Museums*, Lawrence Erlbaum Associates, New Jersey and London.

Leone, M. P. and Little, B. J. (2004) Artifacts as expressions of society and culture: subversive genealogy and the value of history, in Carbonell, B. M. (ed.) *Museum Studies: An Anthology of Contexts*, Blackwell, Oxford, 362–374.

Levitas, R. (2004) Let's hear it for Humpty: social exclusion, the third way and cultural capital, *Cultural Trends*, 13 (2), 1–3.

Lewis, G. (1989) *For Instruction and Recreation: A Centenary History of the Museums Association*, Quiller Press, London.

Littler, J. and Naidoo, R. (2005) *The Politics of Heritage: The Legacies of 'Race'*, Routledge, London and New York.

Lord, P., Doherty, P. and Sefton-Green, J. (not dated) Making connections: informal media education projects for young people, NFER, published by the National Youth Agency, Leicester.

Lyon, D. (1999) *Postmodernity*, second edition, Open University Press, Buckingham.

Macdonald, S. (2002) *Behind the Scenes at the Science Museum*, Berg, Oxford.

Macdonald, S. (ed.) (1998) *The Politics of Display: Museums, Science, Culture*, Routledge, London and New York.

Macdonald, S. (1995) Consuming science: public knowledge and the dispersed politics of reception among museum visitors, *Media, Culture and Society*, 17 (1), 13–29.

Macdonald, S. and Basu, P. (eds) (2007) *Exhibition Experiments*, Blackwell Publishing, Oxford, Malden, MA and Carlton, Victoria, Australia.

Marcousé, R. (1961) *The Listening Eye: Teaching in an Art Museum*, Victoria and Albert Museum, London.

Markham, S. F. (1938) *A Report on the Museums and Art Galleries of the British Isles*, Carnegie United Kingdom trust, Dunfermline.

Marshall, C. and Rossman, G. (1999) *Designing Qualitative Research*, Sage, London.

Marstine, J. (ed.) (2006) *New Museum Theory and Practice: An Introduction*, Blackwell Publishing, Oxford, Malden, MA and Carlton, Victoria, Australia.

Mason, J. (1996) *Qualitative Researching*, Sage, London.

Matarasso, F. (1998a) *Learning Development: An Introduction to the Social Impact of Public Libraries*, Comedia/British Library Board, London.

Matarasso, F. (1998b) *Beyond Book Issues: The Social Potential of Library Projects*, Comedia/British Library Board, London.

McClellan, A. (ed.) (2003) *Art and its Publics: Museum Studies at the Millenium*, Blackwell, Oxford.

McClellan, A. (1994) *Inventing the Louvre: Art, Politics and the Origin of the Modern*

Museum in Eighteenth Century Paris, University of California Press, Berkeley, Los Angeles, London.

McDonald, P. M. (1979) Education, in R. Strathern (ed.) *Rare and Curious Specimens: An Illustrated History of the Australian Museum*, The Australian Museum, London.

McGuigan, J. (2004) *Rethinking Cultural Policy*, OUP, Maidenhead, Berkshire.

McNicol, S., Matthews, G., Kane, D., Lancaster, K., Thebridge, S. and Dalton, P. (2002) *Collaboration between Libraries and Education: Supporting the Learner*, Resource (Council for Museums, Archives and Libraries) and Department for Education and Skills, London.

Miers, Sir H. A. (1928) *A Report on the Public Museums of the British Isles*, Carnegie United Kingdom Trust, Edinburgh.

Miles, R. and Tout, A. (1994a) Outline of a technology for effective science exhibits, in Hooper-Greenhill, E. (ed.) *The Educational Role of the Museum*, first edition, Routledge, London, 87–100.

Miles, R. and Tout, A. (1994b) Impact of research on the approach to the visiting public at the Natural History Museum, London, in Hooper-Greenhill, E. (ed.) *The Educational Role of the Museum*, first edition, Routledge, London, 101–106.

Minihan, J. (1977) *The Nationalisation of Culture: The Development of State Subsidies to the Arts in Great Britain*, Hamish Hamilton, London.

MLA (2006a) *One/ten: Ten Partners, One Voice*, MLA, London.

MLA (2006b) *Museum Learning Survey 2006*, Museums, Libraries and Archives Council, London.

MLA (2004) *Renaissance News*, 3 July. Museums, Libraries and Archives Council, London. www.mla.gov.uk/ resources/assets//R/rennews03_pdf_ 4396.pdf (accessed 29.09.06).

MLA (2003a) *Renaissance News*, 1 August. Museums, Libraries and Archives Council, London. www.mla.gov.uk/ resources/assets//R/rennews01_pdf_ 4394.pdf (accessed 29.09.06).

MLA (2003b) *Renaissance News*, 2 October. Museums, Libraries and Archives Council, London. www. mla.gov.uk/resources/assets//R/ rennews02_pdf_4395.pdf (accessed 29.09.06).

Moffat, H. and Woollard, V. (1999) *Museum and Gallery Education: A Manual of Good Practice*, The Stationery Office, London.

Morgan, W. and McWilliam, E. (1995) Keeping an untidy house: a disjointed paper about academic space, work and bodies, in Smith, R. and Wexler, P. (eds) *After Post-modernism: Education, Politics and Identity*, The Falmer Press, London and Washington, 112–127.

MORI (2001) *Visitors to Museums and Galleries in the UK*, Resource, London.

MORI (1999) *Visitors to Museums and Galleries in the UK: Research Findings*, Museums and Galleries Commission and MORI.

Morris, J. (2005) Missing evidence: why museums should learn from the past, *Cultural Trends*, 14 (1), no. 53, 107–111.

Morris, J. (2003) Pathfinder hubs get the lion's share as Resource distributed funding, *Museums Journal*, 103 (5), 7.

Motylewski, K. (2001) New directives, new directions: documenting outcomes in IMLS grants to libraries and museums, Institute of Museum and Library Services, 1100 Pennsylvania Avenue, DC 20506. www.imls.gov (accessed 22.01.06) or kmotylewski@imls.gov. See also IMLS (not dated), Perspectives on outcome-based evaluation for libraries and museums.

Moussouri, T. (2002) A context for the development of learning outcomes in museums, archives and libraries, RCMG, Leicester. www.le.ac.uk/museumstudies/research/ rcmgpublicationsandprojects.html.

Muddiman, D., Durrani, S., Dutch, M., Linley, R., Pateman, J. and Vincent, J. (2000) Open to all? The public library and social exclusion. Volume 1: Overview and conclusions. Library and Information Commission Research Report 84, Resource (Council for Museums, Archives and Libraries), London.

Museum Education Roundtable (1992) Patterns in practice: selections from the *Journal of Museum Education*, Museum Education Roundtable, Washington, DC.

Museums Association (2003a) DCMS education initiatives could be money wasted, says MA, *Museums Journal*, 103 (3), 13.

Museums Association (2003b) Local support groups to develop leadership skills for museums, *Museums Journal*, 103 (2), 13.

Museums Association (2002) *Code of Ethics for Museums: Ethical Principles For All Those Who Work For or Govern Museums in the UK*, Museums Association, London.

Museums Association (1993) *Responding to Change: Museum Education at the Crossroads*, Museums Association, London.

Museums Association (1919) *Museums Journal*, 19.

Museums Journal (2006) Understanding slavery, *Museums Journal*, 106 (11), 24–29. www.understandingslavery.com.

National Advisory Committee on Creative and Cultural Education (NACCCE) (1999) *All Our Futures: Creativity, Culture and Education*, Department for Culture, Media and Sport and Department for Education and Employment, London.

National Museums Directors' Conference (2004a) *National Museums and Galleries: The Impacts and Needs: A Summary of Findings*, NMDC, London.

National Museums Directors' Conference (2004b) *Museums and Galleries: Creative Engagement*, NMDC, London.

National Museums Directors' Conference (not dated) A manifesto for museums, NMDC, London. www.nationalmuseums.org.uk (accessed 22.01.07).

National Portrait Gallery (1949) *Catalogue of the National Portrait Gallery 1856–1947: With an Index of Artists*, National Portrait Gallery, London.

National Statistics, http://neighbourhood. statistics.gov.uk/ (accessed 22.01.07).

Neighbourhood Renewal Unit (2004) *The English Indices of Deprivation 2004: Report to the Office of the Deputy Prime Minister*, Stationery Office, London.

Newman, A., McLean, F. and Urquhart, G. (2005) Museums and the active citizen: tackling the problems of social exclusion, *Citizenship Studies*, 9 (1), 41–57.

Nicol, G. (2000) *Encompass 1999–2000*, postcard set, ENGAGE, London.

Office for Standards in Education (2003) Expecting the unexpected: developing creativity in primary and secondary schools, HMI 1612, e-publication.

Ogbu, J. (1995) The influence of culture on learning and behaviour, in J. Falk and L. Dierking, (eds) *Public Institutions for Personal Learning: Establishing A Research Agenda*, American Association of Museums, 79–96.

Ohta, R. J. (1998) 'Mine eyes have seen the glory': visitor experience at a controversial flag exhibition, *Current Trends in Audience Research and Evaluation*, 11, American Association of Museums, Committee on Audience Research and Evaluation, Los Angeles, 48–58.

O'Neill, M. (2004) Enlightenment museums: universal or merely global? *Museum and Society*, 2 (3), 190–202.

O'Sullivan, T., Hartley. J., Saunders, D., Montgomery, M. and Fiske, J. (1994) *Key Concepts in Communication and Cultural Studies*, second edition, Routledge, London and New York.

Paris, S. (ed.) (2002) *Perspectives on Object-centred Learning in Museums*, Lawrence Erlbaum Associates, New Jersey and London.

Park Lane Research (1997) NMGM and school trips. Unpublished document for the National Museums and Galleries on Merseyside.

Phillipson, D. (2003) Ivory towers? *Museums Journal*, 103 (3), 25–27.

Pick, G. (2001) *National Survey of Visitors to British Archives*, Public Services Quality Group National Visitors Survey Working Party, London.

Piscitelli, B. and Anderson, A. (2001) Young children's perspectives of museum settings and experiences, *Museum Management and Curatorship*, 19 (3), 269–282.

Pointon, M. (ed.) (1994) *Art Apart: Art Institutions and Ideology across England and North America*, Manchester University Press, Manchester and New York.

Pole, C. and Morrison, M. (2003) *Ethnography for Education*, Open University Press, Maidenhead.

Pollock, G. and Zemans, J. (eds) (2007) *Museums after Modernism: Strategies of Engagement*, Blackwell, Oxford; Malden, MA and Carlton, Victoria, Australia.

Pontin, K. (2001) Represent: an evaluation report for an inclusive project run by Birmingham Museum Service. www.katepontin.co.uk/REP-BRUM.pdf (accessed 19.11.06).

Preziosi, D. and Farago, C. (eds) (2004) *Grasping the World: The Idea of the Museum*, Ashgate, Aldershot and Burlington, VT.

Price, C. (2002) Bodies building, *Museums Journal*, 102 (4), 17.

Pringle, E. (2006) *Learning in the Gallery: Context, Process, Outcomes*, Arts Council England, London.

Prins, D. (2005) The art of memory making, in Atkinson, D. and Dash, P. (eds) *Social and Critical Practices in Art Education*, Trentham Books, Stoke on Trent, UK and Sterling, USA, 67–79.

Prior, N. (2002) *Museums and Modernity: Art Galleries and the Making of Modern Culture*, Berg, Oxford and New York.

Proctor, R. and Bartle, C. (2002) *Low Achievers – Lifelong Learners: An Investigation into the Impact of the Public Library on Educational Disadvantage*, Resource, London.

Qualifications and Curriculum Authority and Department for Education and Employment (1998) Education for Citizenship and the teaching of democracy in schools: final report of the Advisory Group on Citizenship, 22 September 1998 (the Crick Report) www.qca.org.uk/ca/subjects/citizenship/crick_report_1998.pdf (accessed 02.01.07).

Quality Assurance Agency for Higher Education (2000a) *Subject Review Handbook September 2000 to December 2001*,Quality Assurance Agency for Higher Education, Gloucester, www.qaa.ac.uk (accessed 22.01.07).

Quality Assurance Agency for Higher Education (2000b) *Guidelines for Preparing Programme Specifications*, Quality Assurance Agency for Higher Education, Gloucester, www.qaa.ac.uk (accessed 22.01.07).

Ray, L. and Sayer, A. (eds) (1999) *Culture and Economy after the Cultural Turn*, Sage, London, Thousand Oaks, New Delhi.

RCMG (2006a) What amazed me most at the museum today was . . . The impact of museum visits on pupils at Key Stage 2. Flip-book, MLA, London.

RCMG (2006b) The most interesting thing at the museum today was . . . The impact of museum visits on pupils aged 11–18 years. Flip-book, MLA, London.

RCMG (2004) What amazed me most at the museum today was . . . The impact of museum visits on pupils at Key Stage 2. Flip-book, MLA, London.

Rees Leahy, H. (2005) Producing a public for art: gallery space in the twenty-first century, in MacLeod, S. (ed.) *Reshaping Museum Space: Architecture, Design, Exhibitions*, Routledge, London, 108–117.

Rees Leahy, H. (2003) Researching learning at Manchester Art Gallery. Project report for Manchester Art Gallery, www.art.man.ac.uk/museology/ (accessed 05.09.06).

Research Surveys of Great Britain (1991) *RSGB Omnibus Arts Survey: Report on a Survey on Arts and Cultural Activities in G.B.*, Arts Council of Great Britain, London.

Resource (2001) *Renaissance in the Regions: A New Vision for England's Museums*, Resource (Council for Museums, Archives and Libraries), London.

Resource (2000) *Using Museums, Archives and Libraries to Develop a Learning Community: A Strategic Plan for Action*, Resource (Council for Museums, Archives and Libraries), London.

Rice, D. (2003) Museums: theory, practice and illusion, in McClellan, A. (ed.) *Art and its Publics: Museum Studies at the Millennium*, Blackwell, Oxford, 77–95.

Richardson, V. (ed.) (1997) *Constructivist Teacher Education: Building a World of New Understandings*, Falmer Press, London.

Roberts, L. (1997) *From Knowledge to Narrative: Educators and the Changing Museum*, Smithsonian Institution Press.

Roberts, L. (1993) Analysing (and intuiting) the affective domain, in Bicknell, S. and Farmelo, G. (eds) *Museum Visitor Studies in the 90s*, Science Museum, London, 97–101.

Robins, C. and Woollard, V. (2003) *Creative Connections: Working with Teachers to use Museums and Galleries as a Learning*

Resource, Victoria and Albert Museum and Institute of Education, London.

Robinson, M. (1996) *21st Century Dictionary*, Chambers, Edinburgh.

Robson, C. (2002) *Real World Research: A Resource for Social Scientists and Practitioner-researchers*, Blackwell, Oxford.

Ross, A. (1996) The great American numbers game, in Duttmann et. al. (eds) *The End(s) of the Museum/Els limits del museu*, Fundacio Antoni Tapies, Barcelona, 25–52.

Ross, M. (2004) Interpreting the new museology, *Museum and Society*, 2 (2), 84–103.

Ryan, M. (2001) Introduction, in *Museums for 'The People'?: Conversations in Print*, Academy of Ideas, London, 8–9.

Sandell, R. (2007a) Community service, *Museums Journal*, 107 (1), 24–27.

Sandell, R. (2007b) *Museums, Prejudice and the Reframing of Difference*, Routledge, London.

Sandell, R. (ed.) (2002) *Museums, Society, Inequality*, Routledge, London and New York.

Sandell, R. (1998) Museums as agents of social inclusion, *Museum Management and Curatorship*, 17 (4), 401–418.

Sayer, A. (1999) Valuing culture and economy, in Ray, L. and Sayer, A. (eds) *Culture and Economy after the Cultural Turn*, Sage, London, Thousand Oaks, New Delhi, 53–75.

Schroder, K., Drotner,K., Kline, S. and Murray, C. (2003) *Researching Audiences*, Arnold, London.

Scott, C. (2006) Museums: impact and value, *Cultural Trends*, 15 (1), no. 57, 45–75.

Screven, C. G. (1993) Visitor studies: an introduction, *Museum International*, XLV (2), 4–12.

Selleck, R. J. W. (1968) *The New Education 1870–1914*, Sir Isaac Pitman and Sons, London.

Selwood, S. (2006a) Great expectations: museums and regional economic development in England, *Curator*, 49 (1), 65–80.

Selwood, S. (2006b) Unreliable evidence: the rhetorics of data collection in the cultural sector, in Mirza, M. (ed.) *Culture Vultures: Is UK Arts Policy Damaging the Arts?* Policy Exchange, London, 38–52.

Selwood, S. (2002a) Politics of data collection, *Cultural Trends*, 47, 13–97.

Selwood, S. (2002b) Measuring culture, Spiked Culture, www.spiked-online.com (accessed 20/01/2003).

Selwood, S. (ed.) (2001) *The UK Cultural Sector, Profile and Policy Issues*, Cultural Trends and Policy Studies Institute, London.

Smith, R. and Wexler, P. (eds) (1995) *After Postmodernism: Education, Politics and Identity*, The Falmer Press, London and Washington.

Sotto, E. (1994) *When Teaching Becomes Learning: A Theory and Practice of Teaching*, Cassell, London.

Standing Commission on Museums and Galleries (1978) *Tenth Report 1973–1977*, HMSO, London.

Standing Commission on Museums and Galleries (1963) *Survey of Provincial Museums and Galleries* (The Rosse Report), HMSO, London.

Stanley, J., Huddleston, P., Grewcock, C., Muir, F., Galloway, S., Newman, A. and Clive, S. (2004) *Final Report on the Impact of Phase 2 of the Museums and Galleries Education Programme*, Department for Education and Skills, London. www.teachernet.gov.uk/mgep2 (accessed 22.01.07).

Stanworth, K. (1994) The politics of display: a 'literary and historical' definition of Quebec in 1830s British North America, in Pointon, M. (ed.) *Art Apart: Art Institutions and Ideology across England and North America*, Manchester University Press, Manchester and New York, 120–141.

Stephens, M. D. and Roderick, G. W. (eds) (1983a) *Samuel Smiles and Nineteenth Century Self-help in Education*, Nottingham Studies in the History of Adult Education, University of Nottingham, Nottingham.

Stephens, M. D. and Roderick, G. W. (1983b) Middle class nineteenth century self-help – the Literary and Philosophical Societies, in Stephens, M.D. and Roderick, G. W. (eds) *Samuel Smiles and Nineteenth Century Self-help in Education*, Nottingham Studies in the History of Adult Education, University of Nottingham, Nottingham, 16–46.

Storey, J. (1999) *Cultural Consumption and Everyday Life*, Arnold, London and Sydney.

Strahan, R. (1979) *Rare and Curious Specimens: An Illustrated History of the Australian Museum 1827–1979*, The Australian Museum, Sydney.

Taylor, B. (1999) *Art for the Nation: Exhibitions and the London Public 1747–2001*, Manchester University Press, Manchester.

Thistlewood, D. (ed.) (1993) *American Abstract Expressionism*, Liverpool University Press and Tate Gallery Liverpool, Liverpool.

Thomas, A. (1999) The National Gallery's first 50 years: 'cut the cloth to suit the purse', in Perry, G. and Cunningham, C. (eds) *Academies, Museums and Canons of Art*, Yale University Press, New Haven and London in association with the Open University, 207–237.

Travers, T. and Glaister, S. (2004) *Valuing Museums: Impact and Innovation among National Museums*, National Museums Directors' Conference, London.

Trodd, C. (1994) Culture, class and city: the National Gallery, London and the spaces of education, 1822–57, in Pointon, M. (ed.) *Art Apart: Art Institutions and Ideology across England and North America*, Manchester University Press, Manchester and New York, 33–49.

Turner, B. (1984) *The Body and Society*, Blackwell, Oxford.

Usher, R., Bryant, I. and Johnston, R. (1997) *Adult Education and the Postmodern Challenge: Learning Beyond the Limits*, Routledge, London and New York.

Waterfield, G. (1999) A home of luxury and a temple of art, in Olding, S., Waterfield, G. and Bills, M. (eds) *A Victorian Salon; Paintings from the Russell-Cotes Art Gallery and Museum*, Russell-Cotes Art Gallery and Museum, Bournemouth, Bournemouth Borough Council in association with Lund Humphries Publishers, London, 14–23.

Waterfield, G. (1995) The origins of the early picture gallery catalogue in Europe and its manifestation in Victorian Britain, in Pearce, S. (ed.) *Art in Museums*, Athlone, London, 42–73.

Waterfield, G. (1991) *Palaces of Art*, Dulwich Picture Gallery, London.

Watson, J. (2004) *The Isabella Project: Take on Picture, North, South, East, West*, Laing Art Gallery, Newcastle upon Tyne.

Watters, K. and Turner, C. (2001) Proof Positive: a report on research into learners' views on approaches to identifying achievement in non-accredited learning, NIACE, November. www.niace.org.uk/projects/LearningOutcomes /Proof%20Positive%20Final%20Report.pdf (accessed 22.01.07).

Weedon, C. (2004) *Identity and Culture: Narratives of Difference and Belonging*, Open University Press, Maidenhead.

Weil, S. (not dated) Transformed from a century of bric-a-brac, in Sheppard, B. (ed.) *Perspectives on Outcome Based Evaluation for Libraries and Museums*, Institute of Museum and Library Services, Washington, DC, 4–15.

Welsh, P. (2005) Re-configuring museums, *Museum Management and Curatorship*, 20 (2), 103–130.

Wenger, E. (1998) *Communities of Practice: Learning, Meaning, and Identity*, Cambridge University Press, Cambridge.

Wheeler, W. (1997) *The Enlightenment Effect; A Signs of the Times Discussion Paper*, Signs of the Times, London.

Wilkinson, H. (2003a) Measurable results, *Museums Association*, 103 (1), 12.

Wilkinson, H. (2003b) Preaching to the converted, *Museums Journal*, 103 (4), 14.

Williams, D. and Wavell, C. (2001) *The Impact of the School Library Resource Centre on Learning*, Library and Information Commission Research Report 112, Resource, London.

Wilson, D. (1984) National museums, in Thompson, J. M. A. (ed.) *Manual of Curatorship: A Guide to Museum Practice*, Butterworths, London and Boston, 54–58.

Winitzky, N. and Kauchak, D. (1997) Constructivism in teacher education: applying cognitive theory to teacher learning, in Richardson, V. (ed.) *Constructivist Teacher Education: Building a World of New Understandings*, Falmer Press, London, 59–83.

Winstanley, B. (1967) *Children and Museums*, Blackwell, London.

Winterbotham, N. (2005) Museums and schools: developing services in three English counties, 1988–2004. Unpublished PhD, University of Nottingham.

Wistinghausen, M. von, Morgan, K. and Housden, K. (AEA Consulting) (2004) *National Dimensions*, National Museums Directors' Conference, London.

Woodward, K. (2002) *Understanding Identity*, Arnold, London.

Woodward, K. (ed.) (1997) *Identity and Difference*, Open University Press, Milton Keynes.

Worts, D. (1995) Extending the frame: forging a new partnership with the public, in Pearce, S. (ed.) *Art in Museums*, Athlone, London, 164–191.

Yin, R. (1994) *Case-study Research: Design and Methods*, vol 5, Applied Social Research Methods Series, Sage, London.

Index